SOCIAL WORK METHODS AND PROCESSES

Joseph Anderson
Shippensburg State College

Wadsworth Publishing Company
Belmont, California
A Division of Wadsworth, Inc.

Social Work Editor: Curt Peoples
Production Editor: Donna Oberholtzer
Designer: Janet Wood
Copy Editor: Don Yoder
Technical Illustrator: Pat Rogondino

Printed in the United States of America

1 2 3 4 5 6 7 8 9 10—85 84 83 82 81

Library of Congress Cataloging in Publication Data

Anderson, Joseph, 1941–
  Social work methods and processes.

  Bibliography: p.
  Includes index.
  1. Social service. I. Title.

HV31.A4   361.3   80-25431
ISBN 0-534-00955-7

*To those for whom I have served, teachers
from whom I have learned, and students with
whom I have been involved in teaching/
learning situations. What I know I owe to
them. To my family and friends. What I am
I owe to them. And to Him from whom
all things are possible.*

Brief Contents

Contents

Preface

Any author who attempts to create a text is presumptuous. Presumption begins with the idea that one has something to offer to readers. In the searching hours of translating ideas into written words, I have had to rely continually on such presumptions in the creative struggle to contribute what I consider worthy of publication. My painful doubt has been counterbalanced by my belief that this book can be useful.

It is an introduction to social work methods for direct-service practice. It provides a framework for integrating the generic core of social work—the common base—with the generalist use of methods for practice. It presents the concepts behind this core and the principles for the selection of methods based on the needs of consumers and their environment. Since the development of human relations is the basic objective of social work, this book offers a comparative analysis of practice theories for working with individuals, families, groups, organizations, and communities toward that end.

Therefore, this text is designed for the direct-service social worker—either in preparation for practice or in further training. It is designed especially for BSW courses in beginning methods when the objective is to prepare a social worker who can function as a generalist rather than a specialist in specific methods and/or fields. It is also applicable to a beginning-level MSW course geared toward preparation of direct-service workers through what has become known as an "integrated methods," "generic," or "multimethod" approach.

This book has evolved from my concern for the abandonment of practice theory in our search for more effective social work methods. This abandonment has taken two general routes. One is the use of eclectic problem-solving and assessment frameworks that are deemed applicable to all social units—individual through community. This view assumes that there is a single method of practice that applies to both microsystems and macrosystems. Once a system's analysis is completed, the worker can "plug into" the framework all the social units chosen for change. This course comes dangerously close to practice without theory, as generic problem-solving skills are not related to specific concepts of individual, family, small groups, organization, and community processes and appropriate methods for each.

The other trend is the use of people-changing approaches that have evolved outside of social work as a profession. This trend, which is narrow in focus, nudges the idea of social work toward the "fifth profession"—a broad-based psychotherapy. The practice theories in this trend range from gestalt therapy and transactional analysis to yoga, behavior modification, and encounter groups.

I agree with certain assumptions of these competing frameworks: that the *separation* of traditional social work into casework, group work, and community organization has limited our professional effectiveness; that it has dichotomized the person–situation transaction; and that, in many instances, it has been counterproductive in meeting the needs of those we serve. But I also believe that the practice theories behind these traditional methods offer the most effective approaches now available for achieving the goals of the different social units. In our current approaches to practice, we need to assure that the baby is not thrown out with the bathwater.

This book is an attempt to resolve this dilemma by reconceptualizing direct-service social work by means of frameworks that incorporate traditional practice theories. It presents a view of the direct-service worker as a generalist whose work is built on the common foundation of social work's purpose, function, and values. This worker has not only the basic interactional and analytical skills but also a repertoire of a select group of social work practice theories. Therefore, generalist social work is theory-based. Workers use theories to select appropriate methods and then to provide responsible service. This practice permits the testing and further development of theory toward increased professional competence and accountability.

Other assumptions about social work and the needs of students and faculty in a beginning methods course have influenced the scope of this work. First, direct service usually begins with the request of the consumer. Second, the direct-service social worker needs "bifocal vision" to respond to that request in a manner that contributes to the self-actualizing development of both the consumer and his or her environmental systems. The worker must consider working with other consumers (families and groups) in behalf of the individual consumer and others like him or her, or working with indirect consumers (organizations and communities) in behalf of the individual. Third, accountability for professional service is based on the contracts established in social work and on the use of practice theories. Fourth, practice theories that have evolved from social work are currently the most effective approaches available for entry level practice. They have been forged in the heat of serving people in need consistent with social work's purpose, values, and objectives and in the light of a "practice wisdom." The development of these practice theories and the integration of newer theories (gestalt, transactional analysis, reality therapy, social learning) can best be built upon this foundation. Fifth, the key to effective practice is *skill* in providing services.

This skill always encompasses four aspects: knowledge that facilitates professional judgment; knowledge of methods that implement professional action; values that direct professional intent; and personal style. A major goal of this text is to provide a framework in which one's personal style can be asserted individually in skills that are conscious, disciplined, and yet creative—and therefore consonant with social work's purposes in action.

Organization and Features

Part 1—Frameworks—introduces the generic base for social work (Chapter 1) and the framework for the generalist use of social work methods at both the microlevel (Chapter 2) and the macrolevel (Chapter 3). It concludes with the generic principles (Chapter 4) and basic interactional skills (Chapter 5) needed for this practice.

Part 2—Basic Theory and Practice Theory—provides theoretical models for the human development of individuals (Chapter 6) and their systems (Chapter 7). It concludes with a model of practice theory selection, use, and testing in relation to both "espoused theories" and "theories in use" (Chapter 8).

Part 3—Practice Theories—introduces the currently recognized practice theories that inform the generalist methods in action. These include methods for working with individuals (Chapter 9), families (Chapter 10), groups (Chapter 11), organizations (Chapter 12), and communities (Chapter 13). The book concludes with an afterword.

Throughout the book I have used examples plucked liberally from the social work literature. This use of published examples of social work permits the reader to go to original sources for further study. I am indebted greatly to these original works not only for the examples but for many ideas. However, I alone am responsible for their representation and interpretation.

Most chapters are followed by lists of suggested learning experiences, case studies, and supplemental readings that relate to the concepts presented. No single book can cover every aspect of direct-service practice, of course. In fact, no book can teach practice. Practice is learned through doing, thinking about the doing, and relating theory to experience. I hope that the suggested learning experiences can contribute to this process. Discussion of case study material is another important step in the connection of theory to practice. Moreover, our work requires an understanding of such issues as racism, sexism, and other forms of institutionalized discrimination as well as specific knowledge of cross-cultural differences. The material offered at the end of each chapter is designed to enrich the book in these three important areas: learning experiences, case studies, and human diversity.

These are the presumptions which kept me at the task of writing this book. The worth of my contribution can be judged only by its meaning for you. To paraphrase Rudyard Kipling in relation to his own writing: One can only paint the best picture possible on the basis of one's talents, hang the canvas out to dry, and wait for those passing by to stop, examine, and criticize it. My canvas is out to dry and I await the response. I hope it can influence your practice.

Acknowledgements

Finally, no book is ever published without the support and challenge from many others. Among those who contributed to this book are the reviewers of this work in progress. These include William C. Berleman of the University of Washington; Phyllis J. Day of Purdue University; Eudice Glassberg of Temple University; Louise C. Johnson of the University of South Dakota; Bradford Sheafor of Colorado State University; Greta L. Singer of Monmouth College; Patrick Wardell of Pennsylvania State University; and Constance Williams of Metropolitan College, Boston University. Former mentors at the University of Maryland School of Social Work and Community Planning who especially challenged me to clarify my ideas about social work practice are Paul Ephross, Leonard Press, and Daniel Thursz (former dean of the school).

Originally at Duxbury Press, I had the strong encouragement of Jerry Lyons and Steven Keeble. At Wadsworth, this encouragement took the form of direct editorial and production help from those with whom I worked: Donna Oberholtzer, Curt Peoples, Janet Wood, and Don Yoder.

There are two other people who deserve special acknowledgement. William Boor, a friend and colleague at Shippensburg State College, has helped me test out the ideas in this book in the classroom. This cooperative effort provided some useful direction for further clarification in the later drafts of the manuscript. Chris Rhodes Anderson, my wife, has been a great source of inspiration for my work as well as my life. She is truly my most favorite critic, friend, and fan. Her contributions in emotional support, in acceptance of time away from her during this work, and in helping to translate to our daughters why Dad is in his office again are immeasurable. I hope this work is worthy of her efforts, as well as those others who contributed so much to its fruition.

Credits

Excerpt on pp. 6–7 is reprinted by permission.

Excerpt on p. 16 from *Community Organizing* by George Brager and Harry Specht, Columbia University Press, 1973. Reprinted by permission.

Excerpt on pp. 23–24 from *Social Work Processes* by Beulah Roberts Compton and Burt Galaway. © 1975 by The Dorsey Press, Homewood IL. Reprinted by permission.

Excerpt on p. 43 from Andrew Weissman, "Industrial Social Services: Linkage Technology," *Social Casework,* vol. 57, no. 1, January 1976. Reprinted by permission.

Chapter 3, footnote 15, adapted from Francis P. Purcell and Harry Specht, "The House on Sixth Street," *Social Work,* vol. 10, no. 4, October 1965, pp. 69–76. Copyright 1965, National Association of Social Workers, Inc. Reprinted by permission.

Excerpt on p. 59 from William Schwartz, "The Social Worker in the Group," *The Social Welfare Forum,* 1961. Reprinted by permission.

Chapter 6, footnote 14, adapted from Blanca N. Rosenberg, "Planned Short-Term Treatment in Developmental Crises," *Social Casework,* vol. 56, no. 4, April 1975. Reprinted by permission.

Excerpts on pp. 145–146, 147 from Chris Argyris and Donald H. Schön, *Theory in Practice: Increasing Professional Effectiveness,* Jossey-Bass Publishers, 1975. Reprinted by permission.

Excerpt on pp. 161–162 from Florence Hollis, "The Psychosocial Approach to Casework," in Robert W. Roberts and Robert H. Nee, *Theories of Social Casework,* University of Chicago Press, 1971. Reprinted by permission.

Excerpt on p. 260 from Roland L. Warren, *Truth, Love, and Social Change,* Rand McNally, 1971. Reprinted by permission.

Excerpts on pp. 167–168, 271 from Alan Keith-Lucas, *Giving and Taking Help,* University of North Carolina Press, 1972. Reprinted by permission.

But no concept, ideal or otherwise, is lacking
in general significance. Generality is a trait
of all meaning. The individual case is but
a resting place for the movement of thought;
meaning is the trace in verbal behavior left
by the movement itself.

Abraham Kaplan

Truth is a verb!

Buckminster Fuller

Frameworks

1

Chapter One   The Generic Framework

Introduction

Social work is a living, dynamic, complex human activity that has been affected by the reciprocal relationship between the individual and society. It began as an expression of our interdependence as human beings in a stance of "brother's keeper." Social work has evolved into a professional function concerned with connecting the needs and resources of individuals and society in order to contribute to the growth and development of both.

Any book on social work reflects a particular view of this practice in relation to its development. This task requires the identification of the parts of social work and how they fit together into a whole: a *gestalt*. Gestalt is a German word that connotes a pattern, a configuration, a whole—the particular form of individual parts that together make up a total picture.

This book is designed for the beginning-level professional social worker involved in providing direct services. It defines the current nature of this practice in the gestalt of the generalist use of methods and the generic elements of the social work profession. Before proceeding, however, three terms need to be clarified: *generic, generalist,* and *direct service*.

In this book *generic* refers to the elements of social work that are characteristic of all social workers. Generic connotes what is common both to the social worker in the nursing home serving the aging and to the worker at a day care center primarily serving young children and their families. It also includes common elements of practice among such diverse jobs as agency administrator, policy analyst, and direct-service provider. The generics of social work provide the basic professional direction for service.

Generalist refers to the social worker's knowledge and skills for practice. Unlike the specialist, the generalist has a wide range of knowledge, methods, and skills to bring to bear in social work situations. Hence the generalist social worker is similar to the general practitioner in medicine. In social work this generalist practice has been viewed predominantly as the task of the entry level worker.

Direct service refers to specific activities in which social workers help consumers directly. These activities include individual, family, and group counseling; education; advocacy; information gathering; and referral. They also include those aspects of macromethods in which direct services are provided to community groups and organizations. *Indirect services,* on the other hand, focus on the institution of social welfare. They include such professional activities as planning, policy analysis, program development, administration, and program evaluation. Those engaged in indirect services usually do not deal directly with people in need. Rather, they focus on the institutional structure through which services are provided. Currently, specialization for indirect service requires advanced professional education, usually at the MSW level. Preparation for entry-level social work, therefore, is conceived as requiring competence for direct-service generalist practice.[1]

The definition of direct-service generalist practice and the presentation of its methods, processes, and skills are developed throughout the text. This chapter presents a structure of the parts constituting the current generic core of professional social work. Chapters 2 and 3 develop the framework as it relates to generalist practice. This gestalt serves as an organizational scheme for the remainder of the text, which presents theories the generalist can use for the mutual development of individuals, families, groups, organizations, and communities.

The Direct-Service Generalist

Trends and Issues

The concept of the direct-service generalist has evolved as the result of recent historical trends. The first was the growing awareness of unmet needs in our society in the 1960s and 1970s. Another trend has been our growing interest in person–environment interactions regarded as complex biopsychosocial transactions.[2] Despite this interest, our dominant practice theories were still "reductionistic." In other words, there was a strong tendency to view the problems in practice situations as based in the psychology of the client rather than in the biopsychosocial transactions of person and environment. Another trend was the movement of graduate curricula (and students) away from direct-service preparation in many areas of the human services. Graduates quickly moved into such indirect-service roles as supervision and administration. Schools training direct-service workers began to specialize in methods and skills, creating the Ruling Triumvirate—casework, group work, and community organization—which determined much of how practice was to be defined and established.

Along with this specialization of methods arose problems for direct services, problems such as the "law of the instrument."[3] That law defined social problems on the basis of the worker's tools (or specialized method).

(Give little Joey a hammer, put him in a room full of new furniture, and everything he sees needs to be pounded; train social workers for work with individuals alone and most problems are likely to be traced to the individual and demanding change on his or her part.) Other problems arose from the specialization of methods: the use of sick-oriented ("clinical") rather than need-oriented ("service provision") models for practice, for example, and the assumption that social work could be divided between those working for individual change and those working for social change.

These specializations, like the sorcerer's apprentice's broom, began to take over the profession. As a result, the common professional base for practice was severely disrupted. A cursory look at what social workers do and how they define themselves reveals this disunity. There have evolved specializations by field (child welfare, corrections, mental health), specialization by method (casework, family therapy, group work, community organization), specialization by practice theory (diagnostic, functional, gestalt, transactional analysis), and specialization by basic objectives (rehabilitation, correction, socialization, prevention). Picture, if you will, a social worker in a community mental health clinic who works primarily with individuals through a diagnostic casework approach toward rehabilitation; his colleagues and "patients" call him a "therapist." Then picture a social worker in a youth service agency who works primarily with groups through a functional group work approach toward socialization; her colleagues and "members" call her a "recreation director." Now imagine a dialogue between these two on the definition of a social worker! By identifying with their specialization, they may have abandoned a common base from which they can discuss the generic components of social work. Nevertheless, there is in fact a professional identity that coexists with the trend toward specialization in social work.

These recent trends were not without critics from within the profession, however. Many still sought the roots of social work in the earlier tradition of seeking professional unity.[4] Others questioned the illogic behind methods specialization and the split between work for individuals or work for social change.[5] Still others questioned the validity of these trends in relation to minority groups.[6] The challenge progressed beyond the "ain't it awful" concern with institutionalized discrimination (while providing predominately casework services) to direct-service work with both systems and individuals.[7]

Concept of Generalist

A widely used definition of the BSW as a generalist evolved in reaction to these trends and their failure to respond to direct-service needs. The Southern Regional Education Board defines the generalist like this:

> [The generalist] is the person who plays whatever roles and does whatever activities are necessary for the person or family when the person or

family needs them. His concern is the person in need—not specific tasks or techniques or professional prerogatives. He is an aide to the individual or family—not an aide to an agency or to a profession.[8]

There are three assumptions in this notion of generalist social work: (1) the generalist is often the first social worker to see people as they enter the social welfare system; (2) the worker must therefore be competent to assess the needs of consumers and to identify their stress points and problems; and (3) the worker must draw on a variety of methods and skills to serve consumers.

The activities of the direct-service social worker are indeed generalist in nature. The job requires a person who possesses not only a basic knowledge of social work but also the methods and skills required for work with individual, family, group, organization, and community. In this sense, the direct-service social worker is both generic and generalist. For instance, the BSW social worker shares a common base of practice with the MSW practitioner. There are no fundamental differences between the two—the MSW is simply a BSW plus. (The plus is more in-depth knowledge and skills related to particular practice methods and/or fields or to becoming an "advanced generalist.")

Essentially, the BSW generalist has knowledge, values, methods, and skills that are generic to the various fields of practice and upon which advanced training and specialization can build. Consider, for example, this BSW student's description of her field experience:

> As a worker at a children's service, it has been my duty, as I see it, to help strengthen families so that children can stay in their own home and so that that home can be a good home. There are many programs designed to help families, but often families with the need haven't connected with the agency that provides the service. That is where I help.
>
> When I made my first visit to the Korean woman with three small preschoolers, the purpose of my visit was to inform a suspected "abused" wife of her legal rights and to tell her where she and her children could get help if they were in danger. Actually, after we talked for some time it became clear that wife abuse wasn't really a problem she experienced. We talked until we narrowed our discussion to what was really bothering her now. She wanted me to help her to get an abortion and a tubal ligation. Sometimes her husband wanted a baby and sometimes he didn't, but she definitely didn't.
>
> In addition to the problem that was her main concern at present, I could see that her infant set of twins had a problem of their own that needed prompt attention. They had crossed eyes. When I contacted the State Health Nurse, I asked her to talk about the abortion, but I had also asked her to explain the Well-Baby Clinic to the family. This family could obviously benefit from an easing in their medical costs and the children could benefit from additional medical attention. They too were interested in good care for their children as long as I could provide the transportation because the father had to work.
>
> With my intervention, the situation for this family has improved in several ways. I have taken the mother and children to the Well-Baby Clinic for physical and psychological screening. They each had a shot.

After the children were seen, the State Health Department contacted the Pennsylvania Association for the Prevention of Blindness who arranged an appointment with an eye specialist for the twins. The twins have been to the specialist three times now. They each have an eye patch and may require an operation.

After an initial screening visit to Johns Hopkins Hospital, the parents decided against the abortion because she was four and one-half months pregnant. The abortion would have been saline and expensive. Since then I have taken maternity clothes to her. Now they are planning to have a tubal a few days after the delivery. The mother has been to the obstetrician and is fine. Now that a decision has been made, the mother seems to be somewhat calmer with her children.

I will continue to help this family with transportation to Well-Baby Clinic appointments. When I leave I will recommend that a fifth agency become involved with this family. I would like to see the oldest child go to Adams County Day Care Center, if the parents are interested. His language development is poor. He gets no chance to play with children his own age and since his mother will have four children who are all so young, she and the children would benefit from anything that could lessen her tension.

With this family, I have mainly used an approach which articulated the consumer's needs to others in the service network (my agency, other agencies), using primarily methods of consultation and brokerage. This family has received aid for a short time which will affect their lives. All the children will hopefully be healthier citizens for having been checked regularly at the Well-Baby Clinic. The twins are being helped immeasurably. Had they remained cross-eyed they might have lost their vision. They might also have been harassed by their peers. Certainly, they may have had a concept of themselves as unattractive.

The casework service that the mother and father received helped them to stop bickering about the abortion and instead come to a joint decision. Also the mother was better able to use prenatal care. With my help this family is learning to exercise some control over their lives.

The Framework for Direct Service Practice

The aspects of social work involved in the preceding example and explicated throughout this book are summarized in Figure 1.1. The generic base of practice—that is, the common elements—consists of the *purpose, function, focus, objectives,* and *values* of social work. These five elements are generic in that they are essentially the same wherever social work is practiced: They are the professional core. *Knowledge, methods,* and *skills* constitute the changing aspects of practice. Figure 1.1 relates these elements to direct-service generalist practice in terms of *assessment, goals, methods and processes,* and *skills.* The remainder of this chapter elaborates the generic base.[9] The next chapter examines the current parts of direct-service generalist practice.

As Figure 1.1 indicates, the activities of direct-service generalist practice emanate from the common base of social work: the specific configuration of purpose, function, focus, objectives, values, and aspects of knowledge, methods, and skills. Harriet Bartlett has defined social work

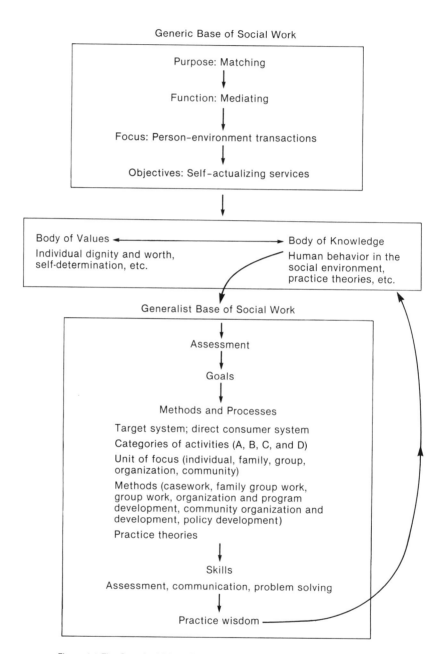

Figure 1.1 The Gestalt of Direct Service Practice

by means of these common components: "Social work practice is recognized by a constellation of value, purpose, knowledge and interventive techniques. Some social work practice shows more extensive use of one or the other components, but it is a social work practice only when they are all present to some degree."[10]

The Generic Base of Social Work

This generic base of social work defines the profession and sets the direction for practice. The base is constant whatever the setting or service. Social work is based on this professional direction, not on a particular agency's prescription for services. Surgeons perform their operations regardless of the hospital. Lawyers carry out their professional obligation regardless of the courtroom setting. The social worker's basic service is the service of the profession, regardless of the employing agency.

Certainly agencies define the consumer and provide the basic resources. But agencies should not dictate the professional function of the social worker. Agencies, and the social worker's rank within them, do affect the worker's activities, of course. The point is that the basic professional stance does not change. Only certain activities for fulfilling professional purpose and function may be altered. Thus the generic base for social work establishes the professional direction and assignment for the social worker, whether that worker is a direct-service generalist or a specialist. In this sense, the generic base is the core of social work, which is continually deepened in professional learning and development.

The Purpose of Social Work

What, then, is the underlying *purpose* of social work wherever it is found? For what ultimate reason does social work exist? As William Gordon suggests, social work is the profession that matches the needs and resources of individuals with the needs and resources of society in order to promote the development of both.[11] Through matching needs and resources, transactions between individuals and their environment can evolve toward greater interdependence and mutual aid—that is, toward greater synergy. *Synergy* describes an individual–society transaction that simultaneously influences the well-being of both.[12] When the matching is actualized in social work, individual developmental needs are met in a way that contributes to the development of the family, group, organization, and community to which they belong.

This synergistic matching directs the practice of *all* professional social workers, including those in direct-service positions. The recent curriculum study of the BSW worker has further specified this general purpose in the following terms:

> Social work is concerned . . . with the interactions between people and the institutions of society that affect the ability of people to accomplish

life tasks, realize aspirations and values, and alleviate distress. These interactions between people and social institutions occur within the context of the larger social good. Therefore, three major purposes of social work may be identified:

1. To enhance the problem-solving, coping, and developmental capacities of people.

2. To promote the effective and humane operation of the systems that provide people with resources and services.

3. To link people with systems that provide them with resources, services, and opportunities. [13]

Thus social work attempts to bring about the synergistic matching of healthy environments and healthy people. And in so doing it creates an institutional and cultural context in which every member has opportunities for individual growth—regardless of class, race, ethnic background, sex, sexual preference, or physical or mental handicap. In short, we build the healthy systems on which we depend for our own growth and development.

The concept of matching is the central perspective from which to view all practice situations. For instance, what are the basic points of matching (and mismatching) of individual and societal developmental needs and resources in the following situation?

Mrs. Woods is a 46-year-old hospitalized terminal cancer patient. The medical staff has withheld from her their prognosis of death within a month, but the family (her husband and three adolescent children) have been told. Her physician has referred her to the hospital social services because Mrs. Woods has been complaining about her family's recent tendency to exclude her from their activities and she has increasingly displayed both angry outbursts toward the nurses and depression when with doctors and members of her family.

Suppose we take a closer look at Mrs. Woods and her situation. Mrs. Woods' basic needs for self-respect, self-determination, and a sense of belonging to the family, hospital, and community, even in the face of death, do not match with the hospital system's needs to protect the patient from unnecessary emotional pain and to follow the doctor's prescription in any decision regarding the patient. Mrs. Woods' needs also mismatch with her family's need to grieve openly for the loss of a member and to use its resources, including Mrs. Woods, for resolving the crisis of death for itself. The responsibility they now share with the physician is the secret prognosis.

Mrs. Woods' need for self-respect, self-determination, a sense of belonging, and dying with dignity do match, however, with the hospital's need to evolve a system of services that contributes to patients' health rather than places more obstructing demands on them. For Mrs. Woods and other terminally ill patients, indeed for all patients, the exchanges between patient and hospital staff are a meshing of the patient's and family's needs for physical well-being with the availability of hospital resources that contribute to this goal. Beyond this exchange is the ultimate need of society to ensure the health of all of its members all of the time, including its dying.

The current resources in Mrs. Woods, in her family, in other patients, in the hospital, and in our society are not being mobilized. That is, they are not directed toward meeting Mrs. Woods' or her social systems' developmental needs so long as information is withheld from patients to protect them from unnecessary emotional pain. To contribute to more mutually beneficial matching, the social worker needs to assume a number of activities that can change the quality of these transactions between people and their environment. In this situation, the social worker would concentrate on influencing the doctor's protective stance, the hospital's policy regarding the patient's right to know, the family's participaton in facing the loss of one of its members, and Mrs. Woods' desire and right to choose how to live and how to die.[14]

The Function of Social Work

The specific function of social work is *mediation.* This function denotes what social workers *do* to achieve their ultimate purpose. Schwartz argues that the primary professional task is to

> *mediate* the process through which the individual and society reach out for each other through a mutual need for self-fulfillment . . . worked out in the specific context of those agencies which are designed to bring together individual needs and social resources—the person's urge to belong to society as a full and productive member and society's ability to provide certain specific means for integrating its people and enriching their social contribution.[15]

This mediating function in social work is hard to define with precision. We have less trouble seeing the medical doctor's function in healing the body—mediating between the physical organism and the environmental influences that contribute to ill-health (unless, of course, the doctor is a psychiatrist and deals with the complex world of mental health and illness). Similarly, we can see the lawyer's function—mediating between individuals and legal institutions. But the word *social* has none of the precision of *medical* and *legal.* Therefore, it is not enough to say that social work treats social problems. Virtually every life problem of every individual in this modern world is, in reality, a social problem in one sense or another. The "social" in social work is more precisely *psychosocial:* the intricate processes between people and their social systems. Two concepts significant for understanding this relationship are *autonomy* and *interdependence.*

The notion of individual autonomy is based on the belief that each individual is unique, separate, alone, and therefore responsible for his or her own existential choices. Klein has applied this concept to social group work: "Responsibility must go along with choice so that . . . members are confronted with the ultimate in freedom: that each man is responsible to himself and that he cannot escape his responsibility by projecting unto others."[16] Individual autonomy therefore refers to the "I-ness" of experience and to all experiential phenomena—self-awareness, self-responsibility, and self-actualization.

While existentially we are separate and autonomous, we are also connected. Donne's classic "No man is an island . . ." remains a profound statement of this human connectedness. We are all interdependent because autonomy is not sufficient for human survival and growth. The satisfaction of our physiological, material, social, and emotional needs requires mutual aid relationships with others. Krill places this concept in the existential perspective:

> To understand existentialism it is essential to have a feel for its conception of man's most fundamental need that distinguishes him as a human being. This may be described as the hunger for unity, belonging, [and] externalization of personality by somehow overcoming the separateness he feels between parts of himself, as well as between himself, others, and the universe as a whole.[17]

The "social" in social work, therefore, involves the concepts of autonomy and interdependence in the relationship between individuals and others in their social system. In our complex society, especially as currently organized with great and unequally distributed power, the function of social work is to mediate the transactions between people and the various systems through which they carry on their relationships with society: the family, the peer group, the social agency, the neighborhood, the school, the job. The mediating function implies not the creation of harmony but the creation of *interaction*. This interaction is based on a sense of matching and draws on the often forgotten stake of people in their own institutions and the stake of the societal institutions in the people they are meant to serve.

This concept of function, based on the premise of interdependence between society and its members, means that we serve not "clients" but "members" in the reciprocal drama of individual and societal development. The communal nature of social work was described by Bertha Reynolds over three decades ago:

> Help must be connected with increase . . . of self-respect, and it must imply the possibility of a reciprocal relationship of sharing within a group to which both giver and receiver belong. . . . It is not hard to take help in a circle in which one feels sure of belonging. It hurts to feel doubtful of being able to repay at all, and by that means to be again in full status as a giving, as well as receiving, member of the group.[18]

This idea of interdependence, or mutual aid, is stated metaphorically in the Hasidic story of the Rabbi who had a conversation with the Lord about heaven and hell:

"I will show you Hell," said the Lord and led the Rabbi into a room in the middle of which was a very big, round table. The people sitting at it were famished and desperate. In the middle of the table there was a large pot of stew, enough and more for everyone. The smell of the stew was delicious and made the Rabbi's mouth water. The people round the table were holding spoons with very long handles. Each one found that it was just possible to reach the pot to take a spoonful of stew, but because the handle of this spoon was longer than a man's arm, he could not get the food back into his mouth. The Rabbi saw that their suffering was terrible.

"Now I will show you Heaven," said the Lord, and they went into another room, exactly the same as the first. There was the same big, round table and the same pot of stew. The people, as before, were equipped with the same long-handled spoons—but they were well nourished and plump, laughing and talking. At first, the Rabbi could not understand.

"It is simple, but it requires a certain skill," said the Lord. "You see, they have learned to feed each other."

In the case of Mrs. Woods noted earlier, where is the mutual feeding? What specific needs, resources, and connections are involved in this mediation? And how can this mediation take place with full respect for Mrs. Woods' individual dignity, worth, and rights to services in a manner that increases her sense of social participation? These are the basic questions to be addressed in every practice situation.

The Focus of Social Work

If the *purpose* of social work is to match individual and environmental needs and resources through the *function* of mediation, the *focus* of social work is on the *person–environment transaction*. This transaction is the point of interdependence where the social worker directs activities in specific situations. Gordon notes that "the central social work focus is placed at the interface between . . . person and environment—at the point where there is or is not matching with all its good and bad consequences for person and environment."[19]

This focus identifies social work as a human relations profession. The phrase *human relations* explains what social work has been doing since its inception, and the profession's persistent objective has been the enhancement of social functioning. Social workers promote this enhancement daily in activities that help people cope with the interpersonal tasks involved in their most common areas of social living: family, school, work, play, neighborhood, community. As Tropp has noted:

> It is in essence the purpose of enhancement and function of helping-to-cope, which, when applied to the area of human relations, converts it into a specific professional service. To claim more than that (as in simply human services) is to include all kinds of work with people. (The taxicab driver does provide a human service, but not one that is intended to help in human relations.)[20]

Social work's primary focus is on human transactions; its basic orientation is toward the growth and development of the people involved. The social worker is concerned with the needs of *all* people—not only the direct-service consumer and family but also the consumer's friends, enemies, peers, boss, mayor, even the service providers. Even in interpersonal conflicts, this transactional focus directs the worker toward mediation that can contribute to the self-respect of all parties involved. A social worker cannot treat colleagues and supervisors as objects devoid of dignity and still respond authentically to service consumers with this basic respect.

Now we can begin to identify the basic human systems in the person/problem/situation/agency context in which Mrs. Woods and the social worker operate. There is the self-system of Mrs. Woods with its developmental needs and tasks. There is also the self-system of the social worker. And there is the interactional system of their relationship, which meshes with the organizational system of the agency. Also involved to various extents are family systems, peer group systems, neighborhood systems, cultural systems, community systems, economic systems, and sociopolitical systems. All these systems are struggling toward both survival and growth. All are involved in transactions with each other as well as with the self-system of Mrs. Woods. And all are potential targets for social work that mediates human relations processes in behalf of both the individual and society.

The Objectives of Social Work

The ultimate objective of social work can be stated simply: to provide services that promote the self-actualizing development of human relations. *Self-actualizing development* refers to the basic process of any life form to become in actuality what it is in potential. In the development of human relations, it is the process of becoming more fully one's self and therefore more fully respecting the selves of others. This actualization includes both personally experienced growth and the development of social skills. It requires the opportunity to experience both one's uniqueness and one's shared humanness.

Social work's concern with individual and social self-actualization manifests itself in the provision of social services. Social services are the means through which social work as a profession translates its purpose and function into a contribution to the social welfare of others. When the agency's resources and the consumer's needs are matched in service delivery, the act transcends the personal relationship between worker and consumer. The service becomes a "cause in function." It simultaneously meets individual needs and contributes to the general fund of resources for increasingly healthful social systems. As a result, people in the general society are better able to meet each other's needs in their daily human relationships. In the words of Harold Lewis:

Every helping act is both a personal and social act, and carries in its elements the core of what we recognized to be cause—i.e., thus Porter Lee's definitions—"a movement directed toward the elimination of an entrenched evil," and function—"an organized effort incorporated into the machinery of community life in the discharge of which the acquiescence, at least, and ultimately the support of the entire community is assumed."[21]

It is toward the provision of these services that social work's purpose, function, and focus direct us and for which our methods and processes are designed.

Methods and Processes

The provision of service (this cause in function) requires methodological skills for influencing individual, family, group, organization, and community processes and goals. The ultimate self-actualizing objective is translated into goals for individuals through the service structure and function, the assessment of their needs, and the use of generic and specific processes derived from practice theories. This work requires a value for and knowledge of human processes. *Process* is generally defined as a recurrent sequence of changes in a particular direction. In practice, social workers must understand process if they are to comprehend transactions and the methods for influencing them. The individuals, families, groups, organizations, and communities served are all involved in developmental processes. Therefore, they embody uniqueness, integrity, wholeness—and also a potential for self-actualization that can be furthered by the social work process itself.

In process-based practice, social work is not the study of a static object—individual, family, group—that can lead to the application of specific techniques to achieve the worker's own preconceived ends. Rather, it is a method for entering into a relationship with others in which there is a mutual and continuous sense of discovery as both parties are changing in the course of the social work process. The intent of the methods is to maximize opportunity for the other (individual, group, community) to achieve its own actualization. Social workers in process-based practice cannot control those being served; they can only handle their own role in the social work process.[22] Therefore, social work is based on the principle established by Heraclitus centuries ago: One cannot step in the same river twice. By necessity, then, social work demands both the rigor of science and the creativity of art. It requires both a general knowledge of and an openness to the experience of the ever-changing processes.

Social work methods should be selected on the basis of the particular processes (individual, group, community) to be influenced in order to achieve the consumer's developmental goals. They must be effective in accomplishing these goals and in influencing the targets appropriate for goal achievement. The use of the generic base and a generalist approach are most appropriate for the direct-service social worker wishing to influence self-actualization.

George Brager and Harry Specht have summarized the relation of methods and processes to each other and to social work in their study of community organizing. In their words:

> Practice consists of method and process, that is what workers do (method) in response to particular behaviors (process). Process is a term which connotes naturalness, an unfolding. . . . Method, on the other hand, implies a set of artificially created procedures. The terms go together because conceptions of processes are necessary to design methods to intervene in them—to encourage, guide, stop, or redirect the process. . . .
> *Process* [in social work practice] is not a natural process, however, but a *social* one. Social processes are intellectual projections of how people are expected to behave in response to problems viewed within a specific framework of values and goals. . . . In effect, then, the description of a social process is a series of questions or hypotheses about how people will behave.
> *Method* is also a series of questions and hypotheses about behavior but it refers to the behavior of one particular actor, that is, the worker. Essentially these are hypotheses that say, "If the worker behaves in a prescribed manner, he will affect the process in a particular way." Thus the role behavior of the worker is the methodology of [social work] practice.[23]

Therefore, the most important knowledge and values for direct service are those that inform social work methods and processes. These include the beliefs and hypotheses (basic theories) that affect our perspective on human development in the social environment and also our means (practice theories) of influencing the transactions between people and their social systems.

Social Work Values

Basic Values

The fundamental value of this profession is the belief in the intrinsic worth, dignity, and importance of the individual human being. Regardless of ability to perform in relation to sociocultural norms and standards, each person is the most valuable of beings, worthy of infinite respect and care, and holding certain inalienable rights as a result of this dignity and worth. No further justification for this dignity is needed than the simple fact of one's human life. The important values emanating from this basic principle are *individualization* (respect for uniqueness), *acceptance* (respect for individual worth and difference), and *self-determination* (respect for individual choice).

Value Dilemmas

At the very least, the values that inform social work require a certain political and ethical climate: The society at large must respect these individual rights, and members must be open to the synergistic balance of individual rights with the rights of others. The potential for this openness lies in the autonomous and interdependent nature of human beings. Yet this mutual growth is more ideal than real for our society and others. Value dilemmas abound. Individual rights and community rights often conflict.

Where, for instance, does the right to public financial assistance end and the right to reasonable taxation begin? Where does the right of a mother who abuses her child end and the right of the child to physical security begin? How can one be an agent for a sociocultural system that institutionalizes discrimination toward certain powerless groups and minorities, such as the poor and the black, or categorizes certain classes of people as worthy or unworthy of opportunities or services? Can one support the values of individual dignity, acceptance, and self-determination for *both* the abusing mother and the abused child? How can self-determination operate where alternatives are unavailable or one is virtually unable to choose, as in the situation of the abused child, the severely mentally retarded, or the hard-core criminal?

Social work values instruct goals and means in the ideal. They reflect faith in the inherent capacity of individuals and their institutions to evolve fully into their autonomous yet interdependent nature. Even when few alternative courses of action are available (as in prisons or mental hospitals), the principle of self-determination demands that social work extend reasonable alternatives and enable the person to exercise choice. Respect for both the individual and the system in the worker's activity is essential— one without the other is insufficient. In other words, we must assume that society needs self-actualizing people in order to achieve its own self-actualization.

Values in Practice

While these value dilemmas will always be a painful paradox for social workers in an evolving pluralistic and democratic society, our professional values constitute a strong base for determining the knowledge, goals, and methods demanded in practice. The variety of methods in generalist social work are the basic means to these ends. Embodied in *all* goals and methods are the ultimate objective of self-actualizing human relations and the principles of individual dignity and worth, individualization, acceptance, and self-determination. Social work values, like all values in the final perspective, are based on faith—faith that human beings, when free to develop and free to choose, will choose not only what is in their own best self-actualizing interest but what contributes to the self-actualizing opportunities of others.

This faith is a cardinal conviction for practice. It is matched only by social work's faith in the scientific method for furthering the competence of the profession. The scientific attitude requires of the social worker certain theoretical and empirical skills. Among these are a knowledge of (yet skepticism toward) current practice theories and procedures, an open-mindedness to new concepts, disciplined thought, and an ability to evaluate events, concepts, hypotheses and practice theories in relation to the self as participant observer and in the evaluation of effects.

These beliefs regarding the nature of people, the purpose of social work, and the main tasks of practice are more than armchair philosophy. Indeed, one series of research studies suggests that it is these very beliefs that separate effective from ineffective helpers.[24] In these studies effective helpers held the following beliefs about people, themselves, their purposes, and their tasks:

1. People do have a capacity to deal with their problems; their actions are essentially well-intentioned rather than evil-intentioned; they possess the utmost of dignity and integrity; they are creative and dynamic rather than passive or inert participants in psychosocial events; their behavior is trustworthy, dependable, and purposeful, rather than capricious or unpredictable; and they are potentially fulfilling and enhancing to themselves rather than impeding or threatening.

2. Helpers are identified with the human condition rather than feeling apart from others and humanity in general; they are adequate to the helping task at hand; they see themselves as essentially trustworthy, dependable, or reliable and as having the potential for coping with events; and they see themselves as possessing dignity and integrity and worthy of respect, not as persons of little consequence who can be overlooked, discounted, and whose dignity and integrity do not matter.

3. The purpose of help is freeing (assisting, releasing, and facilitating) rather than controlling (manipulating, coercing, blocking, or inhibiting); the concern is with broad issues with extensive implications for the future rather than narrow issues with immediate and specific implications; the helping situation requires personal involvement and self-revelation rather than self-concealing aloofness from personal interaction; the focus is on furthering process rather than achieving preconceived goals; and the orientation is toward assisting others altruistically rather than toward narcissistic attendance to their own personal goals.

4. The tasks carried out are directed more to people and their needs than to things (objects, events, rules), and people are approached from a subjective perspective that emphasizes perceptions of reality rather than objective facts of reality.

As these studies and this book suggest, effective practice in the helping professions is a question of the helper's use of self: the particular way the helper is able to combine values, knowledge, and understanding with unique ways of putting this self into operation in the instantaneous responses in practice. Effectiveness is most often the fulfillment of the consumer's goals, the worker's goals, and society's goals, even in the inevitable reality of conflicting values.[25]

Values and Knowledge

As active mediators in the process of promoting synergistic social welfare, social workers apply their knowledge in developing self-actualization. Even though one's information is never complete, the worker must press on, using new sources of knowledge and synthesizing new information. When the information is in doubt, assumptions and values shape the worker's activities. The assumption that each individual has unique and inherent potential guides us in identifying the specific ways to further that person's self-actualization and social participation. Whatever methods are chosen, they must be consistent with our assumption about human nature and our commitment to synergistic self-actualization.

Social work as a career means a constant commitment to effective service. We need to use current theoretical, empirical, and value-based explanations for the phenomena we encounter. Just as our knowledge will change, so will the systems and processes we serve. What must remain steady is a commitment to individual dignity and worth, to self-determination toward self-actualization, and to one's responsibility to be as effective as possible in helping consumers reach their own developmental objectives. After all, social workers must be able to live with themselves.

Summary

Beginning-level instruction in social work is both generic and generalist. This concept of practice has been influenced by changes in the relationship between individual and society, by the failure of specialization to meet social needs during the 1960s and 1970s, and by the development of sophisticated theoretical models for understanding person–environment transactional processes. The *generic aspect* of this base is the combination of purpose, function, focus, objectives, values, and knowledge. These form the permanent basis for social work wherever the profession is practiced, whatever the social worker's position, whatever methods are used.

The *purpose* of social work is the matching, or preventing the mismatching, of individual and societal needs and resources for the autonomous and interdependent development of both people and their social systems. The *function* is the mediating of the transactional processes through which individuals and society connect in their interdependent growth. This mediating deals especially with the human relations needs of a community and its members. The *focus* of social work is on the person–environment transaction, or the point at which people are or are not resources for mutual aid in their current social systems.

The *process* of person–environment transactions determines the specific objectives of practice. The ultimate objective is to provide services that promote the self-actualizing development of human relations. These services must be process-oriented. Goals, targets, and methods (respectively) evolve from the contribution of the helping process to the self-actualizing needs, goals, and resources in individual, family, group, organization, and community processes.

All social work is based on the unwavering belief in individual dignity and worth and the concomitant principles of individualization, acceptance, and self-determination. These values enforce the commitment to service rather than to a particular political or theological ideology. They direct foremost attention to the individual served and to an environment conducive to the freedom, opportunity, and responsibility for fulfilling one's potential for growth and contributing to the growth of others.

This configuration forms the generic base for direct-service generalist practice. Generalists need a variety of methods and practice theories (and a scientific basis for testing them) for achieving their goals. Also required are the unique and generic principles, concepts, and skills to use a generalist methodology. The next chapter presents a framework for organizing the methods and skills for generalist social work. It represents social work's current arsenal in the battle against individual deprivation and social injustice—the major obstacles to the progressive development of both individuals and society.

Suggested Learning Experiences

1. Consider how the classroom for this course could be influenced in a way that matches students' learning needs and resources with the instructor's teaching needs and resources in order to maximize the learning of every student in the class. Be specific about what would be required by you, other students, and the instructor to create this mutual aid system in the classroom. Come to your next class prepared to discuss your ideas and implement them.

2. Consider the teacher of this course as a person who functions as a mediator. What would he or she be mediating *between?* Make a list. Come to class prepared to give specific suggestions how the teacher can mediate the learning situation.

3. State your basic beliefs about (a) people and what they bring to social work service; (b) yourself and what you can offer to others; (c) the

ultimate purposes of social work; and (d) how help is achieved in social work practice. Compare your beliefs to those stated on page 18.

Suggested Case Studies and Readings

Bartlett, Harriet. "Interventive Action." In *The Common Base of Social Work Practice.* New York: National Association of Social Workers, 1970.

This entire book is the best source available on work toward conceptualizing the generics of social work practice. Bartlett's chapter presents particularly illustrative material on basic knowledge and values and how they are used in both microlevel and macrolevel social work.

Encyclopedia of Social Work. Vol. 17 (2). New York: National Association of Social Workers, 1977. Pages 931–984.

This source includes issues and practice implications for work with American Indians, Asian Americans, blacks, Chicanos, Puerto Ricans, and white ethnics.

Heymann, David. "A Function for the Social Worker in the Antipoverty Program." In *The Practice of Group Work,* ed. William Schwartz and Serapio R. Zalba. New York: Columbia University Press, 1971.

This work shows the mediating function of social work in action, as well as other ideas presented in this chapter.

Shapiro, Joan. "Group Work with Urban Rejects in a Slum Hotel." In *The Practice of Group Work,* ed. William Schwartz and Serapio R. Zalba. New York: Columbia University Press, 1971.

This is an excellent example of the establishment of a social work service through the worker's professional direction for use of self. It exemplifies not only the generics of social work in practice but also the personal risks and value conflicts inherent in the profession.

Chapter Two   The Generalist Framework (Microlevel)

Introduction

It is methods that distinguish the "generalist" from the "generic."
While generic connotes the core of all social work, generalist implies a
repertoire of methods for achieving social work's purpose, function, and
objectives in practice. These methods are the application of practice theories selected on the basis of their relevancy and usefulness to the self-
actualizing processes of the service consumer.

Method may be defined as systematic procedures or processes for
obtaining a goal. The systematic nature of a profession's activities is
grounded in its science. Indeed, the ultimate test of any science for any
people-serving profession is its ability to inform methods. Social work as
a profession grew from its ability to translate behavioral and social science
propositions into recognizable and teachable methods for practice. The
social work methods evolved into sets of procedures and skills related to
particular practice theories and to the size of the client system—individual,
group, or community. Thus social work declared its professional identity
primarily through its three service methods: casework, group work, and
community organization.

This triumvirate of methods spurred both professional competence
and professional incompetence when viewed in the light of our basic
commitment to the progressive development of both individuals and society. Certainly the debates within the profession have been far-ranging.
Essentially, however, there is general recognition that the specialization
required to develop these methods has outlived its usefulness for the
direct-service practitioner and at times has subverted our activities away
from meeting the service consumer's needs to achieving narrow methodological goals. Beulah Roberts Compton and Burt Galaway have commented on the issue of methods specialization in social work:

> This has led to training specialists in each of these methods with very
> limited effort to prepare people to assess a person-situation interaction
> except through the colored glasses of their particular methodological
> orientation. Thus community organizers see problems in terms of com-
> munity change, group workers in terms of working with groups, and

caseworkers in terms of individual orientation. Abraham Kaplan noted this same problem in terms of research methodology and formulated a law of the instrument. . . . The conceptualization of social work activities in terms of casework, group work, and community organization leads to a tendency to define problems for intervention in terms of the worker's particular methodological frame of reference rather than a careful assessment of the person-situation interaction.[1]

This book is not an argument against specialization in social work. The nature of social work's professional concerns and the skills required to carry out our function do require a division of labor. A social worker cannot be at a congressional subcommittee hearing on child abuse and simultaneously be present when the school principal refers an abused child to the local service agency. This book is, however, an argument for the direct-service worker's specialization in being a generalist in the organization of activities and methods. For this practice we must organize social work activities and planning in a way that focuses clearly on the mediation of self-actualizing consumer–environment transactions. Given the generalist approach, the law of the instrument can be repealed.

Thus a model is needed to organize the activities of the direct-service generalist in respect to a repertoire and use of methods. This model's orientation comes from the recognition that there are two types of skill involved in social work: skills in knowing what method to use and skills in the actual use of method.

The remainder of this chapter presents a general framework for the selection of methods in direct-service practice and a description of micro-level methods—that is, work with individuals, families and small groups. The framework is organized at the most general level around Allen Pincus' and Anne Minahan's concepts of *client system* (here called "direct consumer") and *target system*.[2] They define client system as "people who sanction or ask for the . . . services, who are expected beneficiaries of service, and who have a working agreement or contract." Target system refers to the "people who need to be changed to accomplish the goals." Figure 2.1, a basic framework for organizing the social worker's activities, is related to the work of Ruth Middleman and Gale Goldberg,[3] who note the importance of indirect-service activities for the direct-service worker. The framework specifies that social work activities include:

1. Work with the individual direct consumer in his or her own behalf (Quadrant A)

2. Work with the individual direct consumer and other direct consumers together in their own behalf (Quadrant B)

3. Work with individual indirect consumers in the service network in behalf of the individual direct consumer (Quadrant C)

4. Work with organizational or community groups of indirect consumers in behalf of several direct consumers (Quadrant D)

Direct consumers are those who are using social services. Indirect consumers are those who benefit indirectly from the services. This chapter focuses on Quadrants A and B—microlevel methods. The next chapter looks at Quadrants C and D—macrolevel methods.

Quadrant A and B Methods (Microlevel)

Quadrant A Methods

In providing direct services, the generalist's work usually begins in Quadrant A, with the expressed needs of an individual consumer of services, and extends to Quadrants B, C, and D according to the demands of the consumer's task. The consumer's task is the translation of a problem into a developmental goal. This task requires the individual to engage in a working relationship with the agency in his or her own behalf. The focus is on the individual; the basic mediating method at this point is some form of casework.

Direct Consumer System

	Individual	Others
	A (Work with individual in own behalf)	B (Work with individual and others in their own behalf)
Individual (microlevel methods)	Unit of focus The individual (individual development) Method Casework	Unit of focus Interactional systems (family and group development) Methods Group work Family group work
Target System	C (Work with others in behalf of individual)	D (Work with others in behalf of individual and others)
Others (macrolevel methods)	Unit of focus Service networks (organizational development) Methods Organizational development Consultation Brokerage (linkage) Advocacy (case)	Unit of focus Classes of people (community development) Methods Organizational development Community organization and development Policy or program development Advocacy (cause)

Figure 2.1 Method Selection in Generalist Practice

Casework has been defined as "a method for engaging a client through a relationship process, essentially one to one, in the use of a social service toward his own and the general social welfare."[4] Casework methods are used most effectively to determine needs and problems in the initial engaging of the applicant to service.

Helen Harris Perlman has specified operations for the social worker using the casework method for problem determination.[5] She notes that direct-service social work begins with a person/problem/place configuration: A person with a problem comes (is brought, or somehow connected) to a place as an applicant to meet with a social worker who may or may not be able to provide the needed service. Problem identification is therefore the first step in the casework process. What is it that hurts, threatens, or frustrates the person? What does the person want to change, or have changed, or get rid of? The applicant's perception of the problem is explored in some detail. This interview serves both the applicant's and the worker's clear perception of the *objective reality* of the problem.

Suppose a child welfare worker visits Mrs. Houser in response to a neighbor's complaint that she has been leaving her two preschool children, Jane, 18 months, and Joe, 2½ years, locked in the apartment alone for half a day or more at a time. On the first visit Mrs. Houser reluctantly lets the worker in, explains that her husband is away, that the children are all right, and that she does not believe she needs a social worker. When the worker remarks that she knows Mrs. Houser is new to the community, Mrs. Houser begins to describe her situation. She moved to the city from Marysville, in the northern part of the state, only three months ago. She is now without friends. Her husband has returned "up north" to log and periodically sends her money on which she manages adequately. She feels unable to go out on the street with the two children and sometimes simply wishes to get away from them. She does not know what else to do. When asked about her knowledge of the neighborhood day care center, she responds that she knows nothing about the neighborhood or the community. Moreover, she expects to be rejected if she looks into such places.

The thread that weaves in and out of this identification and clarification of the problem, sometimes in the forefront of discussion and sometimes in the background, is the expression of the subjective and highly individualized emotional reactions to the problem. This expression releases some of the feelings that may be a central part of the problem. Moreover, it establishes the relationship as a bond between worker and applicant and clarifies the mutual perception of the person's subjective involvement in the problem—the person's experience of the objective reality.

Although the initial problem has been identified and clarified, there is another problem to deal with: the problem of being an applicant. What kind of service is available and under what conditions will it be delivered?

The applicant's first act of self-determination, then, is the choice that this worker in this place will offer the best available means by which to cope with the problem. This is the point at which the person moves from the role of applicant to that of service consumer—the point of contract.

When Mrs. Houser failed to keep an appointment to visit the day care center, the worker began to work with her toward overcoming her fears of using community resources. On the very next visit, Mrs. Houser spontaneously told about the small Indian village in which she had grown up until age ten, the series of foster home placements that followed, and the group home for adolescents she lived in until she married at sixteen. The worker listened sensitively and suggested that these earlier experiences may make it especially difficult to be a single parent with personal needs that young children cannot fulfill. Mrs. Houser elaborated on this topic in terms of her fears and loneliness. Again the worker mentioned the day care center for her son Joe, adding that the center also had a group of mothers who used the center's sewing machine. Within two weeks after this contact, Joe was on the center's waiting list and Mrs. Houser had joined the group of mothers. She informed the worker, "I do not need to talk with you so often. I have some girlfriends now."

This determination of the problem through the casework process establishes the emotional connection between consumer and worker. The ongoing work is built on this relationship. As with the blacksmith, it is the heat that forges the work. While the iron is hot, however, somebody must shape the horseshoe. In this process, the horseshoe is being shaped; the work is beginning. With Mrs. Houser there is a clarified perception of the problem and a better understanding of her place in the situation. There is the expectation of her strengths in the decision to use the service and her responsibility to define needs. There is the provision of services for meeting material needs and for enriching developmental opportunities. Hopefully, too, the process has strengthened emotional and transactional connections between Mrs. Houser and the people in her social network.

This casework process of identifying and defining problems is consistent with a developmental approach to direct-service practice. It places the responsibility for growth and the choice of direction where it belongs (indeed, the only place it can be): in the hands of the individual. This process applies to the involuntary as well as to the voluntary consumer, both of whom begin any growth process, any service use, with resistance to change. Whether consumers request service of their own volition or at the insistence of others, the first task is to recognize the problem of concern. It is the *consumer's* perception of this problem that determines the targets—not the referring organization or the worker. Nevertheless, the worker must be sure the consumer understands the consequences of his or her perception as opposed to others' definition of the problem (court, employer, spouse).

William Reid and Laura Epstein have developed a model of the systematic procedures for this need/problem/target determination:[6]

1.   Elicit the problems with which the consumer appears to be concerned.

2.   Define the problems in behavioral terms.

3.   Rank the problems according to the consumer's major emphasis. If the consumer cannot rank the problems, infer a ranking from the amount of distress expressed in discussions and confirm your ranking with the consumer.

4.   Classify the target problem in one of the following categories:

   a. *Interpersonal conflict:* A problem between two individuals where at least one is behaving in a way the other finds objectionable. ("We fight all the time"; "we don't get along.")
   b. *Dissatisfaction in social relations:* A problem in certain aspects of one individual's interpersonal relations. (I don't have enough friends"; "other kids pick on me.")
   c. *Problems with formal organization:* A problem in an individual's relationship with an organization rather than another individual. ("The court is on my back"; "they won't let me return to school.")
   d. *Difficulties in role performance:* A gap between how an individual performs a social role (parent, spouse, student, employee, patient) and how that person would like to. ("I can't control my children"; I can't hack math.")
   e. *Problems of social transition:* A problem in movement from one social position, role, or situation to another, especially in making decisions in relation to the change. ("We have to decide about having children"; "I don't know whether to stay in school or not.")
   f. *Reactive emotional distress:* An emotional problem in response to a specific event or set of circumstances (death of a family member, loss of status, financial difficulties) in which the individual's major concern is the feelings themselves rather than the situation. ("I'm down because I have lost my job"; "I'm worried about my health.")
   g. *Inadequate resources:* A lack of specific resources (money, housing, food, child care, transportation, a job). ("We have been evicted and have no place to stay tonight.")
   h. *Habit disorders:* A problem in addictive behavior, phobic reaction, concern about self-image, and thought disturbances. ("I can't get through the day without a drink.")

5.   Specify the target problem through further exploration.

For some consumer needs, casework may continue to be the method of choice and most of the worker's mediation will be in Quadrant A. Often, the worker may shift from Quadrant A to Quadrant B activities, where the needs involve "significant others." Targets may point to the focus on group or family developmental systems as many problems involve human relations in primary face-to-face groups in the initiation of social services. The worker must see the applicant's perspective of the problem if adequate service is to be provided.[7]

Nevertheless, before any decision is made in partnership with consumers to focus on the interaction systems of Quadrant B or the units of focus in Quadrants C and D, the activities of Quadrant A are paramount for the engagement of the applicant for service. Consider the worker with Mrs. Brown in the following situation.[8]

Mrs. Brown has eight children. Four are in school and four are of preschool age. Mrs. Brown has been having difficulty with her children and has become increasingly depressed since the birth of her last child six months ago. She has been keeping her oldest child home from school to help her care for the children.

The school social worker has become involved with the family because of the excessive absence of the oldest child. She has referred Mrs. Brown to the neighborhood health center. The community worker with this agency has met with Mrs. Brown to assess the situation.

Apart from the facts related by the school social worker, the direct-service worker discovers the following problems in the course of their initial contact, a home visit:

1. Mrs. Brown feels overburdened by the menial chores of caring for so many toddlers.

2. She feels unproductive and uncreative.

3. She has no significant contact with other adults but desires such contact.

4. Mrs. Brown's relationship with her husband has suffered.

During this assessment, additional barriers to the developmental needs of both Mrs. Brown and her community are noted:

1. Mrs. Brown does not have the resources to hire a caretaker to relieve her of the constant burden of child care.

2. The community has failed to provide a system of day care centers available to all community members.

3. Societal attitudes have defined the role of women as constant caretakers of children.

4. Mrs. Brown feels guilty because she is not fulfilled in this role.

5. Mrs. Brown feels unable to cope with family demands because of her own unsatisfactory childhood experiences.

Mrs. Brown and the social worker discussed needs and resources related to the problem. Both recognized that they could not change Mrs. Brown's childhood experiences, although Mrs. Brown wished this were possible. Too, societal attitudes were not likely to change radically and thus relieve Mrs. Brown's guilt. The worker could meet with Mrs. Brown and through the casework process *perhaps* help her deal with her guilt, but Mrs. Brown would still have the burden of constant child care and the worker might become her only significant source of adult contact. Mrs. Brown placed priority on her need to be relieved of her child care responsibilities for a certain amount of time on a regular basis. The contract for services was thus established: Mrs. Brown and the direct-service worker would work toward some type of day care service.

Up to this point in the process, the social worker's activities have been in Quadrant A (see Figure 2.2). The activities are directed toward the individual, Mrs. Brown, and the target of these activiites is Mrs. Brown's definition of service needs. The focus is on her individual development. The casework method is used to engage her in a service contract promoting her self-actualization. From this specific contract to relieve Mrs. Brown of the obstacles to her own development, the worker's activities shift to other quadrants. There is a brief exploration of the methods and activities of Quadrants B and C before those of Quadrant B are selected.

Direct Consumer System

	Individual	Others
Individual	A (Work with individual in own behalf) Unit of focus The individual (individual development) Method Casework	B
Target System	C	D
Others		

Figure 2.2 Quadrant A

In relation to Quadrant C, the worker checked with her agency and other community groups about the possibility of establishing a day care program for Mrs. Brown and other mothers with similar needs. The agency had limited financial resources. Several local church groups were willing to devote time and space to a day care project, but they did not have the funds for starting one. One church group had obtained federal funds and was planning to open a nonprofit day care center within a year, but Mrs. Brown and her neighbors needed help immediately.

Thus the worker was unable to provide the service through Quadrant C activities. There were no immediate resources in the service network, and the development of a day care program was not a feasible short-term target.

Quadrant B Methods

Quadrant B methods begin when the direct consumer's needs are related to the needs of other direct consumers. Families and other small groups are considered as the primary targets of service to meet selected goals. The worker with Mrs. Brown considered the possibility of mediation in Quadrant B consumer and target systems. What of the *family* as the consumer and target for service? What of other service consumers with the same needs as Mrs. Brown?

The worker noted that the size of Mrs. Brown's family and their interaction patterns had a great effect on her. Could the family reallocate its own child-caring resources to aid Mrs. Brown? Mrs. Brown did not think the family could provide the resources unless she took her oldest child out of school—a solution that created more problems for her than it solved.

Would Mrs. Brown's neighbors be willing to develop a cooperative day care facility? Mrs. Brown and the worker already knew many neighborhood women with a need for day care service. They, like Mrs. Brown, were also engaged with the agency's service through their relationship with the worker. Mrs. Brown and the worker decided they would try to work with these women and organize a cooperative facility in the neighborhood. The worker gave Mrs. Brown their names. She also telephoned them to say that Mrs. Brown would be contacting them about helping with such a facility.

The best method of providing service to Mrs. Brown and the other interested mothers is *group work*. Group work has been defined as "a method for engaging a group . . . in relationship processes with the worker and each other to facilitate use of group experience for achieving individual and group purposes within . . . an agency or service program."[9] In group work the unit of focus is the interactional system of group development. The essence of group work is the mediating influence that enables the group to actualize its potential for mutual aid. Through mutual aid, each member helps every other member to meet his or her needs, to create an environment conducive to meeting those needs, and to match the group's goals and each member's own personal goals. The group in social work evolves around a common goal. The worker must focus on the relationship of each individual to other members, to the worker, and to the group as a whole—always aware that the group's strength lies in the members themselves and their relations with other members.

Regardless of its purpose or the goals of individual members, group process is a powerful medium for the development of empathy, autonomy, and the capacity to choose. Moreover, group process combats alienation through authentic relationships with others.[10] It is the human community in miniature. As Grace Coyle has written: "It seems clear that experience in small face-to-face groups affording opportunity for intimate relationships plays an essential part in the process of human maturation . . . a supplemental social nourishment . . . for those whose lives are for some reason meager or lacking in intimate social relations."[11]

The initial phase of group work begins in the first meeting. The worker needs to create a trusting climate that is both protective and permissive and allows members to approach or avoid one another. The first meeting should be pleasant yet purposeful and should satisfy members' needs—whether the need be information, release of tension, camaraderie, or security. Activities should be noncompetitive, experiences nonfrustrating, and limits nonrigid. Initial trust is built on rules, routines, repetition, and familiarity with tasks and activities. The worker needs to be fair, consistent, explicit about purpose and procedures—and encourage members to achieve their group and individual goals.

The chief purpose of the first meeting is to negotiate a contract. The contract is the agreement, verbal and nonverbal, between group members and the worker about the goal of the group and how they intend to achieve it. The contract establishes the common ground between the members' needs, the worker's goals, and the agency's objectives. Moreover, the contract communicates the worker's belief in democratic partnership and establishes tentative group goals. As William Schwartz has written about this phase in mediating between the group and its members:

> What the worker wants to help bring about in this phase is an opening consensus: from members on what they need, and from agency representatives on what they offer. The worker also wants a partialization of tasks, beginning to break down the work before them into some of the specific jobs of which it is composed. And he seeks to establish some of the ground rules and procedures designed to move them as quickly as possible into a collaborative and independent style of problem-solving.[12]

Having discussed the general nature of group process, let me turn to the details of Mrs. Brown's case. The worker with Mrs. Brown and the other members begins to work through the group process toward the specific goal of organizing and operating a day care center. Five women attended the first meeting at Mrs. Brown's house. All committed themselves to work toward forming a cooperative day care center. They decided on a daily volunteer to care for the others' children in her own home and a daily secretary to keep track of volunteered time. This decision was a deliberate effort to keep everyone involved as an important part of the group. The worker clarified communication among members, commented on the evolving group process, and furnished information on organizational tasks and child-caring concerns. In their second meeting it was decided that each mother would volunteer for extra child-care duties one day per week. If a mother made use of the service, she would tell the secretary the number of hours she left her children and with whom. This mother would then be expected to spend the same amount of time in caring for children of any mother in the co-op. Each mother also agreed to serve as secretary one day a week.

After the co-op had operated a week, the women realized that having a different secretary every day caused confusion in record keeping. It was decided that each woman should be secretary for a week and then turn the record books over to the next person.

The worker encouraged the group to set its own policies during weekly meetings instead of depending on her to do so. As mothers gained confidence and skill, the worker lessened her involvement in the project and met with the group (only when asked) as a consultant.

As the group developed its organization, target goals shifted for Mrs. Brown and other members. Some members, including Mrs. Brown, requested more in-depth counseling. With some the worker was able to provide this service by working with them as individuals (Quadrant A) or with the family (Quadrant B). With others she mediated through referral and brokerage activities (Quadrant C) to ensure that they received appropriate counseling. In time the co-op developed into a day care center with several mothers on duty. At this stage the worker was involved in organizational and program development (Quadrant D). Most of the worker's activities in behalf of Mrs. Brown were also in behalf of other direct-service consumers in the beginning and development of their group, however. By relieving the women of child care responsibilities for a certain amount of time on a regular basis, this mediation allowed them to work on other tasks for personal growth. These methods and activities fall in Quadrant B (see Figure 2.3).

Summary

The direct-service social worker needs both a generic base and a generalist repertoire of methods for effective practice. Before using these methods in practice, however, the worker needs a framework for selecting them appropriately. The framework presented in this chapter is made up of four quadrants depending on the direct consumer and target systems that have evolved from the assessment and the helping process.

Quadrant A involves work with the individual in his or her own behalf. The unit of focus is individual development; the appropriate

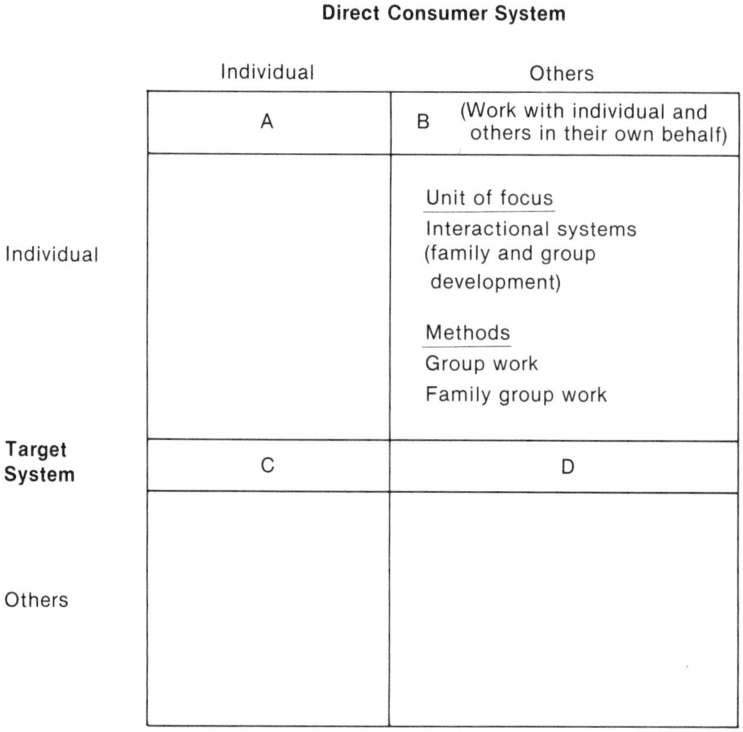

Direct Consumer System

	Individual	Others
Individual	A	B (Work with individual and others in their own behalf) Unit of focus Interactional systems (family and group development) Methods Group work Family group work
Target System	C	D
Others		

Figure 2.3 Quadrant B

method is casework. Quadrant B involves the individual with other direct consumers in interactional systems as targets. The unit of focus is group or family development; the appropriate methods are group work and family group work. Quadrant C involves work with indirect consumers as targets for service to the individual. The unit of focus here is the development of service networks; the primary methods needed to influence this development are consultation, linkage (brokerage), and case advocacy. Quadrant D involves work with indirect consumers as targets in behalf of several direct consumers. The unit of focus is community development; the appropriate methods are organizational development, community organization, policy development, and cause advocacy.

Direct-service work often entails a variety of activities that fall into several of these quadrants. In this chapter we have discussed the micro-level methods for working in Quadrants A and B. Most direct service begins with the casework, family group work, or group work methods and processes of these two quadrants. The work with Mrs. Brown reflects the use of these quadrants in planning practice activities and the major principles for selecting the relevant methods: casework and group work. The next chapter develops this framework further by focusing on the generalist's use of macrolevel methods and processes to provide effective direct service.

Suggested Learning Experiences

1. Imagine some situations in which most of the worker's activities would be directed toward influencing the individual through work with the individual (Quadrant A in Figure 2.1). How many of these situations would also demand activities in Quadrants B, C, and D? What activities are these?

2. Go over the list of situations in the preceding exercise and place each situation into one of the categories developed by Reid and Epstein (see page 28). Study the relationship between the activities in Quadrants B, C, and D and the category you have assigned them. What conclusions do you draw? Do certain situations generally call for particular targets and methods?

3. Consider the additional knowledge and skills needed as one moves from Quadrant A methods and activities (individual as consumer and target) to Quadrant B (family or consumer groups as consumer and target). Make a list of these differences. How are these differences reflected in Mrs. Brown's situation described throughout this chapter?

Suggested Case Studies and Readings

The major classroom learning experiences for this chapter and the next are case studies involving different methods representing a combination of quadrants and diverse consumer groups. The case studies suggested are those in which:

1. the work reflects direct service.

2. the work was done (or could have been done) by a BSW direct-service worker.

3. an assessment framework of some sort is devised from which needs, goals, and targets are chosen and methods selected.

4. at least two methods of the four-quadrant model are used in practice. (All include Quadrant A casework methods in various combinations with other quadrants.)

5. the rationale for selecting methods is explicit enough to permit analysis of the worker's decision-making process in practice.

6. the case studies are available in published sources.

The following list of case study resources is organized according to the methods used and the consumers: work with some combination of individuals, families, groups, organizations, and communities through some combination of casework, family group work, group work, consultation, brokerage, case advocacy, community organization, program or policy development, and cause advocacy.

Work with Individuals and Families
(Quadrants A and B)

Maas, Henry S. "Social Work with Individuals and Families." In *Concepts and Methods of Social Work,* ed. Walter Friedlander. 2nd ed. Englewood Cliffs, N.J.: Prentice-Hall, 1976.

> Two case examples are given, one brief and the other in detail. The first summarizes contact of a child protective services worker with Mrs. Dee Rodgers, a newcomer to the community and a single parent who neglects her two preschool children. The second involves the Coyle family and a public welfare worker. The family at home, Mrs. Coyle, age thirty-two, and three children, Patrick, sixteen, Stephen, fifteen, and Katie, twelve, need help in a number of interactional areas as a result of Mr. Coyle's commitment to a prison honor farm on a morals charge.

Work with Individuals and Groups
(Quadrants A and B)

Garfield, Goodwin P. and Carol R. Irizarry. "The Record of Service: Describing Social Work Practice." In *The Practice of Group Work,* ed. William Schwartz and Serapio R. Zalba. New York: Columbia University Press, 1971.

> The unique contribution of this record is based on its purpose of presenting a model recording system for social work practice. The system reflects the quantity of the work, "process" quality of the work, summaries of consumer and agency primary tasks and problems, and the theory behind the specific practice. These descriptions of the what, how, and why of practice in an individual and group format focus on work to help delinquency-prone youngsters and their families. The work reflects the selection and use of methods for helping Tata Vilar, a twelve-year-old girl, with her strong fears of failure in school and her need for outside help in learning. The study covers a year of individual work with Tata and the first six months of group work with Tata and others with similar needs in the Wanderers, a group of eleven girls between ages ten and thirteen. The group record reflects the work toward creating an atmosphere in which the worker and members can express important feelings and attitudes about each other.

Work with Individuals, Families, and
Groups (Quadrants A and B)

Lokshin, Helen and Georgia Tucker. "Mr. and Mrs. Johnson." In *The Field of Social Work,* ed. Arthur E. Fink, C. Wilson Anderson, and Merril B. Conover. 5th ed. New York: Holt, Rinehart and Winston, 1968.

This record shows a combination of casework, family group work, and to a lesser extent group work in behalf of Mr. and Mrs. Johnson. The Johnsons come to the attention of the worker when both are ill and in the hospital. Mrs. Johnson is seventy-three; Mr. Johnson is seventy-five. Mr. Johnson has glaucoma, arteriosclerotic heart disease, and congestive heart failure. Mrs. Johnson fell and fractured her hip while caring for Mr. Johnson. At the time, they had been living for many years with Mrs. King, a daughter, and her family. Mrs. King, however, did not wish them to return. While casework is used to determine the Johnson's placement needs and decisions, group work is used to engage the couple in the hospital's Rehabilitation Program and lead them toward full recovery. Meanwhile, a series of family network meetings helps them to establish their own apartment with homemaker services.

Introduction

This chapter completes the work begun in Chapter 2 in presenting the
basic social work methods and processes for direct service. Chapter 2
introduced a framework for the selection of methods from a generalist
repertoire and discussed the methods appropriate for working with direct
consumers in their own behalf—casework, family group work, and group
work. These microlevel methods are often conceived as the only ones for
direct-service practice and, indeed, much of the worker's time is spent on
activities that fall in Quadrants A and B of the framework (Figure 2.1).
Effective social workers do not limit themselves to these methods, however. The generalist's repertoire includes approaches for working with
indirect consumers as well. These macrolevel methods are the focus of
this chapter.

When the consumer's goals and the selected targets demand that the
direct-service worker influence organization and community process, the
macrolevel methods of Quadrants C and D are appropriate. These methods
include work with indirect consumers in the service network in behalf of the
individual and work with indirect consumers in the community in behalf of
the individual and other direct consumers. The objectives are organizational and community development and the self-actualizing development of one's direct consumers. Mediation in these larger systems involves
organizational development, consultation, brokerage (linkage), and case
advocacy to influence organizational processes (Quadrant C). It also involves the use of community organization, policy or program development,
and cause advocacy to influence community processes (Quadrant D).

Quadrant C and D Methods (Macrolevel)

Quadrant C Methods

Organizational Development

Social work direct services exist in an organizational context—a fact
that has led to the well-documented emphasis on bureaucracy in social

work practice. Quite often human service organizations are obstacles to, rather than resources for, meeting the individual's needs. In these situations, the direct-service generalist requires the methods and activities of Quadrant C—that is, working with others in the service network toward organizational development in behalf of the individual. The target system for service is the organizational processes of the service network. This target requires mediation within one's own agency or within other human service organizations.

Consider the situation of Mrs. Brown discussed in the last chapter. It is possible that the worker's agency administrator had been considering, but reluctantly, initiation of day care as part of the agency's services. It is also possible that day care services were offered by another agency but its selective policy precluded their use by Mrs. Brown. In either case the worker would need the methods of organizational development, broker-age, and case advocacy to provide service to Mrs. Brown.

Organizational development has been defined as a method "to develop self-renewing, self-correcting systems of people who learn to organize themselves in a variety of ways according to the nature of their tasks, and who continue to expand the choices available to the organization as it copes with the changing demands of a changing environment."[1] Organizational development requires a "sociological consciousness"—that is, the ability to see how institutionalized systems have properties independent of their individual human actors.[2] For instance, structural roles in organizations are created by people, but once established they have great influence on the behavior of those in the organization. Public assistance rules can make the most sensitive worker seem callous in delivering services. These roles and norms can frustrate the manifest purposes of the organization and its social workers. As Ruth Middleman and Gale Gold-berg observe:

> Lectures on racism aimed to change staff attitudes will not affect the work if policies and procedures are racist. Nor will community mental health centers work toward their mandated goals of prevention and serve people in the community so long as the center is paid on a per capita basis for only those who walk into the building for treatment. Nor will children's agencies ever devote much real energy to maintaining children in their own homes, and deliver the material and other resources needed to support this program, so long as child welfare agencies are reimbursed per capita for numbers in foster care or group homes. Nor will medical social workers be able to deal with the gross social problems of massive segments of the population that accompany illness, so long as hospital policy directs major resources to the crises surrounding in-hospital treatment. . . .[3]

Certainly these external forces create an atmosphere of uncertainty in the organizations in which social workers practice and on which they depend for services to consumers. Organizational development is a matter of preparing organizations to face their dilemmas, establish priorities, make choices, and commit themselves to objectives through active participation of members in the planning and conduct of change. Workers initiating organizational development often use external or internal consulting methods, to which we now turn.

Consultation

The direct-service worker's mediating influence on his or her own organization through consultation is well illustrated in the following example.[4] A social worker began her job in the hematology service of a veteran's hospital. The forty men on the ward in which she worked all suffered from terminal blood diseases. In her early casework contacts with these men, the worker discovered serious problems created by their clearly defined patient role in the ward culture. The doctors in their traditional role of knowing what was best for the patients did not share their prognosis with the patient; nor did they allow other staff to do so. In fact, they suppressed patients' questions about their condition and assured them they would get well. The patient's family, however, was given the secret prognosis and the responsibility for protecting him from learning the truth of his illness. The doctors, other staff, and the families all assumed roles that protected them from painful contact with the patients. The patients themselves assumed the helpless role of dependents.

In her individual casework contacts (Quadrant A activities), the worker discovered that patients had many persistent feelings of rejection, isolation, and abandonment. They felt cut off from their identity-enhancing roles of father and husband. They sensed a stigma attached to discussing their feelings and diseases and felt alienated in their human relations. They were aware of questions brushed aside, brusque answers, and deliberate evasions and half-truths. Their fantasies reflected a great deal of despair, hopelessness, suspicion, and distrust.

In her contact with groups of patients and family groups (Quadrant B activities), the worker discovered many conflicts related to interpersonal dissatisfaction. With each other and among family members, patients expressed their alienation in resentment, aloofness, and seemingly noncaring ways. Relatives were often upset and behaved artificially with the patient and with each other. The worker used casework and family group work approaches to resolve these conflicts, but these alone were not sufficient.

She then decided to concentrate her activities on the ward culture itself (Quadrant C). First, she shared the patients' feelings with staff in her consultations with them. The staff's initial reaction was disbelief (denial?). Then they admitted the patients might have such feelings, but they attributed them to the casework exploration itself. Nevertheless, the staff did become more aware of the meaning of the situation to the patients.

The worker began to mediate between the ward culture and the patient to have the prognosis shared with them. One 25-year-old patient whose wife also had a terminal disease needed to plan for his young child's future. He was able to accept his death and capably planned for himself and his family. In fact he quickly became the ideal patient to the staff on the ward. A 30-year-old who was engaged to be married in two months and whose fiancee could not legally be informed of his illness (leukemia) was admitted to the ward. The worker convinced the medical staff that the patient needed to know his prognosis for decision making affecting both himself and his fiancee. With casework help this patient too acted responsibly on this information. Another patient, a 29-year-old, discovered his diagnosis of leukemia when he read a slip of paper he was carrying to the laboratory. At first the doctor claimed it was a secretarial error, but the patient convinced the doctor that he would be relieved to know the truth. He then went to the worker and shared his mixed feelings of shock, relief, and sadness. In the course of this work, he agreed to tape several interviews to teach a different perspective on patient need to the ward physicians. In these interviews he explained how he felt about the life he had left to him and the importance of being able to make choices about his remaining time. He began to help other patients deal with their problems and referred several to the social worker.

These situations and the worker's participation in ward meetings persuaded doctors to begin different ways of communicating with patients and their families. They noted improved relationships. Thus a first step was taken in organizational development in the ward culture (Quadrant D). At this hospital, weekly ward rounds were held for resident assistants to discuss social and adjustment problems and develop plans for resolving them. Since the residents changed every three months, there was an opportunity to introduce them to the new ward approach. It was a year before the situation showed real change. The change was sustained by ward staff after the worker left.

Organizations develop through planned consultation in behalf of individuals, but they also develop by reordering their priorities and reallocating their resources in relation to specific service demands. It is toward this end that brokerage is directed.

Brokerage

Brokerage (or linkage) refers to the methods used to link individuals to community resources. Brokerage tasks and techniques have been studied recently by Andrew Weissman in his social service center at U.S. Steel South Works in Chicago.[5] The brokerage occurs through three prereferral stages: locating appropriate community resources; connecting the consumer to the resource; and evaluating the effectiveness of the resource in relation to the consumer's needs.

Selecting community resources involves a clear statement of the consumer's need, an investigation of the nature, operations, and quality of available resources, and the exploration of options and their conse-quences—including, of course, the one option always available: doing nothing.

Once the resource has been selected with the consumer, the worker connects the individual and the resource. Weissman lists several connec-tion techniques in order of increasing complexity:

1.   The simplest connection involves writing out the necessary facts: the name and address of the resource, how to get an appointment at the resource, how to get to the resource, and a specific explanation of what the consumer may expect once he or she arrives. Here the initiative for contacting the resource, making an appointment, and following through with the appointment rests with the individual. This basic technique works best when people already know what they need but have had difficulty in locating the appropriate resource.

2.   The next step involves providing the consumer with the name of a specific person to contact at the resource. This tactic has one serious drawback: If the consumer contacts the resource and the person the worker has specified is not there, the consumer may give up.

3.   As the complexity of the consumer's problem increases, it sometimes helps to provide him or her with a brief written statement, addressed to the resource, describing the problem and what the consumer wants. It is important that the consumer be involved in writing this statement.

4.   At the next level, the consumer calls the resource from the worker's office to make an appointment. Alternatively, the worker may place the call to ensure that the appropriate person is contacted, but the consumer then carries the conversation. With this technique, the worker is paving the way for the consumer.

5.   There are times when, after the techniques described above have failed, it is necessary for the worker to request a family member, relative, or friend to accompany the consumer to the resource. Occasionally the worker will accompany the consumer, especially when the worker is close to the consumer or anticipates special problems.

There are also specific steps that workers can take to make sure the connections will work to the consumer's advantage. These "cementing techniques" are:

1.   *Checkback:* The consumer is asked to call the worker after the initial contact at the resource to summarize what has been accomplished so far.

2.   *Haunting:* The worker, with the consumer's approval, contacts the consumer by telephone after the initial contact at the resource and after each subsequent contact to check on the success of the referral.

3. *Sandwiching:* The worker meets with the consumer before the initial interview at the resource and then immediately afterward.

4. *Alternating:* The worker meets intermittently with the consumer during the period in which the consumer is involved in interviews at the resource.

These four tactics are used to clear up any misunderstandings a consumer may encounter at the resource agency. The worker may also have contacted an untapped resource for future consumers. In this case the resource and the worker can develop procedures to improve the resource's service to the people the worker represents. A worker might help a resource recognize organizational obstacles to serving a certain group—discovering, for example, that it is hard for those working swing shifts to have an interview at the same time each week.

Follow-up evaluation is essential for three purposes: to make sure the consumer is getting what he or she wants; to determine that the problem is on the way to resolution; and to guide future linkage to the cooperating agency. Therefore, follow-up is the last step in brokerage.

Case Advocacy

Case advocacy, as distinguished from cause advocacy (a method of Quadrant D), is active intercession with organizations on behalf of the individual when there is a conflict of interest between individual and organization. The task of advocacy demands (1) knowledge of the organization's policies, regulations, and administrative structure; (2) specific knowledge of the organization's politics and appeal machinery; (3) knowledge of the possibilities of formal legal intervention in ensuring consumer's rights; (4) knowledge of the organization's informal power structure; (5) knowledge of the external forces to which the organization responds (for example, community leaders); and (6) knowledge of the consequences of escalating issues for the individual and others. Consider the following example of case advocacy by a family service social worker.[6]

Mrs. Adams did not appear for her 11 o'clock appointment one morning at Family Service. She telephoned at 2:30 to explain why. She had an 8 o'clock appointment that morning for her four-year-old orthopedically handicapped son at the outpatient department of the public children's hospital. She had arrived promptly at 8 with her son, accompanied also by her two-year-old daughter. After standing in line awhile to check in and identify herself, she was told to have a seat and her name would be called. After perhaps another forty-five minutes, her name was called and she was directed to another section of the hospital, where she was again checked in and again told to wait. The wait was even longer there, the children were increasingly restless and uncomfortable, and Mrs.

Adams' 11 o'clock appointment at Family Service came and went. The children's lunchtime had also come and gone before mother and children completed the clinic visit. By the time Mrs. Adams and the two small children reached home, it was approaching 2 o'clock. All three were in a state of near hysteria.

The social worker telephoned the hospital's social service department and spoke to the medical social worker, whom she knew personally. She described Mrs. Adams' experience and asked if Mrs. Adams could be served without such a delay in subsequent visits. The medical social worker explained the clinic's operating procedures and defended their rationale, but she assured the Family Service worker that she would find some way to see that Mrs. Adams got special treatment on her next appointment.

This example of case advocacy falls in Quadrant C (see Figure 3.1). In behalf of Mrs. Adams, the worker directed activities to the target of the hospital's organization since this was the source of problems for Mrs. Adams and her children. Thus the methods of Quadrant C include organizational development, consultation, brokerage, and case advocacy. In the next section we examine the methods and activities of Quadrant D.

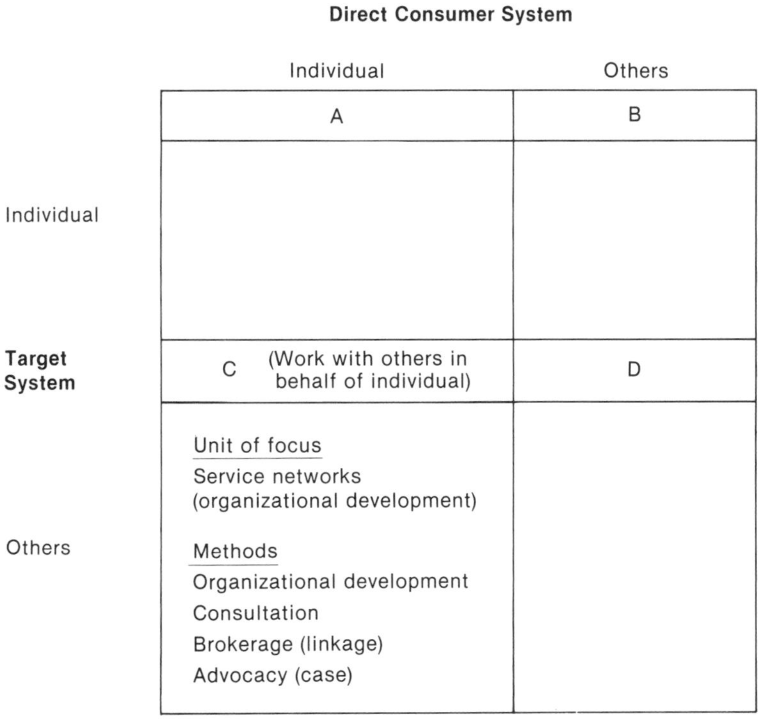

Direct Consumer System

	Individual	Others
	A	B
Individual		
Target System	C (Work with others in behalf of individual)	D
Others	Unit of focus Service networks (organizational development) Methods Organizational development Consultation Brokerage (linkage) Advocacy (case)	

Figure 3.1 Quadrant C

Quadrant D Methods

Quadrant D designates methods and activities in which the direct-service generalist works with indirect consumers in behalf of the direct consumer and others. The unit of focus is community development; the target system is the community process. The methods of choice, along with aspects of organizational development, are community organization, policy development, and cause advocacy.

Community Organization

Community organization is a method of engaging a community and its parts—both groups and individuals—in order to achieve community welfare within the purview of a sponsoring agency.[7] It is concerned with the enrichment and development of social institutions through two related processes: planning and organizing. It is a method of promoting a community's self-actualization. As Murray Ross puts it: "The result of community organizational process, at any stage, is that the community should be better equipped . . . to identify and deal cooperatively and skillfully with its common problems."[8]

Community organization is based on respect for the ability of communities to discover their own purpose and develop into effective mutual aid systems. The method includes extensive use of groups and participatory processes. As Kenneth Pray has noted: "Community organization practice is social work practice . . . if . . . primary concern and objectives relate always to the development and guidance of the process by which people find satisfying and fruitful social relationships, and not to the attainment of specific preconceived products or forms of relationship. . . ."[9]

How can the direct-service provider use community organization methods and processes in practice? Violet Sieder has proposed a well-thought-out answer to this question.[10] Integral to direct service is the use of channels for influencing the work of central planning bodies and creating change in community services in behalf of both direct and indirect consumers. Direct-service workers, through their agencies, are inevitably engaged in interorganizational relations and in the mobilization of community support.

Interorganizational work refers to involvement in joint planning bodies, such as health and welfare councils, to develop the services their separate consumers need. This task requires that the worker have knowledge of available resources (their function, scope, policies, methods, personnel) and skills in interaction with organizations (conference and committee methods, consultation, negotiation, public relations, social action).

The mobilization of community support requires links with community "influentials" (both individuals and groups) and consumer groups who can be informed and mobilized in campaigns for legislation, appropriation, fundraising, and other programs at the community, state, or national level in behalf of direct and indirect consumers. The process of using this support to effect change involves three basic steps: (1) defining the problem by gathering data on service needs through documentation in Quadrant A, B, and C activities; (2) assessing the problem in such basic terms as number affected, geographical clustering of needs, and the personal characteristics of unserviced consumers; and (3) developing and implementing a plan of action through mobilization of community support.

Policy Development

Policy development refers to the establishment of "principles or courses of action designed to influence: (1) overall quality of life in a society; (2) the circumstances of living of individuals and groups in that society; and (3) the nature of intrasocietal relationships among individuals, groups, and the society as a whole."[11] The chief methods for social policy development are strategies for redefining social problems and organizing mutual aid rather than competitive movements. The direct-service social worker is in a strategic position to collect information useful in shaping social policy but must be able to analyze the policy implications of the information and must have ways of contributing this information to policymaking bodies. Specifically, the direct-service generalist is in a position to demonstrate how competitive policymaking obstructs self-actualizing human relations through inequities that deprive large segments of society of support and opportunities for development.

Harry Specht proposes procedures for this direct-service influence on policy development by identifying problems in current policies through case finding, data gathering, and discovering gaps in service.[12] These data are then brought to the attention of others in the basic stages of policy development: analysis (researchers); informing the public (community organizers and public relations experts); developing policy goals (planners and administrators); building public support (lobbyists); legislation (legislative analysts); and implementation and administration (administrators, lawyers). Finally, policy evaluation can only be done full circle. That is, the direct-service worker's continual case finding, data gathering, and discovery of service gaps is the true test of the results of social welfare policy decisions.

Cause Advocacy

Cause advocacy refers to methods by which individuals and others like them are assured rights as a class by organizations. In the preceding section for instance, we looked at the case of Mrs. Adams and her two children. In that situation the worker used case advocacy to assure that Mrs. Adams would have a less frustrating experience at her next clinic visit and hence would not miss her casework appointment. The hospital would continue with its policies, of course. An exception was made for Mrs. Adams only because one hospital social worker agreed to help her and her Family Service worker. She was not helped because her cause was acknowledged as just or out of respect for her dignity, rights, or power. This was an example of case advocacy in which the Family Service worker's power—not Mrs. Adams' power—got better service for one consumer.

Now let us look at a cause advocacy approach to the same situation.[13] First, the caseworker describes the problem to the supervisor and the agency administration. Second, the hospital is contacted by the agency administrator. The hospital confirms that this is the way it operates, explains its reasons, and agrees to talk the matter over with a representative of Family Service and other agencies. Third, other agencies are contacted and their experiences regarding hospital policy are documented. Fourth, a meeting is arranged with representatives of agencies and relevant hospital authorities. Fifth, after learning of the effects of hospital policy on the very families they are attempting to help, and after being challenged to change the system despite some inconvenience to themselves, the hospital revises its clinic scheduling process. As a result of the dialogue process, other results come about—including more effective use of volunteers in the hospital and reorganization of hospital waiting areas. Moreover, since this hospital is a teaching center, fledgling physicians and other trainees were being taught that this disregard for the time and dignity of patients is the approved way to operate. Now they are getting a different message, one that may influence them throughout their careers.

The difference between cause and case advocacy is evident in this example. While case advocacy falls in Quadrant C and benefits the individual—in this case Mrs. Adams and her family—cause advocacy clearly falls in Quadrant D and results in changes that benefit all families affected by the system now and in the future (see Figure 3.2). Therefore, cause advocacy has been advanced as an effective method in combating institutionalized discrimination such as racism and sexism.[14]

A Practice Example

Consider the following example of direct-service work using Quadrant D methods.[15]

"The House on Sixth Street" became a case when Mrs. Smith came to a neighborhood service center to complain that she had had no gas, heat, electricity, or hot water in her apartment house for more than four weeks. She asked the agency for help. Mrs. Smith was twenty-three years old, black, and the mother of four children, three of whom had been born out of wedlock. At the time she was unmarried and receiving Aid to Families with Dependent Children (AFDC). She came to the center in desperation because she was unable to run her household without utilities.

Direct Consumer System

	Individual	Others
Individual	A	B
Target System	C	D (Work with others in behalf of individual and others)
Others		**Unit of focus** Classes of people (community development) **Methods** Organizational development Community organization and development Policy or program development Advocacy (cause)

Figure 3.2 Quadrant D

Her financial resources were exhausted—but not her courage. The center worker decided that in this case the building—the tenants, the landlord, and the circumstances affecting their relation—was of central concern.

A social worker then visited the Sixth Street building with Mrs. Smith and confirmed her charge that the house had been without utilities for more than four weeks. Several months before, in fact, the city Rent and Rehabilitation Administration had reduced the rent for each apartment to $1.00 a month because the landlord was not providing services. However, this agency took no further action. Eleven families were still living in the building's twenty-eight apartments. Since the landlord owed the electric company several thousand dollars, the meters had been removed from the house. Because most of the tenants were welfare clients, the Department of Welfare had "reimbursed" the landlord directly for much of the unpaid electric bill and refused to pay any more money to the electric company. Yet the Department of Welfare was slow in meeting the emergency needs of the tenants. Most of the forty-eight children from the eleven families in the building had not been to school for a month because they were ill or lacked proper clothing.

The worker found the mothers tired and demoralized. Dirt and disorganization were increasing daily. Many of the tenants were afraid to sleep at night because the building was infested with rats. There was danger of fire because the tenants had to use candles for light. The seventeen abandoned apartments had been invaded by homeless vagrants and drug addicts. Petty thievery was common. However, the mothers refused to seek protection from the police for fear that they would chase away every man who was not part of a family in the building. Some of the unmarried mothers had been living with men as one of the few means of protection from physical danger available to them—even though those on public assistance are threatened with loss of income if they are not legally married. The anxiety created by these conditions was intense, disabling, and increasing.

The worker could see that the mothers were not only anxious but fighting mad. Not only did they seek immediate relief from their physical dangers and discomforts, but they were eager to express their anger at the landlord and the public agencies, which they felt had let them down.

The social worker dealt with the situation over a four-month period, using a variety of social work methods as well as the special talents of a community worker, lawyer, city planner, and various civil rights organizations. He functioned truly as a generalist, even helping the families organize their demands for the services and utilities to which they were legally entitled but which the public agencies were failing to provide. Here he used a great deal of both case and cause advocacy.

The mothers showed an ability to take concerted group action, and Mrs. Smith proved to be a natural and competent leader. With support, encouragement, and assistance from the staff, the mothers became articulate and effective in negotiating with various agency systems. In turn, agencies became more responsive to their needs when the mothers began to visit them, make frequent telephone calls, and send letters and telegrams to them and to politicians demanding action.

With the lawyer and a city planner who was an agency consultant, the mothers and staff members explored various solutions to the housing problem. For example, the Department of Welfare had offered to move the families to shelters or hotels. Neither of these alternatives was acceptable to the mothers. Shelters would split up their families, and many of the "hotels" selected were actually flophouses or primarily inhabited by prostitutes.

After a group discussion with the worker, the mothers decided to embarrass the public agencies by dramatically exposing their inadequacies. They would move into a nearby church basement and request that the worker attempt to have their building condemned. At another meeting, attended by tenants from neighboring buildings and representatives of other local groups, it was concluded that what had happened to the Sixth Street building was a result of institutionalized discrimination against the tenants as blacks and Puerto Ricans. The group evolved into an organization. As such, they sent the following telegram to city, state, and federal officials:

We are voters and Puerto Rican and Black mothers asking for equal rights, for decent housing and enough room. Building has broken windows, no gas or electricity for four weeks, no heat or hot water, holes in floors, loose wiring. Twelve of forty-eight children in building sick. Welfare doctors refuse to walk up dark stairs. Are we human or what? Should innocent children suffer for landlord's brutality and city and state neglect? We are tired of being told to wait with children ill and unable to attend school. Black and Puerto Rican tenants are forced out while buildings next door are renovated at high rents. We are not being treated as human beings.

For the most part, during this work, the lawyer and city planner acted largely as consultants. However, as the tenants and worker became more involved with the courts and as other organizations entered the fight to influence policy development, the lawyer and city planner played a more active and direct role.

During this process, tenants in other buildings on the block became more alert to similar problems in their buildings. With the help of the community development staff and the housing consultant, local groups and organizations such as tenants' councils and the local chapter of the Congress of Racial Equality were enlisted and supported the work with the mothers.

By the time the families had been relocated, several things had been accomplished. Some of the public agencies had been moved sufficiently by their actions to provide better services for them. When the families refused to be relocated in a shelter and moved into the neighborhood church, one of the television networks picked up their story. As a result, officials in the housing agencies came to investigate and several local politicians lent the tenants their support. Shortly after the tenants moved into the church, moreover, a bill was passed by the City Council, designed to prevent some of the abuses that the landlord had been practicing with impunity. The councilman who sponsored the new law referred to the house on Sixth Street to support his argument. Quadrant C and D methods met their needs better and assured better service to others.

In the delivery of social services the direct-service generalist is also in a position to influence policy development. Practice contributes to policy development when the service provides access to institutionalized supports to human development—a role that used to be assumed, less formally, by the extended family, the neighborhood, and friends. The worker's activities directed to the establishment of services and their delivery are policy development activities. As Alfred Kahn observes:

In deciding to develop or expand social services, a group, organization, or government adopts a policy—as it does in electing one category of services rather than another for emphasis. Similarly, the designation of organizational forms for the services and the selection of a delivery system for any specific service represent significant policy choices. Such choices have consequences whether or not immediately visible during the choice process, and whether or not the choosing is deliberate or even conscious.[16]

Practice therefore enacts policy through access services, consumer participation in service delivery, and the competence of service providers.

Summary

It is in methods for practice that the generalist is distinguished from the specialist. The direct-service generalist needs a method repertoire consisting of four categories of direct consumer and target systems. These are activities for work with the individual in his or her own behalf (Quadrant A); work with the individual and other direct consumers together in their own behalf (Quadrant B); work with indirect consumers in behalf of the individual (Quadrant C); and work with indirect consumers in behalf of the individual and other direct consumers (Quadrant D). Essentially, these activities require methods for working with individual, family, group, organization, and community processes.

Direct-service practice is most often initiated in Quadrant A, and the casework method is used to determine the problem and the targets for promoting the consumer's self-actualization. The individual's developmental goals determine subsequent foci, targets, and methods. In Quadrant B, the unit of focus is the development of families and groups; the methods of choice are family group work and group work. In Quadrant C, the unit of focus is the development of organizations in the service network in behalf of the individual; the methods of choice are organizational development, consultation, brokerage, and case advocacy. In Quadrant D, the unit of focus is the development of organizations and the community in behalf of classes of people; the methods of choice are organizational development, community organization and development, policy or program development, and cause advocacy. All methods are process-based and all include the use of procedures and techniques related to the helping process.

These methods and activities require the direct-service generalist to follow generic principles and use basic interactional skills as well as method-specific practice theories and skills. Chapter 4 presents the principles and Chapter 5 the skills that are common to all these methods as they evolve from this generalist model for practice. Following chapters introduce the basic theories and practice theories for these methods as they foster self-actualizing human relations.

Suggested Learning Experiences

1. Consider the similarities and differences of work with consumer groups and work with staff groups in organizational development activities in Quadrants C and D. How might aspects of position, roles, statuses, and organizational norms affect behavior in groups in the organization?

2. Describe an effective information and referral system that would allow the social worker to use the brokerage techniques developed by Weissman and summarized on pages 43–44.

3. What other policy changes might produce better service in the public hospital described on pages 44 and 47? List the strategies a social worker could use to implement these policy changes.

Suggested Case Studies and Readings

Work with Individuals and Organizations
(Quadrants A and C)

Fantl, Berta. "Preventive Intervention." *Social Work* 7(3)(1962):41–47.
  Fantl regards much of social work as "preventive intervention." From the perspective of a neighborhood school social worker, she demonstrates these methods in behalf of Tony, an adolescent boy living with foster parents. The public welfare department is planning to place Tony with his father. Tony's father had been released from prison a few months earlier after having served a ten-year sentence for murdering Tony's mother—in Tony's presence when he was three years old. The school counselor calls in the social worker when she learns of this situation through the upset foster parents (who had come to school because of Tony's behavior in the classroom). The worker consults with the counselor and teachers in relation to Tony's situation and needs. She discovers that the public welfare and probation departments had not coordinated services, due to an unfilled vacancy in one and a new worker in the other. The father was without a job, living by himself, and not supervised or supported on parole. Through advocacy in behalf of Tony and his foster parents, the plan was changed to continue the foster family support from the department of public welfare and to have someone work with Tony's father. She then begins work with the foster parents in relation to problems in receiving the foster father's social security benefits as a disabled worker.

Work with Individuals and Communities
(Quadrants A and D)

Council on Social Work Education. "Advocacy in a Community Hospital on the Eastern Shore." Teaching Record 69-340-23. New York: CSWE, 1970.
  This study demonstrates the worker moving from individual cases of racism to community organization and cause advocacy in behalf of all blacks. The strategy affects both the local community and the hospital as a community in relation to changes in institutional policies and practices.

Work with Individuals, Families, and
Organizations (Quadrants A, B, and C)

Hoffman, Lynn and Lorence Long. "A System Dilemma." *Family Process*
8(2)(1968):211–234.
This long, detailed case study involves the Johnsons, a black family
that includes Charles, fifty-two-year-old father; Bernice, mother; a
preschool daughter, Maureen; a fifteen-year-old daughter, Lorna, in
private school; and a nineteen-year-old daughter, Gail, in college.
The study begins when Mr. Johnson is brought to the attention of
the social services department of a neighborhood health center on
New York's Lower East Side. He suffers from dizzy spells at work,
heavy drinking, and the possibility of being evicted from his housing
project unless he lowers his income. In this paradoxical situation,
Mr. Johnson quits his job as a chef, suffers more dizzy spells and
heavier drinking, and experiences severe marital problems. The
worker uses casework, brokerage, and family group work in an
involved effort to help Mr. Johnson and his family negotiate the
various systems affecting his problems and their solutions.

Work with Individuals, Groups, and
Organizations (Quadrants A, B, and C)

"165 Howell Street." In *Teaching Records: Integrative Learning and
Teaching Project,* ed. Louis Lowry, Leonard M. Bloksberg, and Herbert J. Walberg. New York: Council on Social Work Education, 1973.
This record demonstrates work in behalf of individuals and natural
and formed groups of residents in a deteriorating tenement. Detailed
contacts are described in the tenement social system and in the
negotiation of the complex organizational systems impinging on the
residents' lives.

Work with Individuals, Families, Groups,
and Organizations (Quadrants A, B, and C)

Fritz, Dorothy. "Helen Grant." In *The Field of Social Work,* ed. Arthur
A. Fink, C. Wilson Anderson, and Merril E. Conover. 5th ed. New
York: Holt, Rinehart and Winston, 1968.
This detailed case study concerns the placement process in foster
care of Helen Grant, a sixteen-year-old dependent ward of the court
in Philadelphia. The setting is Youth Service, Inc. Work with Helen
includes use of the residential group program, individual casework
contacts, foster family meetings, and a variety of community and
internal organizational resources. The record also includes the involvement of several workers—from intake, through residential
placement, to foster placement. Helen has trouble adapting to structured situations and in her relationships with peers and adults.

Work with Individuals, Groups, and
Communities (Quadrants A, B, and D)

Taber, Richard H. "A Systems Approach to the Delivery of Mental Health
Services in Black Ghettos." *American Journal of Orthopsychiatry*
40(4)(1970):702–709.
   This study uses an ecological systems framework for work with two
   small natural groups for individual and community change. The first
   network is C street adults; mostly women were organized. They deal
   with better and safer recreation for neighborhood children, including
   plans for their own summer play-street program. More extensively
   covered is work with the Nobleteens, a peer system of boys aged
   fourteen to seventeen. The Nobleteens move from ten "black identity" formal interaction meetings to becoming a club. The club provides recreation programs in the neighborhood, runs an odd-job
   service, writes a newsletter, and educates people outside the community about the needs and life-styles of black urban dwellers. In
   addition to advising the club, the worker has individual casework
   contacts with members in crisis. (Three examples are given.)

Work with Individuals, Organizations, and
Communities (Quadrants A, C, and D)

Sitzer, Kurt and Betty Welsh. "A Problem Focused Model of Practice."
Social Casework 50(6)(1969):323–329.
   A particular assessment format is illustrated by work with a specific
   junior high school and other schools to provide basic and preventive
   services to school-age pregnant girls. The work extends to the whole
   community in supporting programs for maternal and infant health
   care, community mental health services, family life education, family
   planning, and resources to meet basic survival needs.

Work with Individuals, Families, Groups,
Organizations, and Communities
(Quadrants A, B, C, and D)

Morales, Armando and Bradford W. Sheafor. "The Social Worker in
Action." In *Social Work: A Profession of Many Faces*. Boston: Allyn
and Bacon, 1977.
   This public welfare worker in a small Midwest community becomes
   involved with Mrs. Karen Baez and her three children while they
   are in the hospital recuperating from injuries received in a fire that
   swept their apartment and killed Mr. Baez and their seven-month-
   old daughter. The worker begins sensitively and knowledgeably with
   Mrs. Baez to help the family deal with the immediate crisis. He
   mediates between Mrs. Baez, the hospital, and family. He gets
   housing, clothing, and home furnishings for the children when the
   family is released from the hospital. He advocates the Baez family

needs for financial assistance within his own agency, at the state level, and with a congressional representative. He organizes a group of influential citizens and hospital representatives to improve the emergency services in the hospital, which were in part responsible for the two deaths in the family. Throughout this work he uses assessments and planned strategies.

Chapter Four　Generic Principles

Widespread

Introduction

Principles and skills are among the generic components of generalist social work methods. As reflected in the framework presented in Chapters 2 and 3, the activities of Quadrants A, B, C, and D include a repertoire of methods for the direct-service social worker. While much interactional skill is needed in applying the methods in Quadrants A and B, in which the direct-service worker is directly involved with consumers, the effective generalist must also master the basic skills needed in Quadrants C and D as well. This wider use of methods is based on certain generic principles and interactional skills—common to practice with all methods—and also specific skills related to each methodological approach (covered in Part 3). This chapter and the next present these generic principles and skills.

Figure 4.1 depicts the domain of the generic principles and interactional skills for generalist methods in the shaded triangle at the intersection of the methods triangles. These generic principles and skills are the core elements, along with the components presented in Chapter 1, in direct-service generalist practice.

In discussing generic principles and interactional skills there is an assumption that the self is the major instrument through which the social worker practices. The professional self as an instrument needs to be used creatively, consciously, and reliably to achieve social work purposes. For effective practice, this instrument needs to be finely tuned in thinking, feeling, and doing in order to promote the simultaneous development of individuals and society. The essential parts of this instrument are the social worker's head (knowledge), heart (values), and hand (skills). The generic principles guide the worker's professional self in direct-service practice.

Alfred Kadushin quotes a Chinese maxim that expresses a pertinent caveat in the use of principles and skills for effective practice: "When the right man uses the wrong means, the wrong means work in the right way; when the wrong man uses the right means, the right means work in the wrong way."[1] This chapter, however, raises a question that Kadushin also raised: What is the power of the right person using the right means in the right way?

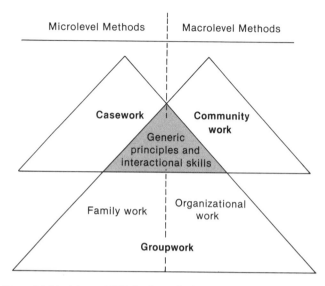

Figure 4.1 Principles and Skills for Generalist Methods

Generic Principles in Use

Generic operating principles instruct the worker in the use of the four-quadrant framework. *Principles* are guidelines for action—basic procedural rules for the conduct of activities. The principles outlined in this chapter are *generic* because they guide the worker's use of methods in all four quadrants. They specify the basic operations needed to influence the self-actualizing processes of people and their environments.

By making these principles and skills specific we can avoid the traditional vagueness of social work guidelines for action that often mark the practice literature. As Scott Briar and Henry Miller have indicated:

> Injunctions to "give support to the client" or to "clarify the client's feelings" are of little use unless the theory specifies in terms of behaviors to be performed by the practitioners how support may be given or how feelings may be clarified. . . . "Support" and "clarification" describe effects, not the actions to be taken to produce them. Such prescriptions amount to telling the practitioner to "make the client feel better" or "improve the client's social functioning."[2]

Therefore, the basic principles are presented in terms of operational definitions and procedures. These principles normally follow a particular order in direct-service generalist practice. This order is not to suggest, however, that they must be used in the sequence presented; the demands of practice will not permit such an abstract plan. Nor will all situations require the use of all these principles. Nevertheless, these principles and their operational definitions do tend to govern much of the sequence of the process of delivering direct services. Certainly the worker would do well to follow these principles in working with most consumers.

Five of these principles are based on the mediating model for generic social work developed by William Schwartz. It was Schwartz who first noted that the function of social work is "to mediate the process through which the individual and his society reach out for each other in a natural need for self-fulfillment."[3] Schwartz sees this function carried out through five generic tasks for the social worker in practice situations:

1. The task of searching out the common ground between the client's perception of his own need and the aspects of social demand with which he is faced.

2. The task of detecting and challenging obstacles which obscure the common ground and frustrate the efforts of people to identify their own self-interest with that of "significant others."

3. The task of contributing data—ideas, facts, value-concepts—which are not available to the client and which may prove useful to him in the attempt to cope with that part of social reality with which he is working.

4. The task of "lending a vision" to the client in which the worker both reveals himself as one whose own hopes and aspirations are strongly invested in the interaction between people and society and who projects a deep feeling for that which represents individual well-being and the social good.

5. The task of defining the requirements and the limits of the situation within which the client-worker system is set. These rules and boundaries establish the context for the "working contract" which binds the client and the agency to each other and which creates the conditions under which both client and worker assume their respective functions.[4]

Finding the Common Ground

The common ground is the interface between the consumer's perception of need and the tasks that connect this need to the social demands (the needs of others) in the immediate environment. It includes the connections between the consumer's need and the worker's service and the connections between the consumer and significant transactional systems: partner, family, neighborhood, school, work. Consider Mark, a fifth-grade student. He is considered a major disturbance in his classroom and was referred to the school social worker because he recently led a group of boys in the room to beat up another child on the playground. The worker needs to seek out the common ground between Mark's developmental needs (in this case perhaps perceived as competence in relation to peer group norms and status) and the school system's demands for classroom achievement. Work with Mark may well attempt to influence both Mark and the school system to connect in this common ground of increased competence in the eyes of peers.

This search for the common ground is pursued through two major activities. The first is to clarify the function of service in relation to the consumer's needs. This clarification requires a clear answer to the question "What are we going to work on together, Mark?" The second is to discover the connection between the individual and his or her transacting systems: "How is our task going to affect your relationship to your peers, your teacher, your family, your neighbors, and so on?"

Challenging the Obstacles

The detection and challenging of obstacles that obscure the common ground is a different dimension of the first task. Aspects of relationships can obscure the connections between people and others in their social systems. Do Mark and the teacher both realize they want the same thing for him—increased competence—but are defining it differently? Does Mark know that he can influence as well as react to the norms of his classroom peer group? These questions attack the obstacles between Mark's needs and those of his teacher and peers.

Obstacles are challenged through three major activities. First is the stage of pointing out these obstacles to the consumer. This information is not based on speculation; rather it is a description of misconnection: "Mark, you and your teacher are not together on your ideas about what is best for you. Mrs. Andrews, you and Mark don't seem to have the same ideas about what he needs." Second, this challenge of obstacles requires feedback on the specific aspects of behavior that prevent mutual satisfaction. Third is the "demand for work" or the consistent expectation that the person will continue his or her own development, even as the obstacles to achievement are being examined. Two questions are continually asked: "Are we working? What are we working on?"

Providing Information

Providing information is the principle of contributing ideas, opinions, facts, and feelings so that the person can see alternatives and choose courses of action. Information is critical to decision making. It can come directly from the worker or it can be drawn from others. For instance, Mark needs to know whether his next serious classroom disturbance will land him in a special disciplinary classroom. He also needs to know how the teacher and the school define "serious disturbance." He can be told that certain behavior is provocative to the teacher or the worker.

The principle of providing information is pursued through two specific activities. The first is the worker's disclosure of ideas, opinions, and feelings. These are always offered as *one* perspective—the worker's—and not as universal truths: "I don't know about others, Mark, but I find myself getting especially impatient with you at times like this, because I think you and Mrs. Andrews do want similar things for you—your achievement of more in school." Second, this principle requires that the information provided, either from the worker or from others, be relevant to the consumer's interest and task. The major question is: "How does this information relate to the purpose and goals of our work together?"

Lending a Vision

"Lending a vision" is the worker's basic contribution to the self-actualizing development of individuals and their social systems. It demands an unwavering faith that people and their social institutions can evolve into mutual aid systems. It reflects the worker's stake in the service provided. The worker with Mark needs to believe in the possibility that Mark's needs and the school system's needs can connect in a manner that satisfies both.

The vision is lent through four major activities: (1) the revelation of faith in the individual's dignity and power to act in his or her own behalf; (2) the revelation of the worker's own investment in the transactions between people and their social systems; (3) the trust in the power of human relations for synergistic growth; and (4) the encouragement of synergistic growth in the individual's specific situation.[5]

Defining Limits

The limits of the consumer–worker system are based on the context of their encounter. There are both institutional and personal boundaries to the working contract and its ongoing negotiation. The service itself places restrictions on the functions, roles, and responsibilities of both consumer and worker. The worker cannot promise Mark time outside of their work time together (on weekends, for instance) without creating consequences for the family systems of both. These boundaries are made explicit in the interests of self-determination and the mutual expectations of their work together.

This principle is pursued through the continual renegotiation of contracts; by specifying the functions, roles, responsibilities, and limits of the work together; and by monitoring work in a way that clarifies responsibilities when they seem obscure. The questions here are: "How are we working? How will we continue to work?"

Being Accountable to the Consumer

Aside from the principles proposed by Schwartz, there are others that guide effective generalist practice. All direct-service social work begins with the principle of accountability to the consumer. The starting point is consideration of the expressed need ("problem") as it is translated into the most pressing developmental task confronting the person. The principle of accountability to the consumer is pursued by determining this task and developing a service contract.

The contract is the explicit understanding and working agreement of the tasks to be accomplished. This open agreement permits the consumer, at least in theory, to hold the worker accountable for the worker's actions. Even though consumers often feel powerless (and frequently may be) to confront the worker about not upholding the terms of the contract, its use does show respect for the individual's rights and encourages partnership in the work together. Service contracts therefore not only contribute to accountability to the consumer but may also reduce the consumer's dependence. Consumers are not expected to enter into a relationship with an unknown worker based on blind trust that their interests will be capably served.

In developing the service contract with Mark, the fifth-grader, the social worker began by stating the teacher's and school's concern and asked Mark if he saw any problems. Mark said the school picked on him. This problem was translated into the task of decreasing the school's pressure on Mark. Mark indicated, with a great deal of zeal, that the problem lay in the teacher's perception of him as "leader of the gang." Another task was determined: Mark and the worker would have to change this perception of him. The stage is thus set for further work that leads to the next two principles: establishing goals and following the demands of the consumer's task.

Establishing Goals

The principle of establishing immediate and long-range developmental goals precedes the selection of service methods. The worker and consumer together consider this question: What needs to be influenced to bring about the desired change? From this question, specific targets are chosen, emphasizing the consumer's most important needs and the resources to be influenced in meeting these needs. Determining goals and targets with the individual should always take into account common and interdependent tasks. That is, these questions are raised: What others need to be influenced to bring about these desired changes? What others have these same needs which require similar tasks to meet them?

In establishing goals with Mark, the worker can begin to see what Mark is willing and able to do to alter the teacher's current perception of him. The worker can also note the worker's own best course of action immediately and later to achieve these goals. The immediate target has become change in the relationship between Mark and his teacher. As the work progresses toward this immediate goal, the longer-range goal of Mark's satisfaction and growth in the school setting and in his social living is determined by following the demands of his tasks.

Following Demands

During the translation of needs into goals and tasks and the identification of the target systems, the worker needs to look beyond the individual to see if others are facing the same tasks. At this point, tasks will call for activities in all four quadrants. The focus is on different units (individual, family, group, organization, or community) at different times. Depending on the units of focus and the goals established in the working contract, different methods are used at different times: casework, group work, family group work, organizational development, brokerage, case advocacy, community organization and development, policy or program development, and cause advocacy.

The social worker with Mark recognized that several other boys in his class appeared to be marking time in school. Their definition of competence, like Mark's, was related to the norms of their peer group, which deviated from those of the classroom. Indeed, a peer group experience that is designed to help them to develop these interpersonal competencies in a mutual aid system could accomplish their primary tasks and free them to use skills more effective for classroom learning. These competencies need to be developed without loss of self-esteem. The group work required contact with those who contributed to their current self-perceptions: their parents and the teacher (Quadrant B). Since Mark needed time for this development, the worker had to influence the policy that further disturbance would result in his transfer to a disciplinary classroom (case advocacy of Quadrant C). Moreover, the neighborhood provided few social supports for the development of cooperative skills in their peer groups. The worker sought to influence the Community Recreation Board to organize satellite programs throughout community neighborhoods that would be geared toward organized peer group socialization activities (Quadrant D).

Maximizing Support

Another basic principle is the maximization of support in the consumer's environment. This principle is closely related to following the demands of the consumer's task and is reflected in the examples of work with Mark and his schoolmates. The emphasis on this principle is stated succinctly by Ruth Middleman and Gale Goldberg:

> The professional helping relationship is a temporary one and an emphasis on changing existing structures and creating new structures to meet human needs recognizes this. The worker does not occupy the central position in the helping process. Indeed, he changes structures and creates structures that can operate without him. In other words, the social worker works himself out of a job.[6]

Life goes on for the consumer after the use of service. The social worker is not a medicine man who hawks his brew as a permanent cure-all. Nor is the social worker a mechanic with a toolbox that can "fix it" forevermore. Rather the social worker mediates processes between the individual and others so that social support is available for dealing with the continuous problems of living. Among these significant others may be specialists offering temporary help. Maximizing supports in the person's environment requires that direct-service workers know their own limitations in helping consumers and their social systems to develop their human potential.[7]

Continuing Assessment

The last significant principle is to continue to base work on assessment and evaluation. This principle requires mutual periodic reviews of the selected goals and targets, the methods and skills used to achieve these goals, and the outcomes of the mutual work. This assessment includes a joint decision about when to end the work together to move on to more independent social living and problem-solving. As the worker and Mark evaluate the changes that take place in Mark and in his situation (especially as resource systems are more available in his home, the school, and the community), they can agree to end this need for social service. Mark can get on to his life tasks of growth and development within his natural support systems, among his "significant others."

The ten principles we have discussed are summarized, this time in sequence, in Figure 4.2 (pp. 66–67).

The Principles in Use: An Example

The practice of a generalist social worker in a county public welfare agency in the Midwest provides an example of these principles used in sequence.[8] The worker, Allen Sutton, first visited Mrs. Baez in the local hospital, after hearing that a flash fire from a gasoline stove in the home (a converted garage) had killed Mr. Baez and their seven-month-old daughter. Mrs. Baez and three other children, who were in the home at the time, were badly burned and taken to the hospital. The first visit with Mrs. Baez occurred with the doctor's approval two days after the worker learned of the tragedy. Her upper body was covered with second- and third-degree burns; her arms were seriously burned from protecting the children from the flames. This physical trauma created a profound emotional depression. Moreover, the hospital had not told her of the deaths and asked Sutton to do so.

In terms of being *accountable to the direct consumer* (Mrs. Baez), Sutton introduces himself and his agency and awaits her response to his presence. Mrs. Baez comments that Sutton is the first person to visit her other than the hospital staff. She then inquires about the health of Mr. Baez and her baby daughter. Sutton recognizes that Mrs. Baez's first problem is to be able to face their deaths and experience the emotions that come with such a loss. He gently informs Mrs. Baez that her husband and daughter died in the ambulance after the fire.

Mrs. Baez immediately reacts by staring in disbelief and angrily accuses Sutton of lying, saying that the nurses have told her that they were improving. Again, he tells her that they did not survive the fire. Mrs. Baez begins to sob deeply and to curse the nurses for their deceit. After some moments of crying while Sutton remains silent, Mrs. Baez inquires about her other three children. Sutton informs her that two of them are off the critical list and the third is definitely improving. Mrs. Baez tries desperately to get up to go to them, finds she cannot, sobs more deeply, and says that she too should have died if she cannot be of help to her other children now.

In *searching out the common ground* between Mrs. Baez's needs and the immediate social demand, Sutton begins to relate Mrs. Baez's feelings to her relationship with her children and to her present inability to care for them (her general lines of connection and current developmental tasks). He comments that although she cannot be of physical help to the family now, certain matters do need her immediate decisions (*establishing immediate goals* in relation to the *long-range goals* of functioning fully as mother and caretaker).

The ensuing discussion develops the service contract, clarifies Sutton's function in relation to Mrs. Baez's needs, determines the immediate target systems, and begins to involve Sutton in a variety of activities requiring a variety of methods as he *follows the demands* of Mrs. Baez's tasks. They first discuss funeral arrangements at Mrs. Baez's initiation. She asks Sutton to make the funeral arrangements and he agrees. When he asks her about a minister, she informs him that Father O'Neil is her priest. He wonders if she would like to see him. She does, and Sutton tells her he will ask Father O'Neil to visit her in the hospital later that evening. Then they talk about the children and their need to know about the deaths. At first Mrs. Baez doubts her ability to tell them. Sutton points out how strong she seems in dealing with this tragedy and suggests she may be stronger by the time the doctor allows her to talk with them on the phone. He urges her to call them, suggesting that they need to know the truth and have her reassurance that she will take care of them as soon as they get well. Sutton also suggests that they need to talk about their feelings with her as she has with him (*providing information to the consumer*).

The next day, with the doctor's permission, Mrs. Baez called each of the children. They were happy to hear from her. Though crushed by the loss of their father and sister, they were reassured about being together again as a family. During subsequent contacts with Mrs. Baez and the children, Sutton continued to *lend a vision* of their ability to help each other through this terrible part of their lives. Moreover, he *continued to define the service contract* with Mrs. Baez *based on continual assessment*, in partnership with her, of her needs, goals, obstacles, and targets. For instance, Sutton told Mrs. Baez that he had contacted her sister, who

Principle	Operational Definition
1. Be accountable to the direct consumer.	Begin with the problem at hand. Develop a service contract with the consumer. Clarify the function of service in relation to consumer need.
2. Find the common ground between the consumer's perception of need and the social demand.	Seek out the connection between the consumer and his or her transacting systems. Translate needs into developmental tasks.
3. Establish immediate and long-term developmental goals.	Determine with the consumer the target systems to be influenced. Elicit the consumer's choice of priority tasks and targets. Determine whether others are facing the same task.
4. Follow the demands of the consumer's task.	Engage in all four types of activity: A: Work with consumer in own behalf. B: Work with consumer and others like consumer in their own behalf. C: Work with others in behalf of consumer. D: Work with others in behalf of consumer and others like consumer. Focus on different units at different times. Use different methods at different times: 1. Casework 2. Group work 3. Family group work 4. Organizational development 5. Brokerage 6. Case advocacy 7. Community organization and development 8. Policy development 9. Cause advocacy

Figure 4.2 Generic Principles of Generalist Social Work

5. Find the obstacles that obscure the common ground.

- Point out obstacles.
- Specify how the consumer's and other's behavior prevents mutual satisfaction.
- Ask for performance of consumer tasks even as obstacles are being examined.

6. Maximize support in the consumer's environment.

- Do not occupy a central position in the helping process; mediate processes between consumer and others.
- Influence change of social support structures as a permanent part of the consumer's life.
- Recognize your own limitations and use specialists when needed.

7. Provide information to the consumer.

- Disclose your ideas, feelings, and values as *one* perspective on the situation.
- Keep authenticity, openness, and information relevant to the consumer's task and interest.

8. Lend a vision to the consumer.

- Reveal your faith in the consumer's dignity and power.
- Reveal your own investment in the transaction between people and their social systems.
- Reveal your trust in the power of human relations.
- Provide hope in the possibility of synergistic growth.

9. Continue to define the requirements and limits of the worker–consumer system.

- Renegotiate contracts on the basis of work.
- Identify specific limits and responsibilities for work.
- Monitor work and clarify responsibilities when they are obscure.
- Establish goals, obstacles, and targets in partnership with consumers through renegotiated contracts.

10. Continue to base work on assessment.

- Use methods and skills pertinent to established goals and targets.
- Evaluate outcomes in mutual assessment.

lived in another community, as Mrs. Baez had suggested, and that she had notified relatives and friends about the funeral. While Mrs. Baez was helped to face her inability to attend the funeral, she and Sutton agreed that some of those attending could visit her in the hospital afterward— her mother, sister, a few in-laws, and Father O'Neil. Sutton made the arrangements.

Mrs. Baez confirmed, too, that she wished to remain in the community. Two weeks after the funeral, Sutton obtained public housing for the family. He also arranged for a neighbor to take care of one of the daughters who was released from the hospital before Mrs. Baez (*maximizing supports in the consumer's environment*), home tutoring for the other daughter who could not return to school for six to eight weeks after being released, and food, clothing, and furniture from such local agencies as the Red Cross and Salvation Army. During this period, he processed all the necessary forms with Mrs. Baez for obtaining social security, medical benefits, and public assistance, which began within thirty days after her release from the hospital (*following the demands of the consumer's task*). Her release took place four weeks after the funeral. Sutton and Mrs. Baez arranged for homemaker services, as she was still unable to use her heavily bandaged hands. While saddened still by the loss of her husband and daughter, Mrs. Baez had by that time regained much of her emotional confidence and concluded that she would make a new life for herself and her children. She was nevertheless concerned, as was Sutton, about presenting her tragic situation to other members of the community to prevent this tragedy happening to others.

This concern led to Sutton's involvement with her in cause advocacy and community organization (Quadrant D of the methods framework). They agreed to describe the conditions in which the Baez family was forced to exist before the fire to various community service organizations, including local clubs and more formal groups. First, Mr. Baez was unemployed yet ineligible for public assistance. Second, they had difficulty existing on his minimum wage before his unemployment. Third, inadequate ambulance and emergency service at the community hospital was partly to blame for the deaths. Mrs. Baez and Sutton spoke to local service groups to initiate a letterwriting campaign to state and federal legislators regarding a review of the state eligibility requirements for public assistance and the need for a higher national minimum wage. Much of Sutton's work was devoted to forming a committee of concerned lay and professional people in the community to study, make recommendations, and take action for improving the emergency preparedness of the hospital. This committee, including key hospital representatives, developed a backup ambulance service with a neighboring community hospital and proposed a building and staffing program to improve the hospital's emergency resources that was approved by the hospital board. As Sutton looked beyond Mrs. Baez's needs to see others facing similar situations, his generalist perspective led to his contribution to both Mrs. Baez's and the community's growth and development.

Summary

The generic principles for the direct-service generalist, who mediates between individuals and their social systems, are the guidelines for using the various methods and activities for practice. The ten principles are:

1. Be accountable to the direct consumer.

2. Find the common ground between the consumer's need and the social demand.

3. Establish immediate and long-term developmental goals.

4. Follow the demands of the consumer's task.

5. Challenge the obstacles that obscure the common ground.

6. Maximize support in the consumer's environment.

7. Provide information to the consumer.

8. Lend a vision to the consumer.

9. Continue to define the requirements and limits of the worker–consumer system.

10. Continue to base work on assessment.

Following these principles leads to a consumer-centered process of determining needs, goals, and targets. And this determination is the prerequisite for the selection of appropriate methods in direct-service practice—methods that can influence the synergistic development of both individuals and their social systems.

Suggested Learning Experiences

1.   Review the operational definitions of the ten generic principles for direct-service social work in Figure 4.2. Can you add any procedures to direct the use of these principles in practice?

2.   Think of some situations when a social worker would not use these principles in the suggested sequence—for instance, when providing information and lending a vision might *precede* establishing immediate and long-term developmental change goals. Can you find any common ground in your examples?

3.   In the case of Mrs. Baez presented in this chapter, what are the major obstacles that obscure the common ground between her perception of need and her social demand? Are there significant obstacles that the social worker does not detect and challenge? If so, what are they?

Suggested Case Studies

The principles discussed in this chapter can best be examined in practice situations. Case studies that lend themselves to the examination and discussion of these principles are listed at the end of Chapters 2 and 3. Five excellent examples are listed here.

Hoffman, Lynn and Lorence Long. "A System Dilemma." *Family Process* 8(2)(1968):211–234.

Morales, Armando and Bradford W. Sheafor. "The Social Worker in Action." In *Social Work: A Profession of Many Faces,* ed. Boston: Allyn and Bacon, 1977.

Purcell, Francis P. and Harry Specht. "The House on Sixth Street." *Social Work* 10(4)(1965):69–76.

Shapiro, Joan. "Group Work with Urban Rejects in a Slum Hotel." In *The Practice of Group Work,* ed. William Schwartz and Serapio R. Zalba. New York: Columbia University Press, 1971.

"165 Howell Street." In *Teaching Records: Integrative Learning and Teaching Project,* ed. Louis Lowry, Leonard M. Bloksberg, and Herbert J. Walberg. New York: Council on Social Work Education, 1973.

Chapter Five   Core Interactional Skills

Introduction

The core interactional skills for direct-service generalist social work, like the principles of the last chapter, are basic to the variety of methods in the social worker's repertoire. Figure 4.1 in the preceding chapter depicts this view. In this chapter these specific skills are described. *Skill* refers to the worker's dexterity in using practice principles and methods. It is the ability to apply knowledge and sensitivity in professional actions. In the case of generic skills, these actions refer to communication and problem solving in the variety of interpersonal relationships through which direct services are provided.

Like the generic principles, these skills are only guidelines—a beginning step in precision for the generalist practice described in this book. They deal with the worker's use of self in personal contacts in behalf of consumers. These communication and problem-solving skills are components of two separate models; one has evolved from within social work and one from outside. In this chapter, they are developed separately before their integration into a single framework for core interactional skills of the direct-service generalist.

Two recent studies have focused on the basic knowledge and skills required of direct-service BSW workers. The first used a national sample of practitioners and educators and a series of meetings for gathering data.[1] Fundamental areas of knowledge were identified: the cultural context of social welfare and social work; human functioning at the individual, group, and community levels; the social foundations of human need; the structure of societal responses to meet human need; and strategies for intervention to achieve change. Fundamental skills were identified also: information gathering and assessment; development of the professional self in interpersonal contexts; practice methods with individuals, groups, communities, and organizations; and evaluation of professional activities.

The second study used a representative national sample of 110 community mental health agencies and survey data to determine essential knowledge and skills for both MSW and BSW job performance.[2] The findings placed similar value on generic knowledge for both MSW and

BSW staff in two areas: knowledge of self and knowledge of community institutions. For BSW staff the generic skills were ranked as (1) interviewing, (2) communication and collaboration with other professions, and (3) diagnosis and assessment. For MSW staff the skills were ranked as (1) interviewing, (2) diagnosis and assessment, and (3) communication and collaboration with other professions.

Both these studies tend to corroborate the importance of core interactional skills for direct-service social work. The two models presented in this chapter—the Carkhuff model and the Shulman/Schwartz model—are instructive for establishing effective working relationships by using the generic principles developed in the last chapter and for the important tasks of gathering information, interviewing and other forms of communication, and engaging others in problem solving.

The Carkhuff Skill Model

From the many studies of divergent theories and helping processes, Robert Carkhuff has discovered that certain characteristics are common to effective helping. These characteristics were first termed "accurate empathy," "nonpossessive warmth," and "genuineness" by Carl Rogers.[3] Carkhuff followed this discovery by embarking on a series of research projects. His research suggests that effective helping is determined by the social worker's ability to provide the essential conditions of the helping process.

As the research progressed, several new dimensions were discovered and scales for their rating developed. Carkhuff has refined, renamed, and standardized the scales of the basic dimensions in a model for helping relationships in interpersonal contacts. This model, though still under revision, seems to stand apart from others because it is based on research and tested hypotheses.

The model is presented below and includes, first, an overview of the goals and phases of the helping process and, second, specific skills within the context of these goals and phases. Taken together, this framework provides a useful picture of the essential conditions of interpersonal relationships for achieving social work practice objectives.

Goals

Carkhuff's model conceptualizes goals to create more competent behavior in others (either direct or indirect consumers). Specific goals arise in the transaction between helper and others in interpersonal situations. The helper controls this transaction by providing the conditions for change through the use of self. This use can be taught, practiced, and used systematically in relation to three procedural goals: others' self-exploration, others' understanding, and others' action.

Self-exploration refers to the gathering of information for mutual determination of the problem and its meaning. *Understanding* is putting together pieces of the problem to gain a new perspective. *Action* is taking steps to correct the problem. These goals are cyclical. If people self-explore, they can gain a better understanding of their concerns—which in turn makes possible a more successful course of action. The action itself provides the ultimate feedback to the person who may need to alter his or her responses to achieve the desired behavioral outcome. The cycle is repeated as often as necessary to lead the person toward the goal (self-exploration ♦ better self-understanding ♦ more competent action ♦ self-exploration).

Phases

These goals indicate two general phases of helping processes: facilitative and initiative. The *facilitative phase* requires the suspension of judgment by the helper in order to establish a base for the skills used later in the *initiative phase* for problem solving rather than problem exploration. Carkhuff states this point succinctly: "Even if you have just fifteen minutes to help, you must use five minutes or so responding (facilitating) to the helpee in order to find out for sure where the helpee is before starting to put the picture together (initiating) and acting upon that picture."[4]

The eight skills constituting the core of effective helping in this general model are empathy, respect, warmth, concreteness, genuineness, self-disclosure, confrontation, and immediacy. Empathy, respect, and warmth are part of the facilitative phase of the helping process. Concreteness, genuineness, and self-disclosure are facilitative-initiative skills. Confrontation and immediacy are initiative skills. Now let us consider the skills of the facilitative phase: empathy, respect, and warmth.

Facilitative Skills

Empathy

Empathy is the most important skill in the helping process. Empathy is the ability to put oneself in another's place or see through the eyes of another. It describes a condition in which the helper understands others through perception and response at least as well as others understand themselves. Carkhuff's scale for measuring empathy refers to a minimum level of effectiveness in which a single interaction (helper's response and the other person's response to it) indicates that the other person is understood at her or his own level of expression in terms of both feeling and content. The deepest level of empathy conveys that the other person is understood beyond his or her own level of immediate awareness. Underlying feelings are identified, and the content is used to complement these feelings in adding deeper meaning to the other person's understanding.

Respect

Respect is demonstration of the helper's belief in the other person's ability to deal with problems given the right help. Carkhuff writes: "Without respect by the helper for some critical helpee characteristics, helping is not possible."[5] This skill is rarely noted as such in communication. It refers to trust in the integrity and potential of others and is therefore often included in responses demonstrative of empathy, warmth, and genuineness. Often its presence is discovered in its absence—that is, the lack of respect shown when the helper gives advice and makes plans for the other person. On Carkhuff's scale, given at the end of the chapter, level 3 refers to whether or not the helper believes in the ability of the other person to enter into the helping relationship. At level 4 there is the communication of a deep valuing of the other person and an intense belief in making sacrifices and bearing the risk of being hurt to further the helping relationship.

Warmth

Warmth, or caring, is primarily demonstrated through nonverbal means. It relates closely to empathy and respect and involves the use of self nonverbally to show attention and interest. At the deepest level (level 4 on Carkhuff's scale) the helper is wholly attentive to the interaction, resulting in the other person's feeling complete acceptance and significance.

Typical Responses

Now let us look at some typical responses demonstrating the various levels of empathy, respect, and warmth. We begin with empathy:

Teenager:		"I'm so shy. I know that's why people avoid talking to me."
Worker:	Level 1.	"Since you know your problem, quit being so shy." [Takes away feeling.]
	Level 2:	"I think you'll come out of your shell when you find a good enough reason to." [Denies feeling.]
	Level 3:	"I guess you feel kind of lonely. Your shyness keeps people away from you." [Includes other's content, identifies feeling of loneliness, and neither adds nor subtracts from other person's statement.]
	Level 4:	"It's depressing seeing others around you enjoying each other while you are left out. You are frightened about your

future if you don't become less shy."
[Contains all the elements of a level 3
response but *adds* underlying feeling
and deeper response to person's concern with the future as well as the
present.]

To illustrate respect, suppose a houseparent in an institutional setting
addresses the worker:

Houseparent: "I am sick and tired of these kids' slop-
                              piness. We've got more to do than pick
                              up after them all day. I wish you would
                              straighten them out about this."

Worker: Level 1:   "I'm here to counsel these kids. I
                              don't have time to do your job for
                              you." [Devalues houseparent as an
                              individual.]

                 Level 2:   "I can't help you with this. I would
                              like to, but if I do it may hurt the
                              relationship I'm trying to build with
                              these kids." [Declines help.]

                 Level 3:   "I can see you have a problem and
                              you're pretty frustrated. Let's talk
                              about what we might be able to do."
                              [Values other and offers help.]

                 Level 4:   "You seem hurt about their taking you
                              for granted. Picking up after them
                              must seem like all you can do for
                              them. I'll try to help. What do you
                              think can be done?" [Takes the other
                              person seriously, treats request non-
                              judgmentally, offers help, and respects
                              other's ideas about the situation.]

To illustrate warmth, suppose a mother confides in a child welfare
worker:

Mother: "I'm really tense lately. I find myself
                              screaming at everybody, including the
                              kids. I don't know why."

Worker: Level 1:   *Frowns in disapproval, pulls back in
                              chair, looks away.*

                 Level 2:   *Stiffly and without expression:* "Why?"

                 Level 3:   *Leans forward in chair with a look of
                              concern:* "You do seem worried about
                              something."

Level 4:   *Moves from chair and puts arms around her:* "You're afraid of what you might be doing to your kids. Tell me more about this and we'll see what we can do to help you."

Facilitative-Initiative Skills

From the base that the helper develops through empathy, respect, and warmth, the other person self-explores to ever-greater depths. This deeper self-exploration is the primary clue to effective use of self through these basic skills. When this self-exploration reaches a plateau, the skills of *concreteness, genuineness,* and *self-disclosure* are necessary. These three skills help to motivate the other person and lead to action. They initiate the problem-solving or planning stages of the action phase.

Concreteness

Concreteness refers to the other person's accurate labeling of feelings and experiences. In Carkhuff's words: "Concreteness enables the helpee to discuss all personally relevant feelings and experiences in specific and concrete terms. Taking a range of forms from direct questions to reflections, concreteness is a catalyst that makes possible full exploration of relevant problem areas."[6] The lowest effective level of concreteness (level 3 on the scale) requires the helper to be at least as specific as the other. Level 4 concreteness is demonstrated by the helper's responding in specific terms and soliciting specificity from the other person. During the earlier stage of the problem-solving process, this solicitation may involve asking for clarification of the other's vague statements. Later, it may entail helping the other person to enumerate clear alternatives, summarizing newly acquired self-understanding, or outlining plans for future action.

Genuineness

Genuineness is authenticity—the ability to be honest with others. The worker's words, in short, are closely related to his or her feelings. Carkhuff writes about the relationship of genuineness to respect and warmth in these words: "In addition to constituting a necessary dimension of the experiential base and indeed the goal of helping, one of the potentially critical dimensions of genuineness is the respect it communicates—we are most genuine with those for whom we care most."[7] He also conveys the relationship of genuineness to self-disclosure: "Although a helper may be genuine and not self-disclosing or self-disclosing and not genuine, frequently, and particularly at the extremes, the two are related."[8] The value of genuineness is related to the degree that it promotes a close relationship between the worker and others. If others recognize the worker's sincerity, they will risk greater genuineness themselves. This bond increases the odds of dealing with real problems, not just those deemed safe or socially acceptable. Level 3 genuineness is reflected in the helper's controlled expression of personal feelings. The worker is neither hiding feelings nor actively trying to label them. Level 4 refers to the congruence between the helper's verbal and nonverbal messages and to the helper's communication of feelings to others in a manner that strengthens the relationship.

Self-Disclosure

Self-disclosure leads to closeness in the helping process under the right conditions. Carkhuff stresses that "the key to the self-disclosure dimension is the word 'appropriate.' It is most appropriate for a helper functioning at a high level to be self-disclosing with a helpee functioning at a high level and least appropriate with a helpee functioning at a low level."[9] The social worker's *timing* of self-disclosure is perhaps more significant here than in any other dimension. At level 3, the worker reveals ideas, attitudes, and experiences relevant to the other person's concerns in a genuine fashion. The helper's feelings are revealed, but his or her uniqueness as a person is not communicated. At level 4, the helper volunteers information about his or her own ideas, experiences, and feelings when relevant to the other's interests and concerns. These expressions involve a degree of risk taking on the part of the helper as they reveal his or her uniqueness as a person.

Typical Responses

Now let us look at some typical responses demonstrating the various levels of concreteness, genuineness, and self-disclosure. To illustrate concreteness, suppose a mother of five is speaking in a family group meeting:

Mother:		"Well, I guess it's normal for brothers and sisters to fight, but I feel like a referee in a tag team wrestling match most of the time."
Worker:	Level 1:	"Yes, my knowledge of child development suggests that fights are normal among siblings." [Relates in the abstract, generally and impersonally.]
	Level 2:	"I guess having a large family today is often some kind of handicap." [Relates to concern but only generally.]
	Level 3:	"Fights among your five children can be hard on you, no matter what the experts say about how normal they are." [Relates to specifics of communication.]

Level 4: "You think the fights might be normal, but I'm not sure you really believe this. What do you believe about their fighting and how does this affect your ability to handle them?" [Uses her terms and seeks more specificity.]

To illustrate genuineness, suppose a ten-year-old group member is addressing the social worker:

Ten-year-old: "You don't like me as much as you do the others in this group. I can tell."

Worker: Level 1:   "Sure I do. You should know that!" [Insincere.]

Level 2:   "I'm sorry you feel that way but I can't pay you any more attention than anybody else in this group." [Preconceived role response, not true feelings.]

Level 3:   "It bothers me that you feel this way about me. What have I done that gives you this impression?" [Controlled expression of feelings, not challenging the relationship.]

Level 4:   "I'm not really sure how I feel about you. I'm glad that you brought this up now so we can talk about it. I have been wondering how you felt about me, especially when I don't let you get your own way in the group." [Congruent, here-and-now, positive and negative, and challenges the relationship.]

To illustrate self-disclosure, suppose a ten-year-old student complains to the social worker in school:

Student: "Whenever the kids pick sides on the playground, I'm always the last one chosen. I'm so clumsy they don't want me. What do you think I should do?"

Worker: Level 1:   "I really don't have any idea. Lots of people get left out of things." [No personal information.]

Level 2:   "I think you'll just have to accept that." [Advice does not reflect personal experience.]

Level 3: "At one time I felt left out at school too. I'm not sure that what I did will work for you. Would you tell me more about your situation? [Volunteers information in general terms.]

Level 4: "You know, when I was in fifth grade no one wanted me on their softball team. It took me a while to get over that. It sounds like you're experiencing the same kind of disappointment I experienced at your age. Maybe we can work this out together." [Expresses self freely and as unique.]

A major strength of the Carkhuff model is his development of helping skills in an *interactive* context. His basic principle is that high-level performance by helpers leads to high-level performance by others in the very same skills. His research has consistently demonstrated that problem solving can both help and hurt in this interactional system: Helpers with low-level skills can *decrease* rather than increase skills in others.

Thus concreteness, genuineness, and self-disclosure are important skills in this context. The prognosis for effective problem solving depends on the degree to which the helper can use the self in these situations. Further, the degree to which others can be specific about the problem (can label it accurately, for instance), can be honest with the helper, and can disclose themselves will determine whether or not they will, in fact, receive help. These skills are built upon those of the facilitative phase and are the basis, in turn, for the initiative phase.

Initiative Skills

Carkhuff regards the facilitative phase as essential, but the initiative action phase is the crucial phase of problem solving. Here the tough decisions are made and the hard work is done. Here the social worker's expertise is most tested. In this phase the helper's toughness and confidence are challenged. The worker must be capable of helping to develop a strategy that will resolve the problem and at the same time provide a method for attacking future problems. The two skills used for this problem solving are *confrontation* and *immediacy*.

Confrontation

Confrontation in this context means informing others about discrepancies in what is being said and what is being done. The value of confrontation is that it provides the other person with another point of view to consider in the process of self-evaluation. Confrontation introduces the possibility of a new reality. Carkhuff further notes that confrontation may be directed toward the other person's strengths or limitations. Level 3 confrontation refers to the helper indicating discrepancies without pointing out their specific directions. Level 4 confrontation requires a response clearly pointing out discrepancies and the specific directions in which these lead. This focuses others' attention on specific contradictions in behavior. It increases awareness of discrepancies and their relation to the problem.

Immediacy

Immediacy refers to what transpires between the helper and the other person. Carkhuff regards immediacy as the bridge between empathy and confrontation. Its value in problem solving, especially in initiation, is in answer to Carkhuff's question: "What is the helpee really trying to tell me that he cannot tell me directly?"[10] Immediacy therefore makes possible the communication of deep understanding in the helper–other relationship when the social worker responds to what is happening in the relationship here and now. Level 3 immediacy is demonstrated when the worker acknowledges the other person's references to the relationship without commital. Level 4 occurs when both accurately, appropriately, and explicitly refer to their transactional system as it exists at the moment.

Typical Responses

Now let us look at some typical responses demonstrating the various levels of confrontation and immediacy. To illustrate confrontation, suppose an aged and secluded resident in a nursing home is speaking:

Resident:		"I've been here two years now and I don't know anybody. I can't seem to make friends here. I think people are only out for themselves. They don't want to hear about some old woman's problems."
Worker:	Level 1:	"That's a shame." [Accepts statement prematurely; ignores discrepancy.]
	Level 2:	"You seem concerned because you haven't been able to make friends here." [Does not refer to discrepancy.]
	Level 3:	"Can you tell me some of the things you've tried to do to make friends?" [Tentative exploration of discrepancy.]
	Level 4:	"You're excusing yourself when you find it difficult to reach out to others

here. You know that you need and want others for friends. As long as you make excuses and write them off as not caring, you will feel this emptiness." [Firm directional statement of discrepancy.]

To illustrate immediacy, suppose a hospital patient is speaking:

Patient: "We've been discussing my placement needs for two weeks now, and I still don't know where I'll be going. You might as well quit coming to see me. In fact, I don't think we can talk about anything today."

Worker: Level 1: "I have talked with the Rehabilitation Center Staff." [Ignores here and now.]

Level 2: "Don't give up. This planning takes time." [Dismisses.]

Level 3: "You're not satisfied with the way things are going. It's not unusual to feel that way when you're afraid of what will happen to you when you leave the hospital." [Open, yet general.]

Level 4: "You're experiencing a lot of frustration because nothing seems to be happening. You're mad at me. It sounds like you don't think I'm willing or able to help you with this placement. Maybe we ought to talk about *that*." [Explicit and current.]

The Carkhuff Model in Summary

Carkhuff's entire developmental model, while somewhat oversimplified considering the dynamics of helping, depends on the timing of the helper. Effective problem solving, regardless of specific goals, unit of focus, method used, or the contact person, involves the art of knowing how and when to respond helpfully. The key to this art of timing is the understanding of one's impact on others—in a word, *empathy*. Empathy is the ability not only to perceive the other's perception of significant events but also the other's perception of the immediate and ongoing transactional process. Figure 5.1 summarizes Carkhuff's developmental model of interpersonal helping skills. It is significant that empathy is first and, as suggested, foremost.

Self-Exploration → Better Understanding → More Competent Action or Direction	
Facilitative Phase (Rapport–Building Phase: helper's humanity emphasized)	**Initiative Phase** (Risk-Taking Phase: helper's toughness and self-confidence emphasized)
1. Empathy (depth of understanding) 2. Respect (belief in dignity) 3. Warmth (caring)	7. Confrontation (pointing out discrepancies) 8. Immediacy (relating to the here and now)
4. Concreteness (ability to be specific) 5. Genuineness (sincerity) 6. Self-disclosure (ability to convey personal feelings)	

Figure 5.1 Key Skills in a Helping Relationship

The Shulman/Schwartz Skill Model

Lawrence Shulman and William Schwartz developed their models for social work skills through application of the five generic mediating tasks (presented in Chapter 4) to practice with groups. It was after the development of these skills for group work that their potential for generalist practice was considered. Just as the mediating tasks are generic principles for direct-service practice, so too are these mediating skills. While Shulman has worked on the identification of these skills, Schwartz has developed them into phases.

Schwartz's Phases of Skills

To Schwartz, the mediating tasks are carried out through skills related to four phases of work: (1) tuning-in, (2) beginning, (3) the substantive work on the problems that brought worker and consumer together, and (4) endings or transitions. These phases apply to the duration of the worker–consumer relationship and to each contact in the helping process.

The *tuning-in* (preparation) *phase* is not the preparation of diagnostic statements or formulation of consumer goals. These are meaningless when workers enter ongoing transactional systems that are in a continuous process of change. Tuning-in requires what Schwartz has called "preliminary empathy"—that is, making oneself sensitive to the subjective world of consumers and their veiled communications. Our prior knowledge about special needs and issues is related to preparation for that action.

The essential questions are: Where might the consumer system be when I enter it? How might my entering affect it?

The *beginning phase* establishes the clear conditions of work in terms of a contract. The needed skills are clear articulation of why applicants need service and the worker's part in providing it; solicitation of feedback and checking mutuality of purpose; and establishment of a partnership with consumers. The essential question is: What are we going to work on together?

The *work phase* involves the worker's skill in carrying out his or her part of the contractual process. The questions now are: Are we working? What are we working on? Here the central tasks are fully carried by the worker. The essential skills are the ability to perceive when work is going on and when it is being avoided; the ability to elicit opposites and challenge ambiguities; the partializing of large problems into manageable pieces; the discovery of connections between small segments of experience; the insistence on talk that is purposeful and invested with feeling; and the ability to demand work that is inherent in the worker's helping function.

The *transitions and ending phase* involves the question: What have we accomplished? The worker's skills require monitoring time, demanding work, partializing problems, eliciting opposites, projecting to the future, and sharing feelings with consumers.[11]

These phase-specific skills can be viewed as "skills of living," useful for anyone in coping with their environmental system. The skills become social work in reference to the mediating function. These skills by definition are interactional and promote the self–system synergy that is the basic objective of social work. Their contribution depends on the degree to which they bring individual needs and societal resources together for the benefit of both.

Shulman's Identification of Skills

Shulman develops his model of mediating skills around two categories: *cognitive* techniques and *transitive* techniques.[12] The cognitive skills involve *knowing*; the transitive skills involve *doing*. Analysis of the skill requires a recognition of (1) the social worker's act; (2) the target of the worker's act; (3) the stimulus that triggers the worker's act; (4) the specific meaning of the stimulus to the worker; (5) the expected result of the worker's act; and (6) the concepts on which the worker bases his or her act. Now let us examine an outline of the skills in the Shulman model:[13]

A. Cognitive Skills

1. *Identifying the common ground:* finding the connections between the individual's needs and the needs of others

2. *Identifying obstacles:* determining how consumers and others obscure their common ground and frustrate their mutual aid

3. *Interpreting clues of verbal behavior:* translating words into a concept of need

4. *Interpreting clues of nonverbal language:* translating body language into a concept of needs

5. *Identifying patterns of behavior:* perceiving repetitious forms of behavior

6. *Contacting one's own feelings:* being aware of the worker's own feelings in the interaction

B. Communication Skills

1. *Stepping up weak signals:* amplifying weak communication (words, tone of voice, body expression) so that it is fully understood

2. *Stepping down strong signals:* reducing another's strong communication (shouting, sarcasm, body expressions) for fuller understanding

3. *Dealing with the theme of authority:* talking about obstacles to interaction presented by authority

4. *Redirecting signal to intended recipient:* indicating for whom the message of a perceived misdirected communication might really be intended

5. *Reaching for facts:* requesting specific elaboration of a communication

6. *Focused listening:* paying attention to communications in order to determine whether work is occurring and what is being worked on

7. *Reaching for feelings in relation to work:* asking for feelings related to accomplishing the task that the worker suspects are present

8. *Waiting out feelings (supporting other in taboo areas):* containing one's response as the other person struggles to express complex feelings

9. *Understanding other's feelings:* responding with empathy

10. *Sharing thoughts and feelings:* expressing one's precise thoughts and feelings engendered by the immediate situation

11. *Seeking out empathic help:* asking others if they can respond to an elusive feeling

12. *Putting the other's feelings into words:* anticipating the other person's feelings

C. Problem-Solving Skills

1. *Clarifying purpose:* explaining the concerns to be discussed

2. *Providing working data:* providing information useful to the other person's decision making

3. *Encouraging feedback:* asking for the other person's ideas on specific subjects discussed together

4. *Confronting contradictions:* providing information that differs from the other person's interpretation of reality

5. *Pointing out obstacles (pointing out illusion of work):* providing information on obstacles to achieving work goals

6. *Pointing out the common ground:* providing information on the mutual needs between parties at the point of conflict

7. *Defining limits:* providing information on the limitation of the other person's activity imposed by the reality of the situation

8. *Defining the contract:* providing information to clarify the responsibilities of work together

9. *Displaying feelings openly:* letting the other person know one's feelings about the situation

10. *Supporting the other's strength:* expressing faith in the other's ability to handle the situation

11. *Partializing the concern:* breaking down a complicated problem into more easily solved components

12. *Making the problem the other's:* holding the other responsible for dealing with the problem within the boundaries of the contract

13. *Waiting out the problem:* not acting and therefore allowing the other person to assume responsibility for work on the problem

14. *Helping the other person to see the problem in a new way:* rephrasing or redefining the problem so that a new perspective may be gained

15. *Contacting "significant others":* meeting directly with others in behalf of the person's needs

Shulman's recent research on the use of these skills with individuals, families, and groups suggests the important combination of rapport-building and problem-solving skills in effective practice.[14] In Shulman's research, certain skills correlated significantly with positive relationships and helpful outcomes. These skills, ranked in order of strength, were "sharing worker's own thoughts and feelings," "understanding the other's feelings," "defining the contract," "reaching for feelings," "providing working data," and "partializing the other's concerns." The problem-solving skills that correlated strongly with helpfulness were "supporting others in taboo areas," "understanding the other's feelings," and "sharing one's own thoughts and feelings." Shulman's data, like Carkhuff's, suggest that effective service is based on the use of core interactional skills—both for establishing empathic relationships and for enabling the other person to take action in areas of concern.

The Shulman/Schwartz Model in Summary

In sum, the Shulman/Schwartz model identifies phases of helping through the use of specific cognitive, communication, and problem-solving skills. These skills enable the worker to establish a relationship in behalf of others. It is this relationship in its sensitivity and purposefulness through which change occurs. Help comes from the worker's conscious and creative use of these skills in the immediate responses to those involved in practice situations. Especially significant are the worker's abilities to both support and challenge the other person through eliciting, understanding, and sharing feelings and through encouragement to act on the basis of this understanding.

Integration of Models

The Carkhuff and Shulman/Schwartz models for basic skills intersect at several points. First, both specify phases in their delineation of skills. Second, both place emphasis on the promotion of human relations and the consumer-centered concept of specific goals. Third, the skills are considered interactional and are related to the communication/facilitative and problem-solving/initiative dimensions common to all interpersonal contact in practice. Moreover, both models are consistent in their view of the mediating function of social work and the implementation of the generic principles described in Chapter 4.

Table 5.1 summarizes these generic skills for the direct-service generalist. Together, these skills are as relevant to one-to-one interviewing and consulting as they are to group discussion. In fact, they are useful in any direct contact with another person in the fulfilling of social work's purpose.

Summary

The generic principles of direct-service generalist practice are put into action through the core interactional skills. Two models for these skills have been developed to integrate phases of the helping process, the generic principles, and the interpersonal dimensions of communication and problem solving. Both the Carkhuff and the Shulman/Schwartz models are promising for their precise and systematic listing of core skills in reference to direct-service generalist practice.

All the principles and skills described in this book contribute to the development of self-actualizing human relations. In Part 1 we have examined the generalist framework, the basic interactional skills, and the

Table 5.1   Core Interactional Skills
for the Direct-Service Generalist

Phase of Process and Generic Principles	Interactional Skills	
	Communication	Problem Solving
Tuning-in (exploration) 1. Accountability to consumer 2. Searching out common ground	*Carkhuff* Empathy Warmth Respect *Shulman/Schwartz* Anticipatory empathy Identifying common ground Identifying obstacles Contacting	*Shulman/Schwartz* Generalizing from experience Connecting segments of experience Identifying patterns of behavior
Beginning (understanding) 3. Establishing developmental goals 4. Following demands of consumer's task	*Carkhuff* Concreteness Genuineness Self-disclosure *Shulman/Schwartz* Clear articulating of need Dealing with theme of authority Seeking feedback on mutuality Reaching for feelings Waiting out feelings Interpreting clues of verbal/nonverbal behavior	*Shulman/Schwartz* Using agency function Clarifying purpose Partializing Sharing own thoughts and feelings Understanding the other's feelings Putting feelings into words Identifying patterns of behavior Pointing out common ground
Work-resolution (action) 5. Detecting and challenging obstacles 6. Maximizing support in consumer's environment 7. Providing information 8. Lending a vision 9. Defining limits	*Shulman/Schwartz* Perceiving work Stepping up weak signals Stepping down strong signals Redirecting signals Reaching for facts Reaching for feelings Reaching for opposites Understanding the other's feelings Pointing out common ground Elaborating Sharing own feelings Clarifying purpose Encouraging feedback	*Carkhuff* Confrontation Immediacy *Shulman/Schwartz* Focused listening Partializing Pointing out obstacles to work Confronting Providing work data Contacting others Seeking empathic help Monitoring time Making problem the other's Sharing own thoughts and feelings Offering alternatives Indicating consequences Putting other's feelings into words Defining limits
Endings or transitions 10. Assessing/evaluating	*Shulman/Schwartz* Reaching for facts Reaching for feelings Reaching for opposites Sharing own thoughts and feelings	*Shulman/Schwartz* Monitoring time Demanding ending work Partializing the past Preparing for immediate future Sharing own thoughts and feelings

relation of both to self-actualizing development. We now turn to Part 2, which presents the biopsychosocial nature of this development as it relates to consumer tasks and social services. Social work practice can be judged, in the end, only on its power to foster these developmental processes.

Suggested Learning Experiences

1. Discuss in class the generic principles and core interactional skills used in the practice examples in Harold Lipton and Sidney Malter, "The Social Worker as Mediator on a Hospital Ward," in *The Practice of Group Work*, ed. William Schwartz and Serapio R. Zalba (New York: Columbia University Press, 1971), pp. 102–118. Identify these principles and skills. Consider how they could have been better used at particular points in the work. Where were they used effectively?

2. Do the following self-help exercise—Helping Oneself: An Exercise in Facilitative Stage Skills—adapted from Gerald Egan, *Exercises in Helping Skills* (Monterey: Brooks/Cole Publishing Co., 1975), pp. 66–67. In this exercise, you are asked to carry on a dialogue with yourself. Choose a problematic area in your life that is relevant to your interpersonal style and your competence as a social worker. Use the Carkhuff skills of the facilitative stage (Shulman/Schwartz early phase) to explore this problem. Do not proceed beyond the early phases; do not confront yourself or start elaborating action programs for yourself.

First study the following example, which involves a beginning worker, untrained, in a halfway house for people who have been in mental hospitals. This dialogue takes place in the worker's mind:

Self:	I'm not so sure I should be working at that halfway house. I've studied a lot of psychology in the last three years of college, but it hasn't been the kind of stuff that helps me with my job. I'm not sure whether I'm helping anybody there or not. I'm a willing worker, but I'm not sure how effective I am.
Response:	You just don't feel prepared to do what you're doing. You work hard, but you still feel inadequate.
Self:	Yeah. I'm pretty much on my own there. I have to figure out what to do. In a sense, I'm trusted. But since I don't get much supervision, I have to go on my own instincts, and I'm not sure they're always right.

Response:	Being left to your own devices doesn't increase your sense of personal adequacy. There's still that what-am-I-doing-here feeling.
Self:	Sure! There are days when I ask myself just that: what am I doing here? I provide day-to-day services for a lot of people. I listen to them. I take them to the doctor. I try to help them participate with one another in conversation and games and things like that. I try to urge them to be responsible for their personal appearance and for the house. But it seems that I'm always just meeting the needs of the moment. I don't feel that I'm helping these people reach any long-range goals.
Response:	You don't feel that there's a great deal of substance or much overall direction to what you're doing, and that's depressing.
Self:	I am depressed. I'm down on myself. Down on the house and the directors. I feel that the most honest thing to do is quit.
Response:	Saying good-bye to the job seems to fit in best with your emotional state right now.

Now write out an example of your own, using a problem in your own development as a social worker.

3. Do the following self-help exercise (Carkhuff action stage; Shulman/Schwartz work phase), also adapted from Egan (pp. 95–97). This exercise is similar to the last, except that it deals with later stage skills as well.

First, continue the dialogue with yourself.

Second, state the problem explored in the preceding exercise. The problem should be relevant to your interpersonal style and competence as a social worker.

Third, use the skills of the facilitative and action stage (or earlier and later phases, especially those of the later phases) to explore the problem further and come to the kind of self-understanding that demands action (although it is not necessary to elaborate an explicit action program).

4. When your self-dialogue is finished, rate the responses that use Carkhuff's skills on the accompanying scale. Use the skill label and number representing effectiveness of use.

Helping Behavior: A Rating Scale

1	2	3	4
Poor	Ineffective	Minimally Effective	Good

Facilitative Skills

Primary-level accurate empathy: The helper communicates an accurate understanding of the other person's feelings, experiences, and behavior from the *other's* frame of reference.

Concreteness: The helper helps the other person speak about specific feelings, experiences, and behavior in specific situations. The helper encourages relevant disclosure rather than storytelling.

Genuineness: The helper is always sincere and does not hide behind professional roles. The helper is spontaneous and open, but does not overwhelm the other person. The helper is not defensive.

Respect: The helper's verbal and nonverbal behavior indicate that he or she supports the other's interests. The helper is initially nonjudgmental but gradually helps the other person place demands on himself or herself. The helper shows regard for the other's individuality and resources.

Action Skills

Advanced accurate empathy: The helper communicates an understanding of what the other person only implies, hesitates to say, or has poorly formulated. The helper helps the other understand himself or herself at deeper levels.

Self-disclosure: The helper is ready to disclose anything that will enable the other person to understand himself or herself better, but in a way that keeps the focus on the other.

Confrontation: The helper challenges contradictions in the other person's life and communication with the helper. The helper invites the other person to explore these discrepancies and challenges the client to employ unused resources.

Immediacy: The helper talks about what is happening in the here and now of their relationship as a way of helping the other person explore his or her interpersonal style from alternative frames of reference.

Suggested Case Studies

The skills discussed in this chapter, and many of the principles of Chapter 4 as well, are put into practice in the following case studies.

Lee, Judith A. and Carol R. Swenson. "Theory in Action: A Community Social Service Agency." *Social Casework* 59(6)(1978):359–369.

Middleman, Ruth R. and Gale Goldberg. *Social Service Delivery: A Structural Approach*. New York: Columbia University Press, 1974. Especially pages 83–150 and 205–210.

Schwartz, William and Serapio R. Zalba, eds. *The Practice of Group Work*. New York: Columbia University Press, 1971.

Shulman, Lawrence. *A Casebook of Social Work Practice with Groups: The Mediating Model*. New York: Council on Social Work Education, 1968.

Suggested Readings

Bowles, Dorcas D., "Making Casework Relevant to Black People: Approaches, Techniques, Theoretical Implications." *Child Welfare* 48(8)(1969):468–475.

Work with the Wright family is presented as an example of working with the life-styles and value systems of poor black families. The family consists of Mrs. Wright, age twenty-four; Mr. Wright, twenty-six and unemployed; and Angela, six; Harry, five; Joyce, three; and Marie, two. The worker is involved in AFDC services in a public welfare agency. Her initial contact with the Wrights comes from Harry's and Angela's frequent absence from school—Mrs. Wright vacillates between helping them get ready one morning and not being concerned on another morning. The example ends with a discussion-provoking list of thirteen special techniques for working with families like the Wrights.

Kadushin, Alfred. "Cross-Cultural Interviewing." In *The Social Work Interview*. New York: Columbia University Press, 1972.

While there are a variety of sources on cross-cultural implications for the use of interactional skills in practice, this source integrates so much of the theory and research that it can stand by itself. It includes material on class, race, sex, and age differences and how they affect the interview. While geared primarily to the worker–consumer contact, many of the implications are relevant to other face-to-face interactions in practice.

Basic Theory and Practice Theory

2

Chapter Six   Developmental Theory

Introduction

Part 2 deals with another generic element of direct-service generalist practice: theory. Chapters 6 and 7 present aspects of basic theory and how it applies to assessment. Chapter 8 introduces the components of practice theories, or interventions. In this chapter we examine basic theory from the generalist perspective in relation to the personality system—that is, individual development. The next chapter explores aspects of theory in relation to social system development.

We in social work have a difficult task because of our dual focus on both the person and the environment. In other words, we need a knowledge base of human behavior in the social environment if we are to analyze transactions between the personality system and the social system. Many authors have written about the problems this dual focus poses for the profession and for individual practitioners.[1] Harris Chaiklin argues that the problem arises from our having to understand the relationships of people as "personality systems" to their environment as "social systems" without a current theory for putting the person and the social system together.[2] That is, we are using two separate concepts of these systems in order to deal with them.

The conceptual unit of the personality system is the *person*. The person is viewed as a system of biopsychosocial needs and creative and coping behavior. Through these characteristics the person's behavioral patterns, regardless of the specific theory, are interpreted. The conceptual unit of the social system is not the person, however, but what occurs between persons—in a word, *interaction*. Patterns of behavior in social systems are interpreted in reference to certain aspects of interaction, such as roles or ecological processes (the way social systems are affected by other social systems).

Direct-service social work, and the assessments on which it is based, therefore relies on abstract concepts. We can see the physical person in an interaction, but we cannot see a personality system or social system— we need *theory* to interpret the behavior of these systems. Meaning is never, by itself, obvious. Only through theory can we interpret these processes. Since a person's behavior contains both personality and social system components, the question we face is: How can we use these concepts to interpret the individual's needs, behavior, and problems in transactions with the environment? To approach this problem we will be focusing on the basic theories that can help us understand developmental processes toward self-actualizing human relations.

Toward this objective the direct-service generalist needs an understanding of human biopsychosocial growth and the place of human relations in this growth. Since direct-service social work methods and processes are used with individuals, families, groups, organizations, and communities, this understanding entails generic developmental concepts and the specific theories of the development of these distinct, yet interrelated, systems. This knowledge constitutes the assessment base for practice.

This chapter presents concepts useful for understanding biopsychosocial processes. It constitutes just one point of view, however, as our knowledge of human behavior and the social environment is forever evolving, forever tentative, and forever limited in its own development. This position, then, is a temporary synthesis between systems and developmental models for human growth. Other syntheses have been attempted, and this chapter and the next stand in the tradition of, yet offer an alternative to, this work.[3] This tradition is a response to Robert Chin's earlier challenge to relate systems and developmental models for change to each other and to point out directions for those involved in promoting change.[4] Together, systems and developmental models form a comprehensive assessment framework for generalist social work.

General Developmental Theory

Life is a developmental process, as evolution is inherent in nature. We are both servant and master of this process. Like other creatures of nature, we are bound by certain genetic laws of development. Unlike other creatures of nature, we alone can spontaneously create our actions and consciously reflect on our actions for personal meaning. The concept of human developmental processes evolves from an understanding of the fundamental laws of development in nature and our human potential.

The seeds of development are sown genetically. At birth, human beings are endowed with the necessary systems for interaction with the world and with self-generative processes that ensure development toward self-actualization. The self is actualized through a continuous growth process—a continuous reintegration into a new and more satisfying sense of self and world. Heinz Werner and Edward Kaplan describe the fundamental *law of the dialectic* in which organisms synthesize their tendencies not only to maintain continuity for survival but also to create the discontinuity necessary for growth: "There is, on the one hand, the tendency of organisms to *conserve* their integrity . . . on the other hand, the tendency to *develop* towards a relatively mature state: under the widest range of conditions, organisms undergo transformation from the status of relatively little differentiated entities to relatively differentiated and integrated adult forms."[5]

Therefore, purposefully directed growth is based biologically in the nature of the human being's existence as body-in-the-world. There is an autonomous and interdependent purpose, direction, and order in the biology of life that extends from the single cell to the cosmos. Consider the magnificent strength in purpose of the human embryo. The embryo grows from 100 to 200 billion cells and from 15 ten-millionths of a gram to 3,250 grams in a nine-month period![6] A recent book by an embryologist, Lewis Thomas, has dealt with this power of the membrane from the single cell to the cosmos. Thomas puts this biological purpose in the following words:

> It takes a membrane to make sense out of disorder in biology. You have to be able to catch energy and hold it, storing precisely the needed amount and releasing it in measured shares. . . . To stay alive, you have to be able to hold out against equilibrium, maintain imbalance, bank against entropy, and you can only transact this business with membranes in our kind of world.

And on the "World's Biggest Membrane":

> Taken all in all, the sky is a miraculous achievement. It works, and for what it is designed to accomplish, it is as infallible as anything in nature. I doubt whether any of us could think of a way to improve on it, beyond maybe shifting a local cloud from here to there on occasion. The word "chance" does not serve to account well for structures of such magnificence.[7]

Several principles of development are relevant to the social worker's use of human relations to strengthen self-actualization within the limitations and potentials of individual capacity and the environment. These are the principles of *orthogenesis, microgenesis, homeostasis,* and *functional analogy.*

Orthogenesis

Werner develops the biopsychosocial gestalt of development through the biological principle of *orthogenesis.* That is, the organism's action systems become increasingly differentiated and hierarchically integrated with later systems.[8] The concepts of differentiation and hierarchical integration reflect the complexity of human development in which both progressive and regressive changes can occur. Human development is not linear but multilinear or spiral. Many selves (biological, psychological, social) arise in parallel. In uninterrupted development, these differentiated selves are related progressively into a hierarchically integrated pattern or gestalt. Regression, by contrast, is characterized by increased de-differentiation and disintegration of this self-gestalt.

Microgenesis

The older selves are not lost, however. They are transformed into newer selves or integrated as subordinates of the current self-gestalt. Therefore, earlier selves are always present as a basis for action. Faced with a novel situation, such as a new stage of biopsychosocial development, we often approach it through a sequence of actions that range from our lowest (earliest) to our highest (most recent) selves. This principle of *microgenesis* describes regression to lower stages to support higher development.

Homeostasis

Within both orthogenesis and microgenesis are self-regulating processes related to the principle of *homeostasis* or equilibrium. Jean Piaget refers to this self-regulation as "formative instability combined with a progressive movement toward stability."[9] According to Piaget, the functional relations within the child's selves are always in disequilibrium but this disequilibrium decreases with development. That is, the child is endowed with self-regulating biological systems that are directed toward establishing equilibrium. Development is the progressive approximation to an ideal state of balance that is never fully reached. Alas, living and growing are an inevitable struggle.

Functional Analogy

Finally, the proposition of *functional analogy* relates this individual development to human relations. This proposition states that earlier stages and systems are the models for later stages and systems. In other words, the tenets of the individual's biological development apply also to that complex biopsychosocial entity called a group or social system.

Werner combined this relationship of biological to social development by proposing that "the personality grows and becomes differentiated in reciprocity with respect to differentiation of the social organism to which it belongs. It develops as it participates in the formation of objective values and as it bends itself to achieve ends established by the group."[10] In other words, he believes that our personality normally grows and becomes differentiated against the growth and differentiation of the social world.

Four Useful Theories of Development

Chapters 6 and 7 present four theories of development that are useful for social work practice toward self-actualizing human relations. The first is Maslow's developmental need theory; the second is Erikson's developmental task theory; the third is a theory of social system development; and the fourth is an integrated theory of stages of group development.

All four theories are complementary representations for the assessment of the person–environment transaction to which social practice is directed. Maslow's and Erikson's theories of individual development are discussed in this chapter; the social systems theories are the subject of Chapter 7.

Maslow's Hierarchy of Developmental Needs

Abraham Maslow's developmental theory centers on a hierarchical continuum of needs.[11] These needs are "instinctoid" in nature. That is, they are biologically based and their frustration leads to ill health and stunted development. The basic needs with which the human organism is born include:

1. Physiological or survival needs (air, water, food, shelter, sleep, sex, contact)

2. Safety and security needs (predictability, control, structure)

3. Belongingness (participation, fidelity, validation) and love (closeness, caring)

4. Esteem (respect, competence, efficacy)

5. Self-actualization (realization of unique potentialities)

Needs must be satisfied according to this sequence. In other words, an individual is not concerned with esteem—nor can social work directed to this goal appeal to one—until one has a minimum and consistent satisfaction of one's survival, safety, belongingness, and love needs.

At any given moment, all five needs are present for the individual but one need is *dominant* in terms of the individual's motivation. The individual's first unsatisfied need in order of priority is that person's dominant need. Lower-level needs must be satisfied before higher-level needs are dominant. Any change in the person, the environment, or both may shift the individual's dominant need along the continuum. The shifting of needs creates that individual's motivation in the situation. Motivation is based on needs, actions, goals, and the energy released to achieve these goals. The energy increases with the intensity of the need. While the person's dominant need may shift from situation to situation, the individual's behavior and energies are seeking at least partial satisfaction of more than one need at a time. The nature of the dominant needs explains the person's connections with people and objects.

If the lower-level needs have been consistently satisfied in most life situations, the person's dominant needs tend to be at a higher level. These higher-level needs then regulate the lower-level needs. If the lower-level needs have not been fulfilled, however, the person's developmental potential may be stunted in immature and energy-consuming behavior patterns geared to satisfying them.

The resources to meet these needs are the human relations and objects in the person's environment. For these needs to be met the environment must furnish the essential nutrients of freedom, justice, orderliness, and challenge. The lower-level needs are survival-oriented and therefore particularly dependent on the external environment for satisfaction. The newborn, for instance, comes into the world with dominant physiological and survival needs requiring responsive mothering. As these needs are fulfilled, the needs for safety, security, predictability, and control arise, requiring an environmental climate marked by stability, dependency, protection, and freedom from fear. Only after these survival needs have been satisfied can the child's higher-level growth needs (belongingness, love, esteem, self-actualization), which were present from birth, directly influence behavior.

Maslow, therefore, conceptualizes the lower-level needs as deficiency needs that are culture-bound and therefore very dependent on the environment for satisfaction. The higher-level needs (which have integrated and subordinated lower-level ones) are in his view growth or *being* needs that often transcend cultural constraints in their fulfillment. The environmental "vitamins" and "nutrients" essential for both survival and growth have led Maslow to the concept of *synergy* as an ideal cultural situation. In a synergistic culture, one's own selfish satisfaction of needs is connected with others in the mutual aid of human relations. The good, therefore, of others is the same as the good for the self.

This theory has many implications for social work practice at both the microlevel and the macrolevel. Our services do not serve if they do not provide resources to meet the variety of basic needs on the continuum. Nor do they serve if our goals are appealing to higher-level growth needs when the dominant needs of a person or group are lower-level survival needs. If our objective of self-actualizing human relations is to be accomplished, work with organization, community, or policy development must be directed toward the provision of resources that guarantee opportunities for meeting lower-level needs. The provision of resources contributing to the meeting of all these developmental needs is essential to the healthy development of both our society and its members. Above all, Maslow's theory proposes that the fundamental need of people is *people*. The self cannot be actualized in a vacuum; it demands autonomous yet interdependent human relations. Maslow's theory is summarized in Figure 6.1.

Erikson's Theory of Developmental Tasks

Erik Erikson has developed a psychosocial theory of age-related tasks that require social resources to promote development.[12] His theory, like Maslow's, is hierarchical and epigenetic (based on the emergent biological growth of the organism). At each of the eight stages of growth, the individual experiences a psychosocial crisis brought on by a physiological

Figure 6.1 Maslow's Hierarchy of Needs

transition. These crises are resolved through the successful completion of tasks that result in a favorable ratio of the positive sense of the self's growth over the negative sense of self that persists throughout a lifetime. This positive sense of self at each stage is the basis for the resolution of later developmental tasks. Table 6.1 summarizes Erikson's "Eight Ages of Humankind." Now let us examine Erikson's stages one by one, beginning with the first stage: trust.

Trust

In the first stage the infant is developing trust in the self, its own capacities, and the selves of others. The infant's needs are "to get" and "to give in return." As one is weaned, one experiences more of a self— separate physically and emotionally from mother and others. While trusting the self and others, the infant has yet enough mistrust of every wish being satisfied to seek increased self-support (*autonomy*).

Table 6.1 Erikson's Stages of
Psychosocial Development

Stage	Needs	Crisis	Tasks	Purpose
I: Infancy (0–1 years old)	Mothering, exploring world and self	Basic trust vs. mistrust	Trusting self and others	Sense of hope
II: Toddler (1–3 years old)	Learning, fantasizing, play, perceiving world and self, security	Autonomy vs. shame and doubt	Interdependent separation of self from others	Sense of self-control
III: Preschool (3–6 years old)	Socialization, learning, play, asserting self in world	Initiative vs. guilt	Purposeful and conscious relating to others	Sense of self-direction
IV: Grade school (6–13 years old)	Intellectual and social challenges and belonging in family, success	Industry vs. inferiority	Purposeful cooperation with others	Sense of competence
V: High school (13–18 years old)	Achievement, partial separation from parents, belonging with peers	Identity vs. identity diffusion	Commitment of self to others	Sense of fidelity
VI: Young adult (18–21 years old)	Self-fulfillment and esteem in adult roles	Intimacy vs. isolation	Loving self and others	Sense of love
VII: Mature adult (21–65 years old)	Self-actualization in life roles	Generativity vs. stagnation	Caring for self and others	Sense of care
VIII: Aged adult (65 years and older)	Continuing self-development, conservation of energy	Integrity vs. despair	Being self with others	Sense of wisdom

Autonomy

Autonomy, in the second stage, comes from the sphincter needs "to hold on" and "to let go." It is the sense of power yet control. The self is still experienced in its separateness, yet there is a need to yield one's own will to the will of others toward acceptance of a developing interdependence. A healthy level of shame and doubt exists to influence the assertion of the self more interdependently and less willfully in the assumption of interpersonal *initiative.*

Initiative

The third stage involves a balance of initiative and guilt. The self becomes more convinced of its separateness and seeks its own direction. The consciousness of self and others in relationships is heightened. The others are more assertively extended beyond mother—to father, grandparents, neighbors, playmates. The guilt experienced when one does not comply with one's own or others' standards for behavior brings on a seeking for competence through *industry.*

Industry

In school, in this fourth stage, the child begins a fresh opportunity to compare the self with others—to appraise one's own difference without loss of self-esteem (inferiority) or loss of the capacity for human relations with peers, teachers, and others. Intellectual, physical, and interpersonal skills expand in cooperative teaching–learning experiences with others. One learns to cooperate with others, follow the rules of the game, and develop close friendships in which both the purposes of self and the relationship can be furthered. The child seeks more of this sense of self toward a personal *identity.*

Identity

The fifth stage in development is adolescence. While seeking an identity within one's peer group, separate from the family, and in the wider world in which one is to become an adult, the adolescent finds new energy, increased powers, and wider opportunities (with less identity diffusion) for this use in human relations, in work, in sports, and in other interests. There is an increased sense of fidelity—a disciplined devotion to shaping one's world and developing relationships based on *intimacy.*

Intimacy

The sixth stage of young adulthood continues the needs for self-esteem, self-fulfillment, and intimacy through home and work roles and the prevention of isolation. The dreams of childhood are weighed against the realities of one's situation in an attempt to make life choices that increase self-actualizing human relations. Loving extends to others in a deepening sense of *generativity* to prevent stagnation.

Generativity

Mature adulthood, the seventh stage, brings a more consistent, less fluid, sense of self, and the self extends to giving more in human relations in the family, at work, and in the community. The sense of responsibility for self, others, and the world deepens. Changes are not as swift unless earlier developmental tasks demand attention. In this case, earlier unresolved crises evolve and need to be resolved in the movement toward *integrity*.

Integrity

The last stage is the aged adult whose physical energy begins disengagement from the wider world to conserve integrity with friends and family. One's life course is rerun in memory with resultant satisfaction or despair. Death, as the end of life, can stand as an affirmation of the journey. The wisdom gleaned on this journey can be left for those who continue the life process on their own varied paths.

An Application of Erikson's Theory

Carol Meyer in her life model approach to social work practice makes excellent use of Erikson's theory in relating social services to the successful resolution of developmental transitions.[13] Table 6.2 shows how Meyer links Erikson's transitional crises to social services and reveals the implications of her model for generalist practice.

Many services function primarily to meet specific developmental needs through the provision of specific resources. These resources can play a great role in the successful completion of life-cycle developmental tasks. They can assist the family and its members, for example, as they negotiate the complex institutions on which they depend for meeting their needs. As Table 6.2 suggests, the baby's needs for responsive mothering toward the development of basic trust depends on the mother's resources in such areas as health, income, and skills for parenting. Income maintenance, prenatal care, hospital services, and well-baby clinic services are among the significant resources available to ameliorate or prevent such problems as inadequate parenting, unwanted children, and neglect and abuse— problems that make the infant's task of developing basic trust difficult indeed. The direct-service social worker is in a key position to help mothers who need these resources.

Thus each developmental stage can be examined in terms of how social services enhance the accomplishment of crucial tasks—both in ame-

Table 6.2 Social Services for
the Transitional Crises

Stage and Transitional Crises	Typical Problems	Social Services
Stage I: role transition for parents, working mothers, absent fathers	Inadequate parenting Unwanted children Neglect and abuse	Income maintenance Prenatal care Hospitals, clinics Well-baby clinics
Stage II: disciplinary and nurturing roles	Abuse and neglect Marital conflict Mental retardation	Child welfare services Day care Homemakers Placement
Stage III: child's separation from home	Inadequate socialization Lack of supervision Behavior reaction	Nursery school care Group care Child welfare Foster care Homemakers
Stage IV: expanding world and increasing stimuli to cope with it	Social and learning failures	School guidance services Recreation Developmental groups Child welfare
Stage V: decisions about sexual identity, work, future	Identity crises Alienation Addiction Delinquency School maladjustment	Youth services Vocational counseling Correctional services Addiction services School services
Stage VI: leaving home, marriage, working	Alienation Marital conflict School or work maladjustment Crime Addiction	Legal aid Marital counseling Family services Correctional services Vocational counseling
Stage VII: household management and child care	Family breakdown, divorce Financial need Parent–child conflict Death of family or friends	Family court services Family services Public welfare
Stage VIII: physical and mental depletion, loss of friends and separation from family, retirement, death of spouse and friends	Sickness Loneliness Social isolation Economic deprivation	Meals on Wheels centers Income maintenance Foster family Institutional care Hospitals Family service

liorating problems that obstruct growth and in preventing problems through the provision of basic resources. For instance, children and youth in Stages II through V require a great many resources, including social services, to enable their basic socialization in developing an autonomous, self-initiating, and industrious sense of self. Without this sense of self-identity, they will be unable in adolescence to make healthy decisions about values, sex, career, and so on. Services often are needed to help the family and other agents of socialization provide the required resources. Moreover, backup formal resources from child welfare services, home-makers, group and foster homes, and so on are needed when the family and other natural resources break down and such problems as behavior reactions, inadequate socialization, and social and learning failures result. Often, then, the direct-service social worker's function, if the developmental objective is appreciated, is to mediate between the individual's developmental needs and society's resources.

A Case in Point

These theories of development, then, aid the worker's understanding of the individual's personality and interactional needs. Now let us look at a case that involves short-term service centering on two developmental crises: identity versus identity diffusion for the adolescent and generativity versus stagnation for the parents.[14] Their developmental tasks and needs provide clear goals for both the worker and family members in their brief experience together.

Alice, aged eighteen, telephones the community mental health agency for an appointment for herself. She is seen four days later. The initial interview reveals that Alice is extremely concerned about her parents and what will happen to them when she goes away to college. She seems preoccupied with her conflict about leaving and her fear for her family's deterioration. (Mr. See, her father, has been unemployed for some years and is drinking heavily.) Her belongingness and love needs are especially strong and related to her family. With some help, Alice agrees to invite her parents to further interviews. The family is eager to be involved.

The first interview yields several important themes: The father reveals a marital rift, reflecting unmet love and self-esteem needs and unaccomplished intimacy tasks; he blames his wife for this rift. Although he complains that his wife will not let him "get a word in edgewise," he monopolizes the discussion. Mrs. See and Alice are upset about the father's unemployment, his drinking, and his chronic depression—these problems affect all of them, but particularly Alice, who identifies strongly with her father. The mother is concerned about the unusual father–daughter closeness to the exclusion of herself (her own self-esteem and love and intimacy needs). Alice is her father's companion and confidante; she "feels his feelings, shares his moods, and stays home to watch over him." Alice fears that her parents will divorce when she leaves for school. She feels she is the glue that holds them together.

Limited background data reveal that the father has had periods of vocational success in the past (self-esteem needs and identity tasks). The mother returned to work after Mr. See lost his job. She is competent and functions well at work (self-esteem and identity). (She had worked for five years early in the marriage, sending her husband through school.) Both parents reveal pride in Alice, their only child. There is a caring parental quality, expressed directly, and there is motivation to "go on with the work here," as related to their developmental task of generativity.

The priorities to work on are Mr. See's current difficulties in functioning and Alice's impending departure—that is, her own difficulties (separate identity) and the impact of this separation on all family members.

The question of employment is explored with Mr. See, and his late-night drinking pattern is revealed. His wife keeps him company in drinking in an effort "to become closer to him" (supporting his alcoholism through her own strong love needs). Much resentment emerges and the father speaks of being unaccepted by the mother. ("She knows I don't like rice, but she has cooked it for me, nevertheless, for the last twenty-five years.") The mother feels more and more unhappy because of the father's depression and because there is no closeness between her and her daughter. Alice expresses her own resentment and anger at her father for "messing up his life."

In the third interview, the worker rearranges the chairs and asks the parents to sit next to each other. Previously Alice had separated them. With more physical closeness, better communication emerges between the parents. As each member of this family is helped toward a better understanding of his or her unique contribution to the family crisis, the shift in family roles becomes a new focus of attention. The father feels unhappy about not supporting his family while the mother has to work. The worker focuses on their needs as reflected in their strengths. The themes discussed are the family's involvement in helping themselves and each other, the parents' sense of pride in and love for Alice, their concern for her future, and their wishes for her success. Slowly the focus changes from Alice to Mr. and Mrs. See's concerns for each other. They recall the good times they have had together, their joint activities, their many friends, their enjoyment in work. A definite improvement in family climate is noted, reflected upon, and used to help members develop more sensitivity toward their own and each other's needs.

The work with the See family demonstrates clearly the worker's theoretical understanding of the transitional conflict and confusion that characterize these stages of the life cycle. Alice seeks her identity both within and outside the family. The Sees reach for their ability to care about Alice, each other, and themselves. The service, in this case delivered through family group work, provides resources for carrying out these developmental tasks as well as the unresolved tasks that were influencing their troubled interaction.

Summary

Basic theories of human behavior in the social environment are necessary for assessment in direct-service social work. Because of the dual focus of practice—on people and their environments—these theories help to explain both personality systems and social systems and their interrelationships in a practice situation. The concept of "development," a useful theme for organizing the theories, is related to social work's major objective of influencing self-actualizing human relations. The general principles of this development are those of orthogenesis, microgenesis, homeostasis, and functional analogy. These principles are based on the fundamental "law of the dialectic," which states that all living systems operate through constant interaction of two opposing tendencies: to remain in a steady state for survival and to change toward higher levels of differentiation and integration for growth.

Two theories useful for understanding individual development are those of Maslow and Erikson. Maslow proposes a continuum of basic needs in a hierarchy from physiological needs and safety and security, through belongingness, love, and esteem, to self-actualization. Much behavior can be understood on the basis of these needs, which are satisfied through people and processes in our environment.

Erikson proposes a life cycle theory of psychosocial development. Like Maslow's theory, it requires successful completion of early tasks through environmental resources before later tasks can be accomplished. Erikson's eight stages from womb to tomb are: trust, autonomy, initiative, industry, identity, intimacy, generativity, and integrity. We need a positive sense of self in these behaviors in each successive stage if our growth and potential are to result in self-development.

The developmental theories of Maslow and Erikson provide blueprints for assessing individual needs and tasks directed toward self-actualizing human relations. Their use requires an understanding of general developmental theory and the specific biopsychosocial stages of normal human development. Social work can be effective in promoting the maximization of human potential in the context of this natural development. As the next chapter reveals, this growth depends on the way in which personal needs match or mismatch with role expectations of the social systems in which people live and grow.

Suggested Learning Experiences

1. Imagine what your life would be like if you had been severely deprived of some of your basic lower-level needs—suppose you had experienced constant hunger, fear for your safety, or not feeling part of a family group (belonging). How could this deprivation affect your current behavior with others?

2. What are the similarities and differences between Maslow's specific needs and Erikson's specific stages of psychosocial development?

3. How could Erikson's differentiation of developmental tasks be used

to establish objectives for social service at a day care center? In an elementary or high school system? In a rape crisis center? In a nursing home for senior citizens?

Suggested Case Studies and Readings

See the references cited at the end of Chapter 7.

Chapter Seven   Social Systems Theory

Introduction

In Chapter 6 we focused on the individual person's development. This chapter focuses on the social system. The conceptual unit of the social system is *interaction*. A social system consists of two or more persons who interact in patterns with each other through position, status, and role relationships and a set of values or norms that regulate matters of consequence to members. It is basically an interpretive statement of the relationship among interacting persons. Social systems, therefore, are structured and have some degree of stability, interaction, reciprocity, interdependence, and identity that makes them significant for influencing behavior and meeting needs.

Social systems are *open*. This means they do not operate in a vacuum. They are also *ecological* in that they transact with other systems in their environment. They interchange processes and resources as well as develop and alleviate tensions with the environment. The generalist social worker needs a system perspective to assess the effects of the social system on its members and the members' effects on the system. This knowledge permits not only comprehensive assessment but also the selection of goals that can simultaneously influence the growth of both individuals and their immediate social systems—the matching purpose of social work.

This chapter continues the presentation of four useful theories of development: (1) Maslow's hierarchy of individual needs; (2) Erikson's theory of developmental tasks; (3) social systems; and (4) group development. The Maslow and Erikson theories of the last chapter develop "longitudinal" concepts of development. They indicate the major needs, which are translated into developmental tasks in the individual's social systems. The two theoretical models in this chapter describe the system's influence on this development. The first, social systems theory, introduces the main sociological variables related to the psychology of individual developmental needs. The second is an integrative model of group development that applies to any of the microcosmic (small, face-to-face) social systems in which people live and grow.

A Social Systems Model

The psychosocial model of Jacob Getzels and Herbert Thelen deals with the "horizontal" growth of people as their needs are met in ecological transactions with their interpersonal and institutional environment. Getzels and Thelen have formulated a theoretical framework of the group that is rich in its conceptualization of interaction within a social system.[1] Their framework is a *model*—in other words, it is a conceptual map for understanding and negotiating the dynamics of any social system. Their model is based on Thelen's earlier work on social and psychological variables in groups and upon Guba and Getzel's work on the social system theory of organizations.

The social system concept involves two classes of independent yet interacting dimensions: the *institutional* and the *personal*. The institutional dimension is linked to behavior through the concepts of institution, role, and role expectation. The personal dimension of activity is linked to the concepts of individual, personality, and need disposition. Understanding behavior requires the use of these sociological and psychological levels of analysis. Now let us examine these two basic dimensions of the social system concept.

Institutional Dimension

The specific institutional relationships are defined as follows. First, all social systems have certain essential functions that must be carried out in certain established ways. These functions have become institutionalized.

Second, the most important analytical unit of the institution is the concept of *role*. Roles are the dynamic aspects of the positions, offices, and statuses within an institution, and they define the behavior of the role incumbents or actors.

Third, roles are defined in terms of *role expectations*. A role has certain privileges, obligations, responsibilities, and powers. When role incumbents put these obligations and responsibilities into effect, they are said to be performing their role. The expectations define what individuals should or should not do so long as they are the incumbent of a particular role.

Fourth, roles are complementary—that is, each role derives its meaning from other related roles. In a sense, a role is a prescription not only for a given role incumbent but also for the incumbents of other roles within the institution and for related roles outside the institution. It is this quality of complementarity that fuses two or more roles into a coherent, interactive unit and makes it possible for us to conceive of an institution or any social system as having a characteristic structure.[2]

Personal Dimension

While the institutional dimension involves the elements of role and expectation, the personal dimension involves personality and need disposition. The concept of *personality* is defined as the dynamic organization within the individual of the needs that govern his or her *unique* reactions to the environment and to expectations in the environment. The central elements of personality are the *need dispositions,* which are defined by Talcott Parsons and Edward Shills as "individual tendencies to orient and act with respect to objects in certain manners and to expect certain consequences from these actions."[3]

The Model

Getzels and Thelen propose that understanding the behavior of role incumbents in a social system requires knowledge of both the role expectations and the need dispositions and their reciprocal influence. Together these elements constitute the motives for behavior. The general model is depicted in Figure 7.1.

Within their framework, an act is conceived as deriving simultaneously from both the institutional and the personal dimensions. Social behavior results as the individual attempts to cope with the environment's expectations for behavior in ways consistent with that person's independent pattern of needs. This proposition is expressed in the equation $B = f(R \times P)$, where B is observed behavior, f is the function, R is an institutional role defined by the expectations attached to it, and P is the personality of the role incumbent defined by need dispositions. The relative influence of role and personality varies with the specific act, the specific role, and the specific personality. In this context, members of a social system may display overt behavior along a spectrum between role and personality. Each system goal, such as a family's need to protect and develop its members, calls for a characteristic balance between these two types of performance.

The behavior in face-to-face social systems (groups) depends on the degree of consensus among members regarding externally defined role expectations and internally defined personality dispositions. This consensus is reached through *selective interpersonal perception.* That is, individuals agree on the institutional and personal dimensions of their behavior

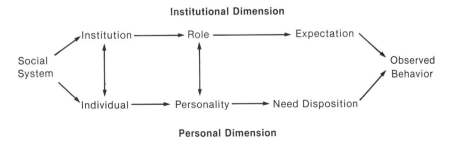

Institutional Dimension

Institution ——— Role ——————— Expectation

Social
System   Observed
                                                Behavior

Individual ——— Personality ——— Need Disposition

Personal Dimension

Figure 7.1 Dimensions of Social Systems

through their mutual perceptions of the interaction. When two role incumbents (such as teacher and student) are said to understand each other, their expectations are in agreement—they match. When they are said to misunderstand each other, their expectations mismatch.

According to this theoretical model, behavior change in a social system usually involves, at one extreme, adaptation of personality to role expectations. This change requires *socialization of the personality*—as when the belligerent man who was recently fired for assaulting his boss is helped to tone down his expressions of hostility to maintain steady employment. At the other extreme, changing behavior may involve the adaptation of role expectations to personality. This change requires *personalization of roles*—as when the man's new boss is persuaded to allow verbal expression of concern in order to prevent physical violence. In attempting to influence change in a social system, the social worker is always attending to these extremes—perhaps emphasizing one or the other, perhaps attempting to reach a balance between the two. The balance between socialization of personality and personalization of roles in a face-to-face social system determines the kind of group that develops and how it meets members' needs.

The small group mediates between institutional requirements and individual dispositions through a certain climate. This climate depends on (1) each individual's *identification* with the goals of the system so that they become part of his or her own needs; (2) the individual's belief that the system's expectations are *rational* if the goals are to be achieved; and (3) the individual's feeling a sense of *belonging* to a system with similar emotional identification and rational beliefs. These are the important psychosocial processes of all social systems: the classroom, the family and other small primary groups, the organization, the community. These dimensions of the group as a social system are presented graphically in Figure 7.2.

This concept directs our attention in practice to the three-way relationships between the individual's role expectations and needs and the group's goals in the various social systems in which they develop. Depending on the match or mismatch of these three variables, we have a model for the analysis of identification, rationality, and belongingness. Belongingness is a real clue for this assessment. When we determine that

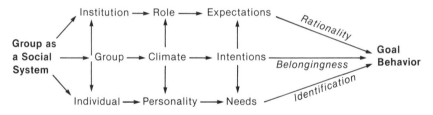

Figure 7.2 Dimensions of the Group as a Social System

a person does not feel a sense of belonging in a social system—family, work, school, agency—we have taken a major step in understanding obstacles to meeting needs and appropriate targets for change. Therefore, we can look closely at the problems in identification with the goals of the system and the rationality of these goals in relation to the needs and role expectations involved.

Thus the social system develops from the transactions between role and personality and presents the image of a system in change. As Getzels and Thelen remark: "It is the image of a group continually facing emergent complexity and conflict (if not confusion) and dealing with these realities, not in terms of sentiment, but in terms of what the complexity and conflict suggest about the modifications that have to be made about the goals, expectations, needs, and selective perceptions of the [members]."[4]

Using the Model

Within the context of developmental needs provided by the theories of Maslow and Erikson, this small-group model suggests directions for a social system's change. Again, as a systems model it is applicable for work with groups and families as well as for organizations and communities in behalf of the individual and others like him or her. The pivotal relationship between needs and role expectations directs our attention, as we have seen, to three major processes: identification, rationality, and belongingness. These three areas of congruence or incongruence reflect the state of person–system matching or mismatching.

This theoretical model is ecological in that no social system exists in a vacuum.[5] It is affected by other systems and affects them in turn. Cultural, racial, and ethnic diversities have a specific meaning both in reference to the larger institutions of which they are part and their own institutional contexts. The dominant cultural ethics in our society intersect with subcultural values in defining goals and role expectations. Thus the assessment and practice questions become: What are the goals in this social system (this family, group, organization, or community)? How are role expectations related to these goals? Do members identify with these goals? To what degree do they experience a sense of belonging to a social system with emotional identification and rational beliefs similar to their own? Work with any social system requires, therefore, that activities be directed toward clarifying goals, role expectations, needs, and selective perceptions for members. This clarification can increase the group's energy and the individual's sense of identification, rationality, and belongingness.

This context, called the *dual perspective,* is especially vital to work with ethnic minorities. The dual perspective, in the words of Delores Norton, is "the conscious and systematic process of perceiving, understanding, and comparing simultaneously the values, attitudes, and behavior of the larger societal system and those of the client [systems'] immediate family and community system."[6] Role expectations, therefore, are always defined by both the institutional systems of the dominant society and the smaller, but no less institutionalized, system of the consumer's immediate family and subcultural environment. Because institutionalized discrimination creates conditions in which society rejects certain role expectations of minority group subsystems, the dual perspective and the specific assessment of mismatching between the role expectations of the dominant system and minority subsystem are requisites for meeting the needs of minority group members. While these general assessments of cultural and subcultural role expectations are most useful when the dual perspective is used for individualizing work with minorities, one important caveat must be made here: No racial or minority label presumes a monolithic group. Individuals perceive reality both consensually and uniquely. Hence the concept of selective interpersonal perception can clarify the meaning of shared racial and minority group experiences for individuals.

The dual perspective suggests that every individual is part of society at large (the "generalized other"), which provides major resources and opportunities and relates to overall status and power rewards. Yet embedded in this larger system and closer to the individual is the nurturing subsystem of the family and immediate community—those "significant others" who influence the person's sense of identity. For example, many role expectations of minority group nurturing subsystems are related to the subsystem's strengths in meeting identity needs. These strengths can combat the devalued status and role expectations inflicted on minority group members by dominant political, economic, and educational institutions in our society in order to sustain the cultural majority.

The social system models presented in this section can help the social worker apply the dual perspective in direct-service assessments and intervention. Its use can help both workers and consumers increase acceptance of human diversity through group and individual differences. As Norton notes:

> It increases awareness of possible and actual points of conflict between the minority client's [or any client's] perspective and that of the dominant society. It enhances awareness of the structural-institutional sources that contribute to the inequality of opportunity for minority groups. When it is utilized, the processes of assessment and understanding should produce results vitally different than at present.[7]

The use of the dual perspective obliges the direct-service generalist to consider the special perspective of the minority group system that prevents stereotyping, misinterpretation, and inappropriate expectations and intervention.

The use of this theoretical model in the assessment framework presented at the end of the chapter can help provide substantive data on which to base intervention. It also ensures a dual perspective when assessing role expectations and needs in relation to the goals of the small group, organizational, and institutional systems that especially affect minorities. Particularly important is the ability to assess the matching of interlocking role expectations—as in the relation of the family as a social system to the dominant community system.

Norton suggests that work with the family as a social system can be based effectively on the dual perspective.[8] Moreover, Ben Orcutt notes in his systems approach to work with families of the poor that changes in any structure or process of the system bring change to the system as a whole.[9] He suggests that the impoverished ghetto family which is alienated from the mainstream of the dominant culture experiences an energy-consuming variety of survival goals at the same time it directs its resources to the achievement of nurturing and socialization goals. These survival goals derive from substandard housing, assaults on members' self-esteem, deprivation of income and opportunity, physical danger from crime and drugs, and inadequate medical care.

Survival goals place a particular strain on the family's ability to develop its resources for higher-level growth. But as Orcutt observes: "With increased input of good housing, medical care, money income, and opportunities for member self-realization and dignity, the exchange processes with the environment can tend to be restorative . . . and family output can become more consistent with the expected role-carrying of the environment, the growth tasks, and higher levels of functioning (differentiation)."[10] Thus institutional resources that free the normal goal-directed energy of the family can increase the identification with, the rationality of, and the belongingness to those parenting, protection, and socialization roles normally demanded of family members in our society. This theoretical model, therefore, places flesh and blood on the skeletal concept of "environmental modification," which has been a traditional component of social work theory.

Orcutt's case example is particularly illustrative of this model's applicability and bears repeating here.[11] Mrs. Reed, a black, 42-year-old, obese mother of ten children, was admitted to a state hospital. Prior to admission, Mrs. Reed, who has an eighth-grade education, resided with her husband and children in a six-room apartment in a deteriorated old building in a ghetto neighborhood. The family received a maximum AFDC grant, and Mr. Reed earned a small income from steady night work. The family managed poorly, as their income provided only basic necessities. (They would currently be characterized as "working poor.")

Mrs. Reed was diagnosed as a chronic schizophrenic. She was hospitalized at the request of the family court when at a hearing both she and her husband were charged with child neglect. Her bizarre delusional responses led to a recommendation of hospitalization. Mrs. Reed spoke of being unable to take care of her ten children, ranging from two-year-old twins to a fourteen-year-old daughter on whom she relied. Her child care was erratic. At times she would not feed, change, or train the twins, nor could she touch or acknowledge any of the children. She refused to prepare her husband's meals and refused sexual relationships, fearing pregnancy. Mr. Reed had withdrawn from her verbally and emotionally, and generally was away from home. He had deserted her four years before but returned when ordered by the court to return home or face a jail sentence.

Mrs. Reed is essentially nonverbal; her voice has a strained, unnatural sound. She distrusts people and is aloof and withdrawn. She complains of the heavy strain of family responsibility. Mr. Reed does not see himself as a helpmate and does nothing to maintain the family or marital relationship, nor does he give physical care to the children. Clinic appointments, school appointments, household chores and management, discipline—all are left to Mrs. Reed. She says she resents this responsibility and her husband's criticism that she is a poor housekeeper, but she does not speak out about it. She tends to withdraw and appears apathetic.

The six school-age children all have learning difficulties and are in special classes at public school. One child, age ten, is severely retarded and cannot dress herself. All the children in the family are functioning below normal expectations. Little is known of Mrs. Reed's early life beyond the fact that she was the youngest of nine children and was born on a farm. She moved to the city with her mother during her teens after her father died. She worked in factories, was self-supporting, and lived with her mother until age twenty-six, when she married Mr. Reed. Her mother has subsequently died, and there is no extended family in the city. In the hospital, in addition to appearing isolated, she evidences some delusional ideas.

This situation is not atypical of the chaos facing urban families from low-income groups using social services in hospitals, public agencies, and the like. In normal development, Mrs. Reed's needs would center on belongingness, love, self-esteem, and nurturing others (generativity). At the same time, her roles demand her to function as a wife and mother when her own needs are unmet. These role expectations block already stunted resources for normal family functions. Mrs. Reed is not alone. Virtually every member of the Reed family is in trouble as they attempt to negotiate the interpenetrating social systems of the family itself, the hospital, the family court, the public welfare department, the ghetto neighborhood, schools, and work. All family members, beginning with the social worker's direct contact with Mrs. Reed, need direct and environmental modification that can free their energies for reexamining their family's goals, role expectations, needs, and selective perceptions toward increased identification, rationality, and sense of belonging. A list of activities in behalf of the Reed family's self-actualizing development would include:

1. Establishing a personal relationship with Mrs. Reed built on empathy, support, and reality that can stimulate her needs for human relations.

2. Mediating between Mrs. Reed and various components of the hospital system to promote a climate for her growth and to tap the health rather than the sickness of her patient status and role.

3. Engaging Mr. Reed in a process of carrying his sole-parent leadership role in the family.

4. Mediating between Mr. Reed and the service network for provision of long-term homemaker service to aid Mr. Reed and the children in caretaking.

5. Mediating between the family and other services—housing, school, family court—as these institutional resources are available for contributing to the congruence of needs and role expectations for individual family members.

6. Working with the family as a group in ongoing assessment and development of their interpersonal relationships to meet individual growth needs and to master developmental tasks.

In sum, social systems theory, as presented here, aids in understanding the relationship between people's needs and environmental demands in any practice situation. Applying these concepts in assessments helps one take a series of snapshots of human behavior in the social environment to aid planning to meet the needs of those involved. It also gives direction for how to influence change in the relevant variables in the system in behalf of members. This change requires an additional model—one that is more like a motion picture than a snapshot of interaction in the social systems with which we work. The fourth and last theory of development useful for assessments—the stages of group development—provides an understanding of how systems evolve into resources for mutual aid of members.

Stages of Group Development

The last theoretical model—the stages of group development—integrates this social system model with the developmental needs and tasks models of Maslow and Erikson. It deals specifically with how people negotiate their own need meeting with the needs of others and the social system they create together. While the model applies to human development in any social system in which people transact their love and work together, it is presented here because of its immediate application to the process of the small face-to-face group. This attention to group process and the influence of a mediator has been the springboard for original and ongoing work on stages of group development in the variety of small groups in social work practice.[12]

Every group has its own unique membership, all involved in complex interaction with each other on the basis of unique developmental tasks and needs. Therefore, each group undergoes a highly individualized development. As members manifest themselves in human relations and contribute to creating an interpersonal microcosm, the complexity and richness of the interaction indicate that the group process will be complex and, certainly to a degree, unpredictable. Nevertheless, there are forces operating in all groups that broadly influence their development toward optimal need-meeting and growth-promoting resources for members.

All members are working out their human natures in a balance of individual autonomy and interdependence. Over and over again in group process, they confront the major existential needs to be separate (autonomy) and to be connected (interdependence) with others in human relationships. These polarities greatly affect the group's development as major process themes, which have been variously labeled as power and intimacy, will and love, difference and closeness, separateness and unity, and the "I" and the "We." These areas of human existence provide the major conflicts for which the structure of group life can provide resolution. They are the basis for the wish/fears—wishes for trust, security, belonging, love, respect, and self-actualization; fears of hurt, rejection, engulfment—which members bring to early group experiences and which arise throughout their process together. At any point, the stages of group development can be viewed as the homeostasis—that is, the balancing—of all the forces that influence members' autonomy (power) or interdependency (intimacy). Every group experience begins with an intensification of members' conflicts regarding power and intimacy.

These existential concerns relate to the two major tasks that confront members of any newly formed group. First, they must determine methods for achieving their primary task—the purpose for which they joined. Second, they must attend to the human relations in the group to create a place for themselves—a place that will not only provide the underlying security and trust for task achievement but also produce the sheer pleasure of group membership. The following sections explain the basic stages of development.[13]

Preaffiliation

In the *preaffiliation* stage the major process is that of involvement before commitment. The search here is for potential resources within the group to meet one's need for trust and security. The two major questions to be answered before involvement are: How is this going to benefit me? What does all this have to do with me? These questions, which crop up in every discussion, often create confusion about personal and group goals. At the same time, members are sizing up one another and the group through an arm's-length process of exploration. They are searching for a viable role for themselves—and are quite often predisposed toward roles that protect them from risk of authentic exposure yet help them develop a sense of belonging. They wonder if they will be liked and respected or ignored or rejected. They want to be able to trust the evolving structure and role expectations—to feel secure, that is, without too much cost to their personal autonomy.

Although members are ostensibly together because of their interest in the group's common goal and will ultimately build trust around their mutual commitment to this goal, the initial social forces involve the establishment of trust through the search for approval, acceptance, respect, or domination. Prospective members use approach/avoidance behavior to explore the question of membership: What are the admission requirements, the price of the ticket to belong? How much must I give or reveal of my prized individuality? Should I involve myself for the gratification promised or remain lonely and left out? Will I feel more hurt if involved and who may hurt me? At a near conscious level they seek answers to wish/fear questions such as these and maintain a constant, often subtle, vigilance for the types of behavior the group expects and approves of.

While the group in the preaffiliation stage is often puzzled, testing, hesitant, so too is it dependent. In groups in social work practice, members overtly and covertly look to the worker for structure and answers, as well as for approval and acceptance. There is always the underlying hope: "If the worker, this powerful significant other, sees me as belonging and OK, then I am OK in this group." Much of the initial communication in the group is directed toward the worker. The worker is surreptitiously glanced at for rewards as members manifest behavior that has gained approval from authorities in the past. At this stage the worker's comments are scrutinized for directives about accepted and unaccepted behavior. Often the worker is given what members think he or she wants; the strong separate self is inhibited from expression. During this stage it is vital for the worker concerned about self-actualizing human relations to reinforce a belief in autonomy and interdependence if these are to be balanced throughout the group process. Among other tasks, this balance requires that the worker reflect in words and deeds that no member is more important to the group than any other member—including the worker.

The content of this stage, and the communication style, are relatively stereotyped and restricted. The social code may resemble that of a cocktail party where social amenities are thrown past each other in the interests of self-protection but also the establishment of initial contact. In fact, the phrase "goblet issues" has been used to refer to group communication at this stage. The analogy refers to the process of picking up a cocktail goblet at a party and using it to peer at and size up the other guests. While group content may be used as a goblet, it also encourages the first forays of contacting others in human relations. Members discover similarities and differences and begin to build the group norms for protection through consensus. This climate establishes a base for cohesiveness—which is needed before members can risk their authentic differences without rejection or judgment by others. It also creates the initial structure, characterized by power and control.

Power and Control

Once the preaffiliation concern is resolved through the decision of members to become involved with each other in the group, structural concerns—*power and control*—tend to dominate. This is the second stage of the formative group. Commitment to the group increases both the wishes and fears for more authentic human relations and intensifies the search for security through the control inherent in position, status, and role. The group shifts from preoccupation with acceptance, approval, involvement, and definitions of accepted behavior to a preoccupation with dominance, control, and power. In Erikson's terms, the crises of autonomy and initiative arise. In Maslow's terms, self-esteem gained from status in the eyes of others and one's own eyes evolves as a dominant need.

The characteristic conflict of this stage is between members or, in practice groups, between members and the worker. Each member is involved in the developmental task of establishing his or her preferred amount of autonomy, initiative, and power. Gradually a status and control hierarchy, a social pecking order, is established. The movement is from "I'm OK. I belong here" to "I'm OK. I *rank* here." The group begins to be stylized through the evolving structure. Communication patterns become established and forces are at work to freeze these patterns for member security in the mutually formed positions, statuses, roles, and norms. High-status members tend to direct their comments to other high-status members. Low-status members participate through those with higher status. The trust at this point is not in other members as people with common developmental needs, but trust in a predictable structure.

This phase can be destructive for some members. Those whose place as low person on the totem pole reinforces already low self-esteem may drop out and be hurt before the group has an opportunity to resolve the hierarchical conflicts of this stage. Subgroups come to the fore as islands of safety where members can ally with others to guard their flanks. The scapegoats and isolates who cannot coalesce into subgroups may be particularly vulnerable to power clique rejection or attack—increasing their fear, loneliness, and isolation in human relations.

The struggle for control is part of the process of every group. It is always present to some degree, sometimes quiescent, sometimes smoldering, sometimes in full conflagration. It is in challenging these structural obstacles to development that a social worker can most strongly influence group process toward self-actualizing growth for members and the group. It is in dealing with the worker's place in this structure that the group finds its own authentic source of power to develop resources for meeting *all* members' needs.

In a practice group, the emergence of ambivalence and hostility toward the worker is inevitable at this stage of development. Members' dependencies are projected on the worker as an omnipotent source of satisfying needs at the same time as their autonomy, initiative, closeness, self-respect, and self-actualizing needs are seeking a climate free from domination and supportive of relationship-building self-expression. If the worker refuses to feed the omnipotent mystique, holds out faith that the members can find their own direction, and expects only that they confront the obstacles to goal achievement, including the worker, the worker can influence a group structure that promotes equal opportunity and freedom for all members. If the group members can express their ambivalence and hostility toward the worker, rather than directing it toward the control of each other, they can begin the aggressive confrontation that may lead to the satisfaction of their security needs for environmental support and protection.

At a certain point the group may discover that the worker functions as a special member because of technical skills and that the worker's contributions can be evaluated for their value to their goal achievement, rather than accepted or rejected because of the authority behind them. At this point the members are ready to discover the unique contributions all other members can make to the goals of the group and the meeting of their individual needs—the basis for intimacy in the group.

Intimacy

The third stage of the formative group is the development of *intimacy* and *cohesiveness*. Following the previous phase of much covert (and often overt) conflict, the group gradually evolves into a cohesive unit. All members come into the group at this stage with some degree of equal importance to each other and to the group as a whole. There is greater morale and a deeper commitment to the group's purpose and goals—including a deeper commitment to dealing with the group's human relations in the service of needs and goals. Mutual trust grows in people and resources rather than in structural power and control. Spontaneous self-disclosure increases, particularly the sharing of feelings of closeness and here-and-now responses to the interaction. The group really becomes a group in the deepest sense of the concept when an absent member is really missed for the first time.

While a mutual aid system in the group is developing for intimacy needs, there is some suppression of conflict-producing feelings. Compared to the previous stage, group interaction seems to be all sweetness and light as the group basks in the glow of its newly discovered unity. Eventually, however, the group's embrace will seem superficial and ritualistic unless authentic differences in the group are permitted to emerge. When fear of authentic feelings is resolved in the interests of mutual aid and self-actualizing development, the group has reached the maturity of differentiation—a state lasting for the remainder of the group's life despite periodic short-lived reappearances of each of the earlier phases.

Differentiation

The *differentiation* stage is marked by dynamic balance of members' needs and the group's needs. Autonomous and interdependent concerns of members are fused. Cohesion remains strong and helps to fuse here-and-now process and content concerns. The processes in a mature work group involve valid communication in which the group as a whole and the individual members are aware of what they are doing together. Members responsibly and spontaneously sense what self and others need to achieve their common developmental tasks, and members are given what they need in proportion to their needs. This consciousness of mutual aid taps resources for individual, interpersonal, and group work through open feedback channels. The group's purpose, whatever the surface reasons for it to be together, moves toward self-actualizing human relations for members. This differentiation occurs until the group separates, members transfer their newfound energy and skills to other social systems, or new members are taken in and thus recreate earlier stages.

Separation

The last stage—*separation*—can come at any time in the group's development. If the group separates after the differentiation stage, members emerge with a strong sense of competence in relation to social systems outside the group. The desire for human relations that satisfy needs begins to outweigh the fears, moreover, and there are higher hopes of matching needs with resources in other life situations. These outcomes in the group are colored by regression to behavior more reflective of the earlier stages in the group. This behavior, based on insecurity, is a last attempt to deny separation through insinuation that members still need each other and, in a practice group, the worker.

If the group terminates during the earlier stages, the reverse is likely: feelings of inadequacy, fears stronger than wishes, increased mistrust in self and others, less faith in self-actualizing potential. The feelings about separation are denied expression even more strongly, and absenses and dropouts are likely to increase.

Often the social work practice group avoids the unpleasant work of termination by ignoring their feelings. The worker must help them keep this task in focus. The end of the group can be a real loss for the worker as well as for members. Both gradually come to the realization that it can never really be reconvened—even if they continue relationships with certain members, the group as an entity is gone forever. It will be missed. For all, it could have been a place of pain, conflict, and fear but also a place of great meaning. Some of life's most poignant and fulfilling moments can occur in the microcosm of a developed group.

Using the Theory

These stages of group development, though useful for work with social systems directed toward self-actualizing human relations, cannot be predicted so rigidly as the preceding paragraphs might suggest. The stages are rarely as well demarcated in practice. At best, the boundary between one stage and another is dim and overlapping. In describing group development, an apt metaphor is that of changing a tire. When it comes to securing the new tire, you begin by tightening all the bolts in succession until the wheel is in place. Then you repeat the process, tightening each bolt in turn until the wheel is secure. Similarly the phase themes of a group emerge to the fore and then recede. The group may return to these phases again and again from a different perspective and deal with them in greater depth toward further progression.

Therefore, this theoretical model perhaps speaks more to developmental tasks than to stages for the group—analogous to Erikson's model for the individual: trust, autonomy, initiative, industry, identity, intimacy, generativity, and integrity. Nevertheless, the model does provide guidelines for the social worker's influence on the natural group process by helping members accomplish their developmental tasks toward individual self-actualization and mutual aid in the interest of achieving group goals. The worker using this model can, in a sense, allow the acorn in individual members and in the group as a whole develop into the oak tree of its fullest potential.

Summary

Developmental theories and social system theories are currently the most useful frameworks for the direct-service generalist who is concerned about interpersonal alienation and self-actualizing human relations. Four theoretical models for understanding the phenomena with which the generalist works are Maslow's developmental needs, Erikson's psychosocial developmental tasks, Getzel and Thelen's social system, and the stages of group development. These theoretical models, which are summarized in the following assessment outline, guide the generalist in selecting appropriate methods and theories for delivering services—the subject of the next chapter.

Outline for Assessment

I. Identification of Consumer (name, age, sex, family and marital status, race, ethnic identity, socioeconomic status)

II. Identification of Problem

   A. Consumer's need or problem
1. What does the consumer say the service need is?
2. How long has this need existed?
3. If this need has existed for some time, what has precipitated the current request for service?
4. What parts of the need are viewed by the consumer as falling within the consumer's responsibility, within the social system's, or within both?

   B. Significant others' (family, school, referral agencies, community) view of the need for service
1. What do the others involved say the service need is?
2. How long do they think this need has existed?
3. If this need has existed for some time, what has precipitated their current concern?
4. What parts of the need as a problem are viewed by them as falling within the consumer's responsibility, within their social system's, or within both?

   C. Worker's view of the need for service
1. What do you think the need or problem is?
2. How long do you think this situation has existed?
3. What do you think precipitated the immediate need for service?
4. What have the consumer and significant others done about the need to this point and how do they feel about these efforts?

   D. Need or problem to be worked on
1. On what problem does the consumer place priority for work together?
2. What problem do you judge as critical for beginning the work together?
3. How does this problem relate to your professional function? To your agency's service function? To existing resources of the consumer and his or her social system?

III. Identification of Person–Situation Transactions

   A. What are the consumer's major developmental needs reflected in the current situation? (Maslow model of needs)

   B. What are the consumer's major developmental tasks reflected in the current situation? (Erikson model of tasks)

C. What is the relationship between these needs and tasks and the role expectations with which the consumer is faced in relation to the current problem? (Getzels and Thelen's points of matching or mismatching)

1. What is occurring in *rational* understanding (social system's goals in relation to role expectations)?
2. What is occurring in *identifications* (social system's goals in relation to developmental needs)?
3. What is occurring in the sense of *belonging* (social system's role expectations in relation to developmental needs)?
4. What is occurring in relation to the mutual perceptions of members of the system in these areas?

IV. Primary Group Influences on Problem

A. What is the developmental stage of the family in relation to the current service need? (Pre-affiliation, power and control, intimacy, differentiation)

B. What aspects of the family's development relate to the current service need and resources to meet the need?

C. What is the developmental stage of the other primary groups in relation to the current service need?

D. What aspects of these groups' development relate to the current service need and resources to meet the need?

V. Organizational Influences on Problem

A. What organizations are involved (directly or indirectly) with the consumer's service needs?

B. How are these organizations functioning as social systems in relation to the consumer's service needs? (Include your own agency.)

1. What are their goals?
2. How do these goals relate to the consumer's role expectations? (Rationality)
3. How do these goals relate to the consumer's developmental needs? (Identification)
4. How do these role expectations relate to the consumer's needs? (Belongingness)
5. What mutual perceptions are involved in these areas?
6. What resources do these organizations have in relation to the consumer's needs?
7. What obstacles exist in linking consumer to resources?

C. What is the current stage of development of these organizations in relation to the consumer's service needs?

VI. Community Influences on Problem

    A. What processes relate to the community's development as a social system in relation to the service needs?
1. What are the community's goals?
2. How do these goals relate to the consumer's role expectations?
3. How do these goals relate to the consumer's needs?
4. How do these role expectations relate to the consumer's needs?
5. What mutual perceptions are involved in these areas?

    B. What is the community's current stage of development in relation to the consumer's service needs?

VII. Identification of Goals

    A. What goals are to be worked on?
1. What are the short-term goals (most immediate changes in current situation)?
2. What are the long-term goals (the state at which consumer and worker believe to be the end of their work together)?

    B. What primary targets are focused on to reach these goals?
1. What goals will be sought by the individual in behalf of his or her own development?
2. What goals will be sought by the individual and other consumers together (families and groups) in their own behalf?
3. What goals will be sought by others in the service network (organizations) in behalf of the individual?
4. What goals will be sought by others (community) in behalf of the individual and other consumers?

VIII. Plan of Action

    A. What is the current contract for service?
1. What are the consumer's roles and responsibilities?
2. What roles and responsibilities do I have?

    B. What methods and practice theory approaches will be used to reach what goals?
1. What casework approaches toward what goals?
2. What family group work approaches toward what goals?
3. What group work approaches toward what goals?
4. What organizational development, brokerage, and advocacy approaches toward what goals?
5. What community organization and policy development approaches toward what goals?

IX. Evaluation

    A. What has been accomplished thus far in reference to service goals?

    B. How have the methods been appropriate to the current goal accomplishment?

Suggested Learning Experiences

The basic learning activities for this chapter are those that teach students to use the assessment framework in practice—for example, assignments to assess student experiences in the field and vicarious case study experiences. Any of the case studies noted to this point can be used for students' assessments. Moreover, other assessment frameworks could be used in identifying needs, problems, goals, targets, and direction for intervention planning and implementation. Two comprehensive frameworks of this sort are the following: Beulah R. Compton and Burt Galaway, "Outline of Problem Solving Model," in *Social Work Processes,* ed. B. R. Compton and B. Galaway (Homewood, Ill.: Dorsey Press, 1975); Max Siporin, "Outline for a Social Study," in *Introduction to Social Work Practice.* New York: Macmillan Publishing Co., 1975.

Suggested Case Studies

In addition to the case studies cited in earlier chapters, the following three works are useful for applying the assessment framework discussed in Chapters 6 and 7.

Leader, Arthur L. "Innovations in Family Casework Services." In *The Field of Social Work,* ed. Arthur Fink. 6th ed. New York: Holt, Rinehart and Winston, 1974.

    This presentation includes four separate examples of family casework. In the first situation, a quick-response unit helps Mr. G., fifty-eight, Mrs. G., fifty-nine, and daughter Janice, twenty-one, to open up needs and communications in the family group in six meetings. The second example involves service with a crisis unit when a staff member finds a homeless woman, Mrs. K., on the street and through casework and brokerage helps her return to employment, find housing, and reestablish communication with her distant children. The third case study involves a group session of five boys and girls aged fourteen to seventeen who formed a natural group around the agency's mobile van in a neighborhood where adolescents tended to roam aimlessly. The six formal meetings are concerned with common feelings of alienation, parental rejection, and problems with identity. The fourth study describes the combination of group and family group work methods used with three boys and two girls aged four-teen to eighteen. The members had similar patterned roles and conflicts in their natural families, felt isolated, and were to varying degrees involved with drug use.

Lokshin, Helen and Darya Penn. "Some Aspects of Serving Older Peo-ple." In *The Field of Social Work*, ed. Arthur Fink. 6th. ed. New York: Holt, Rinehart and Winston, 1974.

Two case studies are presented in this source. The first concerns two sisters, Mrs. Sachs, sixty-five, and Mrs. Love, seventy-nine, who come to the hospital's outpatient clinic. Both are helped to meet their needs and are linked to community resources to sustain their life in the community. The other case involves John Kelly, a 76-year-old who was hospitalized. Work with Mr. Kelly individually, with his adult children, and with hospital staff is described in fairly rich detail. Included are some ideas for group and community work with the aging.

Orcutt, Ben A. "Family Treatment of Poverty Level Families." *Social Casework* 58(2)(1977):92–100.

This case study of a poor white family, reported by a worker in a residential treatment center, details the individual and family group work as well as significant work with the agency service network. James A. is an eight-year-old boy who ran away from home, set fires, wet the bed, and missed school. He was living with his mother (a 28-year-old divorcée) and his younger brother, five-year-old Jerry, supported by AFDC. Mrs. A. has a great influence on James's be-havior. Through family group meetings and Mrs. A.'s involvement with the worker in learning about James through service network personnel, she begins to respond differently to James.

Chapter Eight   From Basic Theory to Practice Theories

Introduction

This chapter is a response to the current call for accountability in social work practice. I believe that this trend will increase the demand for clearly conceptualized practice theories that can be tested in action by every social worker. At the very least, social work requires an understanding of the elements of practice theories and their relationship to basic theory and research.

This chapter introduces the reader to the elements of practice theory and offers guidelines for selecting, using, and testing practice theories. Moreover, it prepares the reader for the social work practice theories presented in Part 3. In this sense, then, the chapter does respond to the present demands for accountability and the increased emphasis on theory-based practice that is likely to follow. You cannot evaluate your practice without a clear explication of the ends toward which it is directed and the means through which these ends will be achieved—in a phrase, a "practice theory."

Suppose you were to overhear a student interviewing a social worker for a class assignment to discover what practice theories are being used in the field. You might hear something like the following contrived but likely dialogue:

Student:	What practice theories do you use in your work?
Worker:	What do you mean by "practice theories"?
Student:	Well, Dr. Anderson says they are more or less formalized systems of propositions, or principles, explaining what you do in the particular events you experience in practice. He says what you do in practice is based on these propositions you have about how you

can influence particular events in particular ways.

Worker: How long has he been in his ivory tower? If professors would come out into the real world, they would be less concerned about theories. Theories look fine in books, but I have so much to do in a hurry that I find little practical value in them. When you're on the firing line like I am, you don't have time for theorizing.

Student: You mean you don't use *any* theories in your practice?

Worker: Oh, I use some ideas but I don't think you can call them theories. When I first started working, after I got my degree in social work, I used a lot of what I learned. But I found myself thinking so much about what the books told me to do that it got in the way of my really being with people and understanding their point of view. Now I have no preconceived notions about what I do. I take my leads from them. I try to understand how they are perceiving reality, what they want from me, and I use this understanding as a basis of a relationship in which I give them acceptance and support and help them see what they can do to get what they want.

Student: (With typical student perceptiveness and delight at discovery.) Hey! That sounds like one of the practice theories Dr. Anderson has mentioned and that I've read about. . . .

Worker: You don't understand at all! Just wait until you get out here in a full-time job. You'll discover that the books can't help you much. Even if you try to apply your "theories," they will get in your way or won't help you know what you need to do to help others. You'll see. . . .

The worker in this dialogue is making several invalid assumptions. It is likely that he does not *think* he is behaving in accordance with a theory of practice. It may also be true that Dr. Anderson does not fully appreciate the difficulty in using theories in practice. However, it is not necessarily true that theories are an obstacle to understanding and responding to an individual's needs and realities. Nor is it true that the student will learn a single unified practice theory that applies to every event experienced in practice—there is none. Nor can it be true that the worker is not using a practice theory. Most of our experiences of reality are filtered through a meaning process that is in essence a "theory." Michael Polanyi terms this process, when it is not consciously recognized, "tacit knowledge."[1] When it influences professional behavior, it has been called *theory in use* versus the more formally stated *espoused theory*.[2]

Scott Briar and Henry Miller speak directly to the point of the impossibility, naiveté, and danger of the assumption that one can work without theory.[3] They note, for instance, that social workers have often disagreed about the place and importance of theory in casework practice. One side claims that theory is essential. The other side argues that theory should be left at the doorstep and not be allowed to intrude into the encounter between worker and consumer, so that the worker presumably can approach the client unencumbered by the concepts and categories of a theory. To Briar and Miller, this issue is a false one. The atheoretical position is simply naive. The choice for the worker is not *whether* to have a theory but *what* theoretical assumptions to hold. All social workers require assumptions to interpret practice events and behavior, including their own. These assumptions frequently are not stated formally; they are "implicit theories of personality." Thus, Briar and Miller regard the call for practitioners to be atheoretical as simply an argument that theory ought to be implicit, not self-conscious.

It is difficult, however, to defend this position favoring the use of implicit theory. By definition, implicit theory is not susceptible to scrutiny and objective validation and therefore cannot be distinguished from mere personal bias ("All consumers should be like me."). These weaknesses of implicit theory are particularly serious for a profession in which a significant portion of activity involves forming judgments and impressions about people on the basis of which decisions are made that affect their lives in critical ways.

Definition of Practice Theory

Theory has been defined in many ways. In sociology, Robert Merton has defined theory as the "logical interrelationship between propositions"[4] and Talcott Parsons has defined it as a "system in the present sense . . . of logically generalized concepts of empirical reference."[5] In psychology, Carl Rogers refers to the *tentativeness* of theory in his description of it as a "fallible changing attempt to construct a network of gossamer threads which will contain the solid facts."[6] In social work, Joel Fischer writes of theory as "a more or less formalized explanatory conceptualization of the relationship of variables."[7] Theories, then, are an organization of hypotheses (propositions) and concepts that explain the relationships among variables in observed events (or "facts").

In essence, practice theory is the *system* from which we can be systematic in our approach to practice. Donald Ford and Hugh Urban deal with practice theory as system in their comparative study of theoretical approaches to psychotherapy.[8] They define practice theory as a system in the following terms:

> The term *system* has three principal meanings, all of which apply to our problem. First, a system is a method of classification, or codification, a taxonomy, a classificatory scheme. To be systematic, we must define a set of classes into which the phenomena or events of concern may be placed and thereby differentiated from one another. Second, a system is a regular method or order. To be systematic is to be methodical, orderly, and consistent in following a set of procedures. Third, a system is a collection of objects, facts, ideas, or principles related in some fashion to form a coherent whole. In this sense, to be systematic is to operate within a coherently related framework: in this latter sense, the terms system and theory may be synonymous.[9]

In line with this relationship of theory to system, the following definition is proposed: *Practice theory is a more or less formalized system of propositions, hypotheses, or practice principles, including their concepts, which systematically explains the nature of, establishes our relationship to, and proposes our procedures for influencing observed events in practice situations.* In this sense, practice theory is a map of the territory of practice. The map is not the territory, of course. It is a certain organization of symbols that helps us travel, or negotiate, the territory.

Value of Practice Theories

Noted in the work of Briar and Miller, and of others concerned about the uses of theory for practice,[10] are a number of reasons for the deliberate use of practice theories. Like any tool, including scientific tools, theories do not have an intrinsic value. A tool's worth is in its *usefulness*. This is the axiom of pragmatic science: A difference to be a difference must *make a difference*. What difference does the deliberate use of practice theories make for the generalist social worker?

First and foremost, theory predicts outcomes and thus guides responsible choice. In the decision to use Procedure A, Procedure B, or Procedure C to bring about Event Z, theory informs our educated guess that one procedure is more likely to get the desired result than another. It is the best compass to tell us where to go to get what we want. It prevents the comic-tragic situation of the airplane pilot with a broken instrument who radios the control tower that he doesn't know where he is or where he is going but is going to double his speed to get there faster! In the conscious formulation of action linked to expected outcomes, the social worker is involved in a theory-testing and theory-building process. It is in the testing and building of theory that practice moves away from the guesswork that attacks every new situation by reinventing the wheel through laborious experimentation. Our commitment to provide the best possible resources to those we serve demands an ability to predict the outcome of our efforts.

Closely related to the prediction of outcomes is our accountability to the consumer and to the society that sanctions our practice. Practice theory allows us to evaluate our practice and improve its effectiveness. Evaluations include both efforts and effects. _Efforts_ refer to what we have done and our rationale for doing so. _Effects_ refer to the results of this action. An evaluation of efforts and effects holds us accountable for determining how our knowledge, our use of this knowledge, and our own idiosyncrasies have influenced the achievement (or nonachievement) of outcomes. Above all, we can determine whether we have helped or hurt consumers, how we have helped or hurt, and what we can or cannot do for the individual and for society.

Moreover, theory spotlights the parts of reality that influence events. It indicates the variables we must observe and comprehend in practice situations. In this case, theory protects our sanity and enables us to act. An attempt to see and understand _everything_ in every event would leave us in a catatonic state, lost in the mysteries of existence, and immobilized.

Theory also allows us to anticipate the outcome of novel situations and to judge the relationship of variables in these situations. Our spotlight can move from stage to stage and player to player to show us the main action for understanding the play. To the extent that the theory is sound, unexpected developments should not overwhelm us. With theory, therefore, we should experience fewer surprises in our practice.

All these benefits increase the reliable and consistent use of the self in practice situations. Moreover, we can use practice theories to determine what is common and what is unique about each situation. This consistency is not antithetical to our values of self-determination and individualization. In fact, the consistency of a theory's use ensures that we view each consumer and his or her situation as _both_ similar to and different from any other.

In using practice theories in new situations, we are able to determine the theory's limits (and our own) and discover the gaps in our practical knowledge. We can determine, moreover, what we can work on and what we cannot. It is as important to know what we do not know as it is to know what we do know. We may stop blaming ourselves for being human.

Practice theories can increase our confidence in being human, though. In the awesome responsibility of giving oneself to the cause of another, practice theories can lessen our doubt and ease the painful experience of our human vulnerability. In fact, our belief in theory—even a theory that is unsound or unused—can reinforce our faith that we have something to offer in a potentially overwhelming situation. The danger of this faith, of course, is that consumers may use our beliefs, rather than our competence, to bolster their own confidence in dealing with a potentially overwhelming world. But if our direction is in the use of our practice theories, as well as their tentativeness, consumers may also use our service for their own answers. Nevertheless, practice theories can be an anchor in the stormy sea of otherwise confusing realities.

Furthermore, practice theories allow us to communicate what we do. To the degree that our theories are formalized, we can explain our activities to others, demonstrate our propositions, and enter the professional arena where our activities càn be evaluated by others. If our theories are sound, others can profit from our experience in their own practice. Thus we can serve unseen and unknown others. If our theories are unsound, we can profit from others' scrutiny. Thus we can serve better those we do know and are directly concerned about.

Finally, our theoretical concepts and their testability can serve as a base for analyzing other theories. We can choose other theoretical explanations to increase our effectiveness in practice. At least our awareness of practice theories and their empirical verification can lead us to fuller understanding and perhaps modification of our own use of theories. We can take in the new without totally relinquishing the old.

Current State of Practice Theories

Social work educators have played too many self-defeating games in helping students develop useful practice theories.[11] These classroom games have affected our theory testing and theory building, which can come only from the real world of practice. The games range from having students find the precious pony of their own theories by shoveling their way through a stable full of reading assignments to teaching students to ask "Who says?" about every theoretical formulation in the hope they will discover that theory is linked to vested sociopolitical interests and therefore an important game-of-games.

What we really need is the development of theory-based accountability for competent practice. Part 3 provides a comparative introduction to social work practice theories for study, use, and testing in practice. This chapter provides the framework for learning *how* to study, use, and test these theories. Ideally the student will have mastered at least one practice theory for each major unit for practice—individual, family, group, organization, and community—as a base for future theory and practice.

Selecting Practice Theories

In social work, our practice theories are influenced by our values, purposes, and objectives. They are also filtered through a logical deductive and inductive process as we apply basic theory to the phenomenon we serve: human behavior in the social environment. While basic theory (presented in Chapters 6 and 7) directs our systematic assessment of people–environment transactions, practice theory relates to our assumptions about development and change and directs our systematic influence (or "intervention") on events in transition. Figure 8.1 depicts this general process of applying basic theoretical systems for assessment and intervention to events. It is the logical connection of these ideas, as one reads this

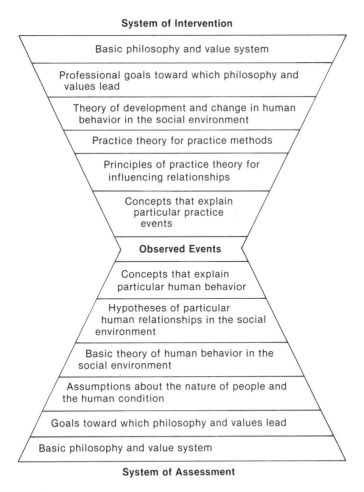

System of Intervention

Basic philosophy and value system

Professional goals toward which philosophy and values lead

Theory of development and change in human behavior in the social environment

Practice theory for practice methods

Principles of practice theory for influencing relationships

Concepts that explain particular practice events

Observed Events

Concepts that explain particular human behavior

Hypotheses of particular human relationships in the social environment

Basic theory of human behavior in the social environment

Assumptions about the nature of people and the human condition

Goals toward which philosophy and values lead

Basic philosophy and value system

System of Assessment

Figure 8.1 Framework for Practice Theory

figure from bottom to center and top to center, that serves as the framework for linking assessment to intervention in practice theories. This framework includes elements and their order for those basic and practice theories that can inform social work practice.

Figure 8.1 shows the general framework for selecting, using, testing, and building social work practice theory. So far, the theory developed in

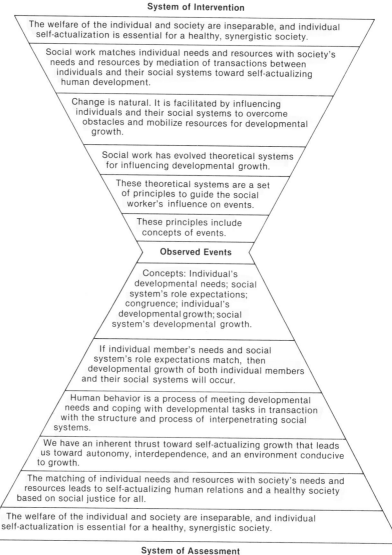

System of Intervention

The welfare of the individual and society are inseparable, and individual self-actualization is essential for a healthy, synergistic society.

Social work matches individual needs and resources with society's needs and resources by mediation of transactions between individuals and their social systems toward self-actualizing human development.

Change is natural. It is facilitated by influencing individuals and their social systems to overcome obstacles and mobilize resources for developmental growth.

Social work has evolved theoretical systems for influencing developmental growth.

These theoretical systems are a set of principles to guide the social worker's influence on events.

These principles include concepts of events.

Observed Events

Concepts: Individual's developmental needs; social system's role expectations; congruence; individual's developmental growth; social system's developmental growth.

If individual member's needs and social system's role expectations match, then developmental growth of both individual members and their social systems will occur.

Human behavior is a process of meeting developmental needs and coping with developmental tasks in transaction with the structure and process of interpenetrating social systems.

We have an inherent thrust toward self-actualizing growth that leads us toward autonomy, interdependence, and an environment conducive to growth.

The matching of individual needs and resources with society's needs and resources leads to self-actualizing human relations and a healthy society based on social justice for all.

The welfare of the individual and society are inseparable, and individual self-actualization is essential for a healthy, synergistic society.

System of Assessment

Figure 8.2 Main Propositions for Practice

this book has proposed certain social work values, purposes, and goals. This theory includes the basic concepts of individual and social systems operations and developmental growth as a base for the generalist's use of practice theories. If we insert the major theoretical propositions for practice into Figure 8.1, we get a structure like Figure 8.2.

The Concept of "Concepts"

The pivotal part of these systems for social work practice is the *concept* and its value in theory. It is therefore pertinent to elaborate here on the concept of the "concept." A concept is defined by one dictionary as "something conceived in the mind; an abstract idea generalized from particular instances." It is a unit of meaning—a term that categorizes the variables in particular events. Concepts are boxes of abstraction in which we put concrete events for organizing them, thinking about them, generalizing among them, and systematically doing something with them. Let us look at some concepts relating to the life and events of Farmer Brown as depicted in Figure 8.3.

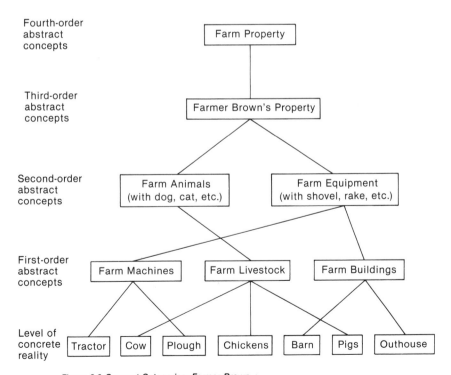

Figure 8.3 Concept Categories: Farmer Brown

Semanticists warn that the word, or concept, is never the same as the thing it denotes. Farmer Brown has fifty cows, and cow_1 is not cow_2 is not cow_3 . . . cow_{50}. Cow is an event in process and cow today is not cow tomorrow. And if our business is cows, this difference can make a difference. The Wintu Indians, for instance, have an economy based on cattle raising and they have a staggering number of names for that category of Farmer Brown's we have simple labeled "cow."[12] Nevertheless, Farmer Brown can ask us to go milk a cow without having us go to his chickens, pigs, or outhouse. The concept is concrete enough to denote the thing to which it refers. A theory is only as good as its concepts and their ability to denote concrete reality. This denotation is the ultimate function of concepts—the recognition of the difference between a "cow" and a "presenting problem" of a "consumer" in a "social work" "practice situation" when we see one. In fact, the inevitable use of concepts means that reality is never a matter of "seeing is believing." It is quite the contrary: "Believing is seeing."

The semanticist Wendell Johnson tells an instructive tale about a theory with the weak concept of "plogglies." According to this theory there were once two very perplexing mysteries, over which the wisest men in the land had beaten their heads and stroked their beards for years. But nothing came of all this. The two mysteries continued to plague everyone.

The mysteries were these: Whenever people wanted to find a lead pencil they couldn't; and whenever anyone wanted to sharpen a pencil the sharpener was sure to be filled with shavings. It was a most annoying state of affairs, and after sufficient public agitation a committee of distinguished philosophers (social workers?) was appointed by the government to carry out a searching investigation and, above all, to concoct a suitable explanation of the outrage.

One can hardly imagine the intensity of the deliberations that went on among the august members of that committee. Moreover, their investigations were carried out under very trying conditions, for the public, impatient and distraught, was clamoring ever more loudly for results. Finally, after what seemed to be a very long time, the committee of eminent philosophers appeared before the chief of state to deliver a brilliant explanation of the twin mysteries.

It was quite simple after all. Beneath the ground, so the theory went, live a great number of little people called plogglies. At night, explained the philosophers, when people are asleep, the plogglies come into their houses. They scurry around and gather up all the lead pencils, and then scamper over to the pencil sharperner and grind them all up. And then they go back into the ground.

The great national unrest subsided. Obviously, this was a brilliant theory—with one stroke it accounted for both mysteries. The only thing wrong with it was that there aren't any plogglies.[13]

There are other problems with the plogglie concept. It is not a concept that can be tested and used to predict outcomes. This shortcoming opens up its irresponsible use by irresponsible others. Shamans and medicine men, ancient and modern, can use plogglies (and do!) for controlling and influencing others. Plogglies make for a perfect alibi because of their unpredictability and utter invisibility. No matter what happens in practice, it can always be explained *after the fact* by this powerful concept by saying, as solemnly as possible, "Well, that's how it goes with plogglies." Some of the major concepts in social work may very well be plogglies. Depending on how we conceptualize change, we may use such concepts as "heredity," "environment," and "human nature" to explain—afterward— why the outcomes we predicted did not occur. We may too often agree with Popeye's patented plogglie that developmental growth did not occur because "I yam what I yam and that's all I yam—I'm Popeye the sailor man."

Not only are such concepts weak and irresponsible because of their inability to predict outcomes and be subjected to verification. They also are useless for practice. So what if there are plogglies? We cannot do anything about them. They are too ingenious to catch. Maybe we had better devise a theory based on concepts that help us to plan a strategy to empty our pencil sharpeners every morning and keep a fresh supply of pencils on hand. In social work practice we need to select theories that conceptualize events in a manner that will help us develop those parts of our thinking, feeling, and doing self that make a difference in human relations.

Formulating Practice Theories

The formulation of a personal practice theory requires a knowledge of self, a knowledge of practice theories, a knowledge of the demands of practice situations, and a knowledge of building and testing theories. The following ten steps may aid this process:

1. *Sharpen* awareness of your own feelings, values, beliefs, expectations, thought processes, and other characteristics relevant to your own practice theories ("theories in use"). In short, you need to know your own style. There is sufficient research to indicate that one's style is inevitably linked with one's theories in predicting behavior in practice situations.[14]

2. *Seek* information about various theories, old and new, for social work practice. Find theories that have evolved from social work experience before looking to developments in other professions that may or may not apply to social work.

3. *Study* existing theories. Examine their major assumptions, their compatability with your own personal style and values, their links to basic theory in human behavior in the social environment, the quality of research supporting their propositions, and their current uses in practice (where, with whom, for what problems, by whom, with what results?).

4. *Set* a theoretical framework that addresses itself to the components of a theory for social work practice. (See Figure 8.1.)

5. *Screen* out theoretical formulations that are totally incongruent with your personality and style.

6. *Select* dimensions and procedures that fit your personality and style, but remember that you may need to change this style and your practice theories as you evaluate the results of your practice. Include the selection of practice theories which can base the variety of methods you need to use for generalist practice: casework, family group work, group work, organizational development, brokerage, case advocacy, community organization and development, policy development, and cause advocacy. Be sure that the theories are free of plogglies and therefore verifiable and useful.

7. *Synthesize* what you select—both within your practice theory systems and with your own style and theories in use.

8. *Subject* your evolving practice theories to practical application.

9. *Shift* your theories according to your experience with them. Test your theoretical propositions against the facts of practice.

10. *Stabilize* your practice theories as time and experience accrue. But remember that theory can be slavishly followed to the point that it becomes an albatross rather than a compass.

Testing Practice Theories

The testing of practice theories begins in the concise and consistent nature of the theory itself. Testing demands an ability to explicate the theory—that is, to organize the propositions of both the espoused theory and the theory in use and to define their relationship to each other. Chris Argyris and Donald Schön offer a scheme for testing practice theories (Figure 8.4).[15] Let us see how it applies to espoused theories.

Espoused Theories

In using this system the first step is explication of the espoused theory and its internal consistency. This process includes a statement of the relationship among the various hypotheses and concepts of the practice theory. Let us take, for instance, theories that have evolved from recent methodologies for growth groups. Both theories claim to explain how a worker can influence group process toward self-actualization for members. The first theory, based on Carl Rogers' work, is related to a basic encounter group methodology.[16] The second, based on Fritz Perls' work, is related to a group-based sensory awareness methodology.[17]

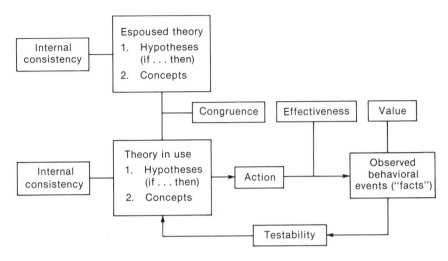

Figure 8.4 Scheme for Testing Practice Theories

The underlying assumption of the Rogerian theory is that an encounter group can generate "a psychological climate of safety" through the leader's avoidance of judgment and nondomination of the experience. This assumption of safety leads to the following ten hypotheses (see Figure 8.5):[18]

1. If you *feel safe within the group,* then you will exhibit *freedom of expression.*

2. If you exhibit freedom of expression, then you will provide genuine *communication* to others.

3. If you genuinely communicate your ideas and feelings to others, then others will return genuine *feedback* to you.

4. If you receive genuine feedback, then you will increase your *empathy* with others.

5. If you increase your empathy, then you will increase *self-knowledge.*

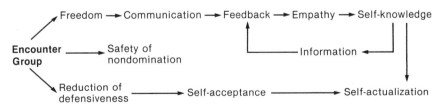

Figure 8.5 Rogerian Encounter Group Theory

6. If you feel safe in an encounter group, then you will exhibit a *reduction of defensiveness.*

7. If you exhibit a reduction of defensiveness, then you will have greater *self-acceptance.*

8. If you receive empathy-increasing feedback, then you will obtain new *information* on other modes of being.

9. If you receive new information on other modes of being, then you will increase *self-knowledge.*

10. If you exhibit self-knowledge and self-acceptance and have information on other possible modes of being, then you will be more likely to achieve *self-actualization.*

The second theory, gestalt sensory awareness theory, can be contrastingly diagrammed as in Figure 8.6. The underlying assumption of this approach is that the leader can provide sensory awareness experiments that lead to increased perceptions of self. This assumption leads to the following eight hypotheses:

1. If you participate in the *leader-initiated experiments,* then you will increase your *sensory awareness of present experience.*

2. If you increase your awareness of present experience, then you can be guided to *experience* the *polarities* inherent in conflict.

3. If you experience the polarities of conflict, then you will *integrate* these *opposites* in your personality.

4. If you integrate these opposites, then you will *increase* your *excitement* or energy.

5. If you participate in the leader-initiated experiences, then you will increase *sensory awareness* of your *resistance to awareness of present experience.*

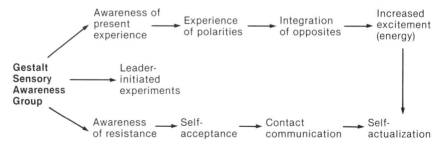

Figure 8.6 Gestalt Sensory Awareness Group Theory

6. If you increase your sensory awareness of your resistance to awareness of present experience, then you will increase your *acceptance of self* in the present.

7. If you increase your acceptance of self in the present, then you will *contact* the objects of current needs in the group through *communication,* or behavior.

8. If you act on contact communication of current awareness and have increased energy to bring to behavior, then you will be more likely to achieve *self-actualization.*

One can test these two espoused theories. Their propositions and concepts have been stated in such a way that one can follow the procedures of both approaches in similar situations. If one could find a clear way to observe whether "increased self-actualization" was reached for members of these two groups, one could test whether these practice theories work and perhaps even indicate whether one method works better than the other to achieve the predicted outcomes. The author did just that testing in some recent research.[19] With "increased self-actualization" interpreted as decreased feelings of interpersonal alienation, an increased sense of self-autonomy, and increased interpersonal empathy among group members, the encounter group was more successful than the gestalt group with young adult volunteers for a growth group experience of a short twelve-hour duration. The major process variables that affected outcomes were predicted in the Rogerian theory: member-to-member empathy and acceptance in the group.

Theories in Use

Theories in use are harder to explicate than espoused theories and must be drawn from reflection on actual practice. Argyris and Schön have developed a method for analyzing theories in use vis-à-vis espoused theories and testing them in practice.[20] They suggest the following assignment for social workers:

> Please describe a challenging intervention or interaction with one or more individuals that (1) you have already experienced or (2) you expect to experience in the near future.
>
> If you have difficulty with either of these conditions, try a hypothetical case in which you doubt your effectiveness.
>
> Begin the description with a paragraph about the purpose of your intervention, the setting, the people involved, and any other important characteristics.
>
> Next, write a few paragraphs regarding your strategy. What were your objectives, how did you intend to achieve them, and why did you select those goals and strategies?
>
> Next, write a few pages of the dialogue that actually occurred or that you expect to occur. Use the following format.

On this side of the page, write what was going on in your mind while each person in the dialogue (including yourself) is speaking.

On this side of the page, write what each person actually said or what you expected him to say. Continue writing the dialogue until you believe your major points are illustrated. (The dialogue should be at least two pages long.)

Finally, after you reread your case, describe the underlying assumptions that you think you held about effective action.

In the work of Argyris and Schön is an example of a social worker who used this assignment to identify her theory in use and increase her effectiveness in practice. The example is given with comments on the relation of this theory to her practice. The worker is trying to help a person who does not seem to be changing his behavior. She writes, "I feel annoyed with him and pretty determined either to cut off our interaction, delve more deeply into his problem, or demonstrate to him that he is in fact not interested in changing at all. The last alternative is fine with me. I dislike wasting my time on futile activity."[21] At this point, we see that the social worker (1) has already decided the course the next session should take; (2) has attributed characteristics to the consumer without telling him so that he can confirm or deny them; (3) has decided that the responsibility for failure lies with him and therefore does not explore her own role in the apparent failure; (4) assumes that she is responsible for the consumer's behavior; and (5) denies responsibility for her sense of failure. (She states that she dislikes having her time wasted, but a more accurate statement might have been "I dislike being with a client I cannot help because I feel that I have been partially responsible for wasting my time.")

Later the worker writes, "I knew that I had to be very much on top of the situation so that we would not fall back into our old ways of interacting. I tried to keep my objectives in mind all the time and I tried to push myself to think and evaluate clearly because I knew he did not want to hear what I had to say, and I could slip backward in a weak moment." Here the worker assumes that she, rather than the consumer, is in control. However, the social worker's purpose is to promote growth and responsibility. Her dilemma is that she is faced with a person whom she feels unable to help unless she violates her principles.

Looking more closely at her theories in use, we find that although the social worker claims to dislike people who are dependent, passive, and weak, she selects tactics that reinforce these characteristics. Perhaps she wants people to exhibit such characteristics so she can accept her predisposition to control others. She may even have selected a theory in use that minimizes the probability of being confronted on this issue by either the consumer or herself. Her assumption that the consumer is not going to grow could be a self-fulfilling prophecy.

A concluding dialogue reflects these problems with her theories in use:

Social Worker:	You seem to want or expect personal change to be easy.
Consumer:	No, I don't. I expect it to be hard but I know it's for my own benefit. But you must understand I have to work within certain constraints . . . [cut off by social worker].
Social Worker:	Why? You're working within "certain constraints" now and you're not going anywhere. You're saying you [must] accept these constraints. That doesn't make any sense; you can't change yourself and not expect to challenge your environment.
Consumer	Why not? I mean, it's me that has to change if I want this to happen. I can't expect the world to change for me.
Social Worker:	Yes, that's true but as I have told you many times you can make the world change so that you can live more fully in it.
Consumer:	I guess you're right. I know I don't have much self-discipline. That's one of my real faults that I can't do anything about. But now that I see my father coming apart at the seams, I want to change before I get to be like that, too.
Social Worker:	How much do you want to change? Enough to commit yourself to a job? Enough to risk some arguments with your wife?
Consumer:	Well, I'd like to teach young people something in psychology or religion or history.
Social Worker:	How do you think you could go about getting what you need to be a teacher for those subjects?
Consumer:	I don't know. I guess I'd have to get a teaching certificate, but that's impossible.
Social Worker:	Why?
Consumer:	I didn't even finish college.
Social Worker:	Well, so what? Go back to school.
Consumer:	I'm too old. I'd be laughed at.
Social Worker:	Now, you know that's not true. People go back to finish up all the time. As I've said before, if you really want to, you can do anything.[22]

This social worker, having used this assignment, may be in a position to test how much her espoused theories, her theories in use, and her own idiosyncrasies may affect her service to this person (and surely to others, too). In this approach she may *choose* among the options for achieving her objectives in conjunction with the consumer's needs. This returns us to the value of *conscious* use of practice theories.

Now let us turn to a story that summarizes the major purpose of this chapter. You may recall A. A. Milne's account in *Winnie-the-Pooh* about what happened one morning when Pooh Bear went tracking in the snowy woods. Piglet saw him going along with his head down and asked what he was doing, and Pooh said, "Tracking." When Piglet wanted to know "tracking what?", Pooh said he didn't know because you never could tell with paw marks. So Piglet joined him since he didn't have anything else to do until Friday anyway. The paw marks they were following led them round a spinnet bush, and they were going along wondering whether the creature they were tracking might turn out to be a Woozle or a Wizzle, when suddenly it appeared that whatever it was had been joined by another Woozle or Wizzle—and to their mounting astonishment they found as they continued that they were evidently pursuing more and more Woozles and Wizzles.

In fact, Piglet became so befuddled that, judging the time to be twelve o'clock, he was suddenly moved to recall he had something to do between the hours of twelve and five past twelve, so he left Pooh Bear to his tracking. He who tracks and runs away will live to track another day— this seems to have been Piglet's way of sizing up the situation. And so it was Pooh who made the great discovery. After a while he stopped going around the spinnet bush, and looked closely at all the tracks made by the many Woozles and Wizzles, and he looked at them for a long while because he was a bear of very small brain. Then he carefully placed his own paw snuggly down into one of the Woozle tracks! And when Pooh Bear did that he did a very remarkable thing from which he learned a very important lesson. Pooh Bear got wise to himself.[23]

Wendell Johnson has this to say about the story: "What Pooh Bear had learned, only partially no doubt, we can learn in significant measure as we become more and more aware of what we are doing, going round and round the spinnet bush of human knowledge, engrossed in the feverish and sometimes frightening pursuit of the inky paw marks of Truth. . . . And when wisdom comes, as very occasionally it does, it reveals itself in the wry smile with which we admit that the tracks we follow are the tracks we ourselves have made."[24] Our wisdom in social work is to be found in the continuous tracking of our practice theories and their contribution to our use of self—our major instrument for effective practice.

Summary

While social workers may deny their use of theories in practice, all practice is based on theory. The direct-service generalist is using either informal theory or theory that is formal and conscious—or, more likely, both. The questions for the practitioner are not *whether* to have a theory but *what* theories to use and *how* to use them.

Formal practice theories hold no intrinsic value but can pragmatically aid the worker and consumer in several ways: (1) by helping us to predict outcomes; (2) by holding us responsible for evaluating our services; (3) by directing us to pertinent aspects of practice; (4) by helping us adjust to novel situations; (5) by contributing to the reliability and consistency of our work; (6) by helping us to see gaps in our knowledge; (7) by contributing to our confidence; (8) by their communicability to others; and (9) by their use as a basis for evaluating new theories.

Social work practice theory, though it has certainly germinated, has yet to bloom. In fact, the recent movement toward undisciplined eclecticism has made theory-based accountability for practice very difficult. Social work education bears a major responsibility for this growing conceptual anarchy through the games that educators play in teaching practice theories. Social work students must be taught how to select, use, and test the theories that have grown out of social work *practice*.

Practice theory is therefore a system that directs systematic practice— a more or less formalized set of principles and concepts that explains the events we observe in practice, establishes our relationship to them, and proposes procedures for influencing them. Basic theory is a system for assessment; practice theory is a system for intervention.

The pivotal point of these two theoretical processes is the concept of "concept"—an abstract idea about concrete events. A concept allows us to categorize, organize, think about, generalize about, and act on events in process. The validity and utility of our concepts determine the strength of the foundation on which our practice theories are built. "Plogglie" concepts must be exposed and discarded in both our theories in use and our espoused theories.

Ten steps are useful for formulating a personal practice theory. These steps are organized through the words sharpen, seek, study, set, screen, select, synthesize, subject, shift, and stabilize.

Both espoused theories and theories in use must be tested in practice. Espoused theories can be tested by analyzing the relationship of concepts to each other. Theories in use can be tested through the recording process developed by Argyris and Schön. Once we understand what parts our espoused theories, our theories in use, and our idiosyncrasies have played in our practice, we are in the position of Pooh Bear discovering his own tracks. We can get wise to ourselves.

The chapters that follow in Part 3 are designed to contribute to practice wisdom. They introduce alternative frameworks for comparing, selecting, and integrating social work practice theories for an interlocking and disciplined approach to generalist practice. Two kinds of models are used: those that constitute practice theory for the generalist and those that have evolved from within social work as a profession.

Suggested Learning Experiences

The major activity suggested to enhance learning the concepts of this chapter is the use of the Argyris and Schön assignment to relate one's theories in use to the espoused theories covered in Part 3.

Suggested Case Studies

Two case studies noted earlier are particularly useful for identifying and discussing both espoused theories and theories in use in direct-service practice: Henry S. Maas, "Social Work with Individuals and Families," in *Concepts and Methods of Social Work,* ed. W. Friedlander, 2nd ed. (Englewood Cliffs, N.J.: Prentice-Hall, 1976); Armando Morales and Bradford W. Shaefor, "The Social Worker in Action," in *Social Work: A Profession of Many Faces* (Boston: Allyn and Bacon, 1977). An excellent example of a direct-service worker's experience related to both theories in use and espoused theories is found in Martin Bloom, *The Paradox of Helping: Introduction to the Philosophy of Scientific Practice* (New York: John Wiley and Sons, 1975), pp. 144–154.

Practice Theories

3

Introduction

When the "consumer system" and the "target system" are both the individual as in Quadrant A of the methods framework of Chapter 2, the method of choice is casework. Practice theories for the casework method fall into a variety of categories, but generally there are four primary approaches: psychosocial, functional, problem-solving, and sociobehavioral.[1]

The *psychosocial approach* is grounded in the basic psychoanalytic theory of Freud and its ego psychology. The *functional approach* is grounded in the will psychology of Rank,[2] symbolic interaction theory, and the theoretical branches of existential humanistic psychology. The *problem-solving approach,* which stands between the psychosocial and the functional, is grounded in the pragmatic theories of Dewey[3] and has been influenced by ego psychology and the symbolic interactionists. The *socio-behavioral approach* is grounded in the works of the social learning theorists. All these approaches have used elements of social systems theory as a framework for integrating the sociological and psychological dimensions of transactions between the individual and the environment.

These practice theories inform the casework method in their essential agreement with the definition of casework offered in Chapter 2 and repeated here: Casework is "a method of engaging a client, through a relationship process essentially one-to-one, in the use of a social service toward his own and the general social welfare."[4] The essential characteristics of these four casework practice theories are examined in the following section. The chapter concludes with a brief summary of each of these four theoretical approaches.

Classification of Casework Theories

Several frameworks have been proposed in the social work literature for a comparative study of casework theories for the purpose of selecting approaches for practice.[5] These frameworks range from the complex 79-item checklist of Joel Fischer to the seven questions of Scott Briar and Henry Miller: (1) past, present, or future most determinant of behavior?;

(2) nature–nurture emphasis?; (3) intrapsychic *versus* social influence assumptions?; (4) unit (personality part, personality as a whole, interpersonal) of behavioral analysis?; (5) is behavior knowable?; (6) amenable to scientific test?; and (7) capacity to generate principles for intervention? Most of these frameworks for comparing theories assume that the theories which are consistent with professional values, specific in their principles for practice, and empirically validated through research should be selected for use in practice.

For most of these frameworks, this is a most unfortunate assumption. No practice theory for casework stands superior to the others when subjected to this scrutiny. We are left, therefore, with the claims of practitioners regarding the value of these approaches in their own experience. I am reminded of a recent experience in my doctor's office. I was reading a review in a health magazine about the mixed findings on the relationship of mass dosages of vitamin C to colds. The article generally concluded that there is no definitive evidence either to support or refute the use of vitamin C to prevent colds. I turned to my own experience and noted that I had not had a cold in several years, since I had started taking vitamin C. At that moment, I closed the magazine and looked up, only to discover, for the first time, the sign in the doctor's waiting room: "WHEN EXPERTS DISAGREE THE IGNORANT ARE FREE TO CHOOSE!"

In an exaggerated manner, perhaps, this situation is the one we face in selecting casework practice theories. We are free to choose. But how can we choose with less ignorance? If we had only one weapon to cut through this indecisiveness it might well be the question: What are the *consumer's* goals? Methods are systematic procedures for reaching a *goal*. In practice, then, the choice of casework approach can best be made on the basis of our knowledge of the individual's goal and the practice theories directed toward achieving that goal.

Goals

Donald Krill has developed a goal-based framework for selecting the appropriate practice theory.[6] In his view the major problems in selecting practice theories are the extremes of dogmatic marriage to one theory or the anarchy of using informal theories. The first extreme leads to the prejudicial application of such "plogglie" concepts as "untreatable" or "unmotivated" to all who do not respond to the theory's application. The second extreme creates a situation in which all consumers are treated alike—according to the worker's own system. Both problems lead to the nonresponsive situation in which the choice of theories creates the choice of goals. Krill suggests a way out of this dilemma: There is a relationship between consumer goals and the many approaches of different practice theories. In other words, specific techniques are more or less appropriate for the achievement of specific goals.

Krill's framework consists of six categories based on his concept of "client modifiability"—that is, the goals of the contract related to the consumer's needs and tasks:

1. Sustaining relationship: the consumer "wishes to endure an unchangeable situation and have available a helping person who cares and understands his situation."

2. Specific behavioral change: the consumer is "interested in changing a specific behavior or an isolated symptom."

3. Environmental change: the consumer seeks general improvement in an environmental activity.

4. Relationship change: the consumer seeks general improvement in significant relationships.

5. Directional change (personalizing values): the consumer "wishes to establish direction (meaning) in his life."

6. Insightful analysis: the consumer "seeks extensive and thorough rational-emotional self-understanding."

When consumer-oriented goals are specified to this degree, both in theory and in practice, we are in a position to discover the appropriateness of a practice theory for our use in casework. Moreover, both the nature of the goal and the approach suggest other elements for comparison: the personality dimensions that must be tapped to achieve the goal, the theory's value assumptions, the time it will take, the worker's basic stance, and the specific techniques needed. Finally, workers can evaluate practice theories by looking *inside* the theory at its specific principles for practice methods and its empirical status and by looking *outside* the theory to determine the type of consumer to whom it tends to be directed.

The major personality dimensions toward which these theories are directed are emotionality, cognitive, intrapsychic, interpersonal, and behavior (symptom). The major time dimensions are short-term crisis intervention (one to five contacts in one to two weeks), short or moderate term (five to twelve contacts in two to four months), and long term (a number of periodic contacts spread over five or six months to years). The worker's primary stance may be viewed as teacher, helper, or guide.

Values

There are a number of values related to the goals of particular practice theories. Eight important values help to distinguish the separate approaches: (1) belief in the predictability of human behavior; (2) belief in our basic autonomy; (3) belief in our basic interdependence; (4) belief in individualization in practice; (5) belief in purposeful expression of feelings in practice; (6) belief in controlled emotional involvement in practice; (7) belief in nonjudgmental acceptance in practice; and (8) belief in self-determination in practice.[7]

Techniques

Casework techniques have been classified in a series of research studies by Florence Hollis and others.[8] The categories and examples of these casework techniques are:

1. Sustainment: "I understand how you feel."

2. Direct influence: "I think you should tell her so."

3. Exploration/description/ventilation: "How did you feel about it?" "How old were you then?"

4. Person–situation reflection: "Your reaction to him was unexpected."

    a. Reflection on others or the environment: "Your mother won't let you go." "The clinic gives free care."
    b. Reflection on the effect of the consumer's behavior: "When you act that way, he changes."
    c. Reflection on the nature of the consumer's behavior: "Your need for attention from him is obvious." "You seem angry today."
    d. Reflection on the interpersonal cause of the consumer's behavior: "He seems able to get you angry very easily." "When he acts like that, how do you feel?"
    e. Reflection on the consumer's feelings and behavior in relation to personal or social values: "If you make that choice, will you be living up to yourself?"
    f. Reflection on treatment or the worker–consumer relationship: "What do you think counseling is all about?"

5. Reflection on personality patterns or dynamics: "You expect others to mistreat you."

6. Reflection on early life: "You and your father avoided each other."

These techniques are emphasized differently in the various casework approaches. The emphasis depends on the approach's assumptions about human behavior and change and the primary goals to which the theory is addressed.

Phases

The generic phases of social work methods and processes have been identified in a number of sources.[9] While their labels for the phases may differ, these sources generally agree on the following sequence: (1) intake; (2) establishment of a working relationship; (3) assessment; (4) determination of goals for change; (5) selection of an interventive plan; (6) establishment of a contract; (7) sustaining of work; (8) evaluation of work; and (9) termination of service.

Empirical Status

Fischer suggests that the major criteria for determining the empirical status of a practice theory are its emphasis on empirical testing, its success in measuring aspects of theory, its clarity about the determination of outcome, and its success in validating effectiveness. Briar and Miller make the special point that the nature of the consumer is a vital component for casework practice and theory. While much casework theory has derived from voluntary individuals who request a counseling service and is therefore directed toward this type, social workers require theories applicable to others to whom they provide a large number of services—involuntary consumers (family courts, child welfare, corrections), dyads (lovers, husband–wife, parent–child), or families as a unit. Other consumer types include children, adolescents, the severely disturbed and the mentally retarded. The question here is: With whom does this approach work?

A Comparison

Table 9.1 compares the four primary casework practice theories on the basis of the major elements outlined above. Each element of each theory is rated for its emphasis. From this comparison emerges a clearer conception of the similarities and differences among these approaches and their applicability to both consumer-oriented goals and preferred worker styles. In the remainder of this chapter we will take a closer look at each of these four casework practice theories.

Psychosocial Approach

The foremost developer of psychosocial casework theory is Florence Hollis.[10] Other important contributors have been Gordon Hamilton,[11] Charlotte Towle,[12] and Annette Garrett.[13] Recent contributions have come from Norman Polansky,[14] Gertrude Sackheim,[15] and Francis Turner.[16] The primary proposition of this approach is: *If a social worker accurately assesses the person-in-situation gestalt, then he or she can devise and implement a specific treatment plan to alter the person, the environment, and/or the relationship in behalf of the individual.* In this sense, the psychosocial approach has been termed a "medical model" of casework. That is, the major responsibility for determining the problem and the treatment is based on the knowledge and expertise of the worker.

Table 9.1 Characteristics of
Casework Practice Theories

Characteristic	Psychosocial Approach	Problem-solving Approach	Functional Approach	Sociobehavioral Approach
Goals				
Sustaining relationship	L	M	H	L
Specific behavioral change	L	M	L	H
Environmental change	M	L	L	L
Relationship change	L	M	H	L
Directional change	L	L	H	L
Insight	H	M	L	L
Value dimensions				
Predictability of behavior	H	M	L	H
Autonomy	M	M	H	L
Interdependence	M	M	H	H
Individualization	L	M	H	H
Expression of feelings	H	M	H	L
Controlled emotional involvement	M	M	H	L
Acceptance	M	M	H	M
Self-determination	M	M	H	M
Main dimensions tapped				
Emotionality	M	M	H	L
Cognitive	M	H	L	L
Interpersonal	M	M	H	M
Intrapsychic	H	M	L	L
Behavioral	L	M	L	H
Time dimension				
Crisis intervention	L	H	M	M
Short term	L	H	L	H
Long term	H	M	H	L
Worker's stance				
Teacher	M	H	L	H
Helper	H	M	M	L
Guide	L	M	H	M

	C1	C2	C3	C4
Techniques				
Sustainment	L	M	M	L
Direct influence	M	H	H	H
Explanation/description/ventilation	H	M	M	L
Person–situation reflection	H	M	M	M
On others or environment	M	M	M	H
On outcome of behavior	M	M	M	H
On nature of behavior	M	M	M	H
On cause of behavior	L	M	M	L
On behavior in relation to values	L	H	L	L
On worker–consumer relation	H	M	M	L
Reflections on personality patterns	M	L	H	M
Reflections on early life				
Phases in work sequence				
Intake	M	H	I	M
Establishment of working relationship	M	M	I	L
Assessment	H	M	I	I
Determination of goals	M	M	L	I
Selection of plan	I	I	L	I
Establishment of contract	M	L	M	M
Sustaining of work	I	M	L	I
Evaluation of work	M	L	L	M
Termination	L	L	I	I
Empirical status				
Emphasis on empirical testing	M	M	L	H
Success in measuring aspects of theory	I	I	L	I
Clarity about determination of outcome	L	M	L	I
Success in validating effectiveness	L	M	L	M
Consumers				
Voluntary	I	I	I	M
Involuntary	L	M	I	M
Dyads	M	L	L	L
Families	M	L	L	I
Children	M	I	L	M
Adolescents	M	I	I	I
Severely disturbed	M	M	I	I
Mentally retarded	L	L	L	I

H = high emphasis; M = moderate emphasis; L = low emphasis.

Goals

The major goals toward which this approach is directed are personality-changing insight for the consumer or modification of the consumer's relationship to specific persons or specific environmental demands. To determine the consumer's needs and the effects of change, the worker must focus on the intrapsychic dimension of the personality—that is, on the id, ego, and superego as they relate to environmental determinants. The primary focus, however, is on the cognitive, emotional, and interpersonal dimensions. These are tapped largely in relation to the consumer's ego as it mediates between superego demands ("conscience") and the drives of the id, as well as the external realities that affect this organization of the personality.

Values

The primary values behind this concept of human behavior include the predictability of behavior and the importance of the expression of feelings in relation to change. Secondary values include belief in the balance of the individual's autonomy and interdependence, belief in the worker's controlled emotional involvement with the individual, and acceptance of the individual's behavior as reasonable. In assessment and treatment, the individual's functioning is consistently compared against generalized norms, placing conditions on the use of the value of individualization. Self-determination is also a conditional value, as the worker has a responsibility to work toward goals that will change the consumer's person-in-situation gestalt—even though these goals may not be recognized or accepted by the consumer. Too, the worker is responsible for restricting the consumer from choosing actions that the worker believes would harm the individual or others. The worker's basic stance is therefore that of a helper with certain teaching functions.

Techniques

The major techniques used for both assessment and treatment are *person–situation reflection* and *exploration/description/ventilation*. In assessment, these techniques are based on three interrelated processes: dynamic, etiological, and clinical diagnoses. *Dynamic* diagnosis deals with both the worker and the consumer gaining insight into, specifying, expressing feelings about, and reflecting on the problem and the points of stress in the consumer's personality, relationships to others, and environmental demands. *Etiological* diagnosis uses similar techniques to arrive at an understanding of the historical background of the present problem. *Clinical* diagnosis is the worker's classification of the present problem into a category related to the individual's personality (psychiatric disorder, social class, and so forth). The category can then be used to prescribe specific treatment.

In treatment, the worker uses techniques pertinent to the assessment-based goals and plans. Most often, these techniques are reflections concerning others and the environment, the consequences of certain behavioral patterns, the relationship of behavioral responses to the consumer's personality and interactions, and the transfer of early life reactions into present situations.

Focus

The psychosocial approach also places particular emphasis on the use of defense mechanisms and their influence on the person–situation interaction. Moreover, much of the work is based on the assumption that current problems are caused by transference. *Transference* is the nonconscious carryover of past problems to present relationships—including the casework relationship with the worker. Insight and corrective emotional experiences can resolve the problematic aspects of these transferences and free the individual to devote libidinal or instinctual energy to more mature personality organization and fuller social functioning in love and work.

Phases

The main phases of work in the psychosocial approach are assessment, selection of interventive plans, and sustainment of work. There is less emphasis on intake, establishment of a working relationship, specific goal determination, contracting, and evaluating results. And there has been very little emphasis on termination.

The procedures during assessment require systematic thought and the gathering of specific information related to determination of the treatment plan. The tenor of these assessment operations is reflected in the following example presented by Hollis:

> A client claims he is going into debt because his rent is too high and he cannot find another place to live. To find the source of his trouble one must first compare his rental with the normal range of rentals for his income. Without this one cannot know whether the problem is in fact a disproportionately high rent or is some misconception on the client's part. It may be that his income is too low to cover his necessities even though his rent is not abnormally high. Here again a norm is applied in arriving at an opinion about the adequacy of his income. If in fact the income is adequate and the rent too high the problem is still not defined. Why has he not moved to a less expensive place? If he says he has tried but has been unable to find such a place, several alternatives are open. What is the rental situation in the community? Is it really extremely difficult to find suitable living quarters for the amount the client can afford? If so, he may need help in looking for a cheaper rental.
>
> If the measurement of the rental situation against our knowledge of reality tells us it is not very difficult to find suitable quarters, the question becomes, Why can he not solve this realistic problem for himself? Now the possibilities broaden and various systems in which the problem might

lie must be explored until a reasonable definition of the problem is reached. The worker is now considering what factors might cause a person to be unable to locate suitable living quarters when his income is sufficient and housing in his price range is available. What about the social system? Is his race or ethnic group or social class or the size of his family making it difficult for him? Here the worker uses both the client's description of his house hunting experiences and his own knowledge of social attitudes usually found in the neighborhood. If the answer does not seem to lie here, the worker asks himself, Does the trouble lie partially or wholly within the individual himself? Does he seem to lack knowledge of where and how to look? If so, why might this be? Is he a newcomer? Does he have difficulty speaking English? Is there a lack of intelligence? If no clues are found in these possibilities, does he lack initiative? If so, is it because he is physically ill? Depressed? Discouraged? Mentally ill? Again observations are evaluated against knowledge of ordinary behavior, and causative elements are looked for in terms of our knowledge of what is likely to cause the trouble the client finds himself as having. If the trouble now appears to be partially within the person—in the personality system—we must look more closely not only into his personality but also into his family system, or perhaps into his friendship system or his employment system, looking always at his interactions—his transactions—with other individuals in these systems.[17]

The worker using the psychosocial casework approach needs to do a great deal of problem solving in the helping situation. This process extends throughout: experience of event, inference, normative classification, generalization, response, event. It includes the planning and sustaining of treatment in conjunction with ongoing diagnosis.

Empirical Support

The empirical status of psychosocial casework theory is strong in the testing of techniques but weak in the assessment of outcomes. This weakness can be traced to vague definitions of success and the difficulty in measuring the major goals of personality reorganization through insight.

Consumers

Psychosocial theory has derived primarily from work with adult voluntary consumers. Its procedures include specific directions for working with dyads and families as a unit, although its literature is short on examples of this work. Some use is made of the approach in working with children and youth as well as with adults. There has been very little study of its applicability to the severely emotionally disturbed or the mentally retarded. Moreover, there is little emphasis on the involuntary consumer, as the assessment approach demands a great deal of cooperation. The approach assumes some motivating tension, or anxiety, and in the voluntary consumer resistance is generally conceived as the ego's fear of facing itself.

Problem-Solving Approach

The problem-solving theory of casework practice is traced directly to the works of Helen Harris Perlman.[18] Its applicability to crisis intervention has been particularly studied by Howard Parad[19] and its short-term use by William Reid and Laura Epstein.[20] Among the recent contributors who have expanded parts of the theory to work with families and other systems are David Hallowitz[21] and Kurt Spitzer and Betty Welsh.[22] The primary proposition of this approach is: *If a social worker can engage the consumer in a systematic problem-solving process in relation to the present problem, then the consumer can develop problem-solving skills for dealing with future problems in behavior and relationships.* The problem-solving approach can be viewed as an "educational model." The process and its outcome are related to the learning of problem-solving skills for dealing with the inevitable problems in living.

Goals

The major goals of the problem-solving approach are closely related to the consumer's problem in the person/problem/place/process configuration. Though goals are often determined by the agency's function, they usually include increasing the consumer's insight as a basis for understanding the problem and acting on it. The emphasis is on changed behavior in both relationships and social roles. As Perlman states this: "The primary goal of the problem-solving model, agreed on between client and caseworker, is to help the person deal as effectively . . . as possible with the present problems of social task and relationships he now sees, feels to be stressful, and finds insuperable without outside help."[23]

To achieve this goal, the worker focuses on the cognitive and rational dimensions of the consumer's ego. The work is geared chiefly to sustaining, supplementing, and fortifying the ego's functions to partialize reality, think about it, consider alternatives for action, and act on the facts of the situation. The other dimensions of the personality—emotionality, interpersonal, intrapsychic, and behavioral—are tapped only in reference to their influence on the consumer's perception of activities related to the goals of the problem-solving process. These dimensions are even less a part of the approach's short-term crisis intervention models and short-term task-centered models.

Values

The underlying values regarding human behavior and change concern faith in pragmatism and faith in the person's becoming more competent. Value is placed on the predictability of the problem-solving *process*, not on the prediction of specific behavior. There is some emphasis, moreover, on the individual's autonomy balanced with his or her interdependence in social roles. The worker–consumer relationship is valued for its contribution to the problem-solving process. There is individualized focus on the consumer's problem-solving capacities and an emphasis on shared feelings and acceptance that "warms" the intelligence, "sustains" the spirit, and "motivates" problem-solving work. Self-determination is moderately valued and conditional. While trust is placed in the consumer's identification of what "hurts" and what he or she wants to do about it, there is also an assumption that you cannot be self-determined until you can choose on the basis of increased consciousness of needs, goals, and alternatives. These values and the primary learning goal of increased skills in problem solving require that the worker carry a basic teaching function with secondary emphasis on helping and guiding. Hallowitz refers to this basic activity as assertive counseling, which includes confrontation, taking a stand, giving suggestions, and assigning "homework."

Techniques

The major techniques the worker uses in the service of problem-solving goals cover the spectrum of sustainment, exploration/description/ventilation, and person–situation reflection with a great deal of direct influence. Information-gathering techniques are predominant in the initial stages, and there are reflections on the objective and subjective facts of the present problem: "The first part of the casework process, as in all problem solving, is to assert and clarify the facts of the problem. The second aspect of casework problem solving grows out of . . . the ongoing eliciting of facts: it is 'thinking through the facts.' "[24] Facts are gathered by enabling the consumer to seek solutions to problems within self and situation. As Perlman proposes:

> The problem-solving model has from its inception held that central to the helping process is the engagement of the client's capacities to see and feel himself not only as problem-carrier and victim but as having within himself the powers for problem-solving, . . . for becoming aware of how his choices and decisions can affect his problem. So the client is from the first led to express, to explain, to speculate, to suppose, to see relationships, and to consider ways and means, reasons, actions, and consequences. In brief, he is rehearsed in the mental-emotional work of problem-solving.[25]

Focus and Phases

In relation to this emphasis on engagement of the person's motivation and capacity, the problem-solving approach attends greatly to the intake phase of the work sequence. The first problem confronted is that of moving from "applicant" to "consumer." The relationship is established during this work, and assessment is narrowly focused on those parts of the consumer's motivation, capacity, and opportunity that relate to the present problem. The relationship is oriented toward work and based on this reality. While transference is dealt with as it occurs, the idea is to manage the relationship in a way that avoids transference. In this process, the emphasis is on the contract for work with its specification of roles and responsibilities.

Specific goals for change are secondary to the engagement of the consumer in purposeful problem solving. The immediate target is to make it less necessary for consumers to protect themselves (both against their problem and against their fear of the agency or of change) and more possible for them to reinforce their efforts to cope with the problem. The sustaining and evaluating phases of the work are not dealt with specifically in the theory, largely because of its process orientation and the assumption that the problem-solving means and the problem-solving goals are synonymous. Nevertheless, the internal phases of the process are concluded by the consumer's choices and decisions and by renegotiation of the contract for subsequent problems. The termination phase is not considered in the theory, except for mutual recognition that the consumer has been helped to decide on a course of action in relation to the present problem.

Empirical Support

Empirically, the model has been tested in its short-term use. Results indicate a specific set of procedures that can be identified in relation to particular results. For certain purposes, especially in relation to interpersonal problems, the outcomes have indicated its effectiveness.

Consumers

While this theory derives primarily from work with voluntary consumers and is mostly applied in this context, it has also been used with involuntary consumers with particular focus on engaging them in the process of solving the problem of their "involuntariness." Some studies have found the approach useful for working with hard-to-reach multiple-problem families, although the theory is not designed for working with the family as a unit. There is little documentation of its use with children or those whose egos are overwhelmed by reality, such as the severely emotionally disturbed. Some reports indicate its use with adolescents and the mentally retarded.

Functional Approach

Jessie Taft[26] is the founder of the functional casework approach. Early contributors to the practice theory were Virginia Robinson,[27] Kenneth Pray,[28] and Anita Faatz.[29] More recent contributions have come from Ruth

Elizabeth Smalley, Harold Lewis,[30] and Alan Keith-Lucas.[31] A special perspective on its use with involuntary consumers is found in Shankar Yelaja.[32] The primary proposition of this approach is: *If a social worker can use the agency's function as a purposeful and conscious context for providing the individual a therapeutic relationship, then the individual can use the concrete reality of the helping situation to engage the core of the self and set in motion an authentic process of growth.* Functional practice theory evolves from a "growth model." The worker's major responsibility is to use his or her self in providing a relationship in which consumers can discover, reaffirm, and tap the growth impulses of their true selves, or at least the sense of true self sufficient to mobilize their own resources to deal with their specific problems in social living.

Goals

The major goals of this approach center on a sustaining relationship in which directional growth in the consumer's use of self in relations can be achieved. The emotional and interpersonal dimensions of the consumer's personality are the principal foci. The psychological base for these goals derives from the view that the push toward life, health, and fulfillment is paramount in human nature. Moreover, it is held that individuals are capable of modifying both themselves and their environment according to their own changing purposes and within the limitations and opportunities of their changing capacities and changing environment. The emotions in this process are the energy source for making growth choices and the basis for the inevitable crisis that precedes growth: "Only at points of growth crisis, where the pressure for further development becomes strong enough to overcome the fear of change and destruction, is the ordinary individual brought to the necessity of enlarging his hard-won integration."[33]

This crisis and its concomitant opportunity for growth are achieved through relationships with others. In relationships, the individual is consistently seeking a dynamic balance between the need for dependence on others and the opposing need for the development of independence through the organization of the will. This will finds expression in emotion: "There is no factor of personality so expressive of individuality as emotion. . . . The personality is impoverished as feeling is denied, and the penalty for sitting on the lid of angry feelings or the feelings of fear is the inevitable blunting of capacity to feel love and desire. For to feel is to live, but to reject feeling through fear is to reject the life process itself."[34]

Values

Because our basic nature is assumed to be uniquely individual and creative, functional theory places very little value on the predictability of human behavior. The strongest values involve the consumer's balancing of autonomy and interdependence within his or her unwavering, creative, self-determined purposes and growth. The acceptance of the person's developmental growth is conditional by virtue of the worker's own affirmation of individual difference. Both controlled emotional involvement and the purposeful expression of feelings are highly valued in practice. The worker's basic stance is that of guide. That is, the consumer's journey into the self and the world is channeled through the worker's instrument of self in rendering a specific service connected to the consumer's need.

Techniques

The techniques for the functional approach range from sustainment to exploration/description/ventilation, depending on the worker's perception of the consumer's goals in the here and now of their relationship. The specification of techniques is not part of this approach. Rather, the emphasis is placed on the worker's bringing his or her own self, fully owned and affirmed and with disciplined containment of one's will to direct the consumer's life, to an interpersonal encounter with the consumer. Workers use their understanding of the time phases (beginnings, middles, and endings) of process and the agency's policy to establish a relationship in which the consumer "tries to accept, to reject, to attempt to control, or to modify that function until he finally comes to terms with it enough to define or discover what he wants, if anything, from the situation."[35] In this process, resistance is expected as consumers will reject any interference with any phase of their life before they themselves are ready to abandon it. This "counterwill" in opposition to the will of others, and against reality in general, carries the strength of the consumer's positive will of determined growth.

Focus

A general outline of procedures for this helping process has been proposed.[36] Keith-Lucas identifies the essential helping factors as the degree of reality, empathy, and support offered in the helping relationship. The techniques are conceived as ways of continuously expressing that "This is it (reality)"; "I know that it must hurt (empathy)"; and "You don't have to face this alone. I am here to help you if you want me and can use me (support)." With these elements and such qualities as courage, humility, and concern at the core of the process, the worker using a functional approach is generally instructed to:

1. Start with the request as it comes to you.

2. Respond to feeling rather than to literal content.

3. Recognize feelings even before they are expressed.

4. Listen rather than explain or instruct.

5. Hold fast to your function as helper. Do not take over the helped person's decisions, but do not allow him or her to control the conditions of help.

6. Make clear, as soon as possible, both the conditions of service and authority and the roles of everyone concerned.

7. Set limits, if possible, particularly time limits.

8. Help the person express what he or she wants and then work together to get it.

9. Allow the person you are helping to fail if he or she wants to.

10. Do not defend a reality you cannot change or do not intend to change.

11. Formulate the helped person's problem from time to time as you see it.

12. Partialize the problem.

13. End the interview at the point where a decision has been made.

14. Leave something to work on next time.

15. Test decisions by requiring action to confirm them.

16. Start each contact with the helped person's specific feelings at that time.

17. Introduce one's own difference from the other person when:
    a. There is a firm base of empathy and support.
    b. The difference is an important part of the helped person's reality.
    c. There is an element of challenge or a patent contradiction in the picture being presented.
    d. You are prepared to help the person with his or her reaction to it.

Phases

In the theory of functional process, there are three basic phases of practice: intake (beginning); establishment of a relationship; and ending. There are no "middles." Consistent with Rank's concepts of psychotherapy, Taft concludes that once the individual is using the service in relation to his or her growth interests, the ending phase of help has begun. The approach does not emphasize such phases as assessment, determination of specific goals, selection of an interventive plan, sustainment of work, and precise evaluation of work. Rather, the idea is to set in motion a consumer-centered process of using the relationship to deal with social reality toward self-actualization. Beginnings and endings are conceived as unique microcosms of the consumer's dependence–independence conflicts and are used for enabling the consumer to reaffirm autonomous and interdependent growth through experience of feelings, will, and authentic self.

Empirical Support

The individualistic perspective of this practice theory and its emphasis on creative, self-determined growth have not supported empirical verification of its effectiveness. The case study approach with its emphasis on the uniqueness of the individual and its basic assumptions regarding human growth in creative life processes and the relationship encounter for help has been substituted for quantifying aspects of the theory, specifying behavioral outcomes, and validating effectiveness through measurement.

Consumers

More than other approaches, the functional theory is based on work with involuntary as well as voluntary consumers. Special concepts of the use of authority in practice (such as in children's protective services or in prisons) have arisen from this tradition. Also, the emphasis on the consumer's use of the helping relationship to experience, own, and affirm personal feelings has contributed to the application of the approach to a wide range of consumers—children, adolescents, adults, the severely disturbed, the mentally retarded. The individual focus in the helping relationship has restricted its use with dyads, family units, and other interactional systems.

Sociobehavioral Approach

The foremost proponent of sociobehavioral casework practice theory—the behavior modification approach—is Edwin J. Thomas.[37] Other major contributors are Richard Stuart,[38] Morton Arkava,[39], Derek Jehru,[40] and Arthur Schwartz and Israel Goldiamond.[41] Most of the behavior modification techniques have been developed outside of social work by such theorists as Frederick Kanfer and Jeanne Phillips[42] and Albert Bandura.[43] The primary proposition of this approach is: *If the social worker uses the principles and techniques of behavior modification, then the individual will decrease the frequency of less desirable behavior and increase the frequency of more desirable behavior in modifying self, situation, or both.* In this sense, the sociobehavioral approach is based on a "technology model." The worker's major responsibility is to apply the appropriate behavior modification techniques in the behavior-modifying plan.

Goals

The primary goal of this approach is specific behavioral (symptom) change. This goal often requires a concomitant change in specific aspects of the person's environment. While the emotional, cognitive, and intra-psychic dimensions of the consumer's personality are assumed to be operating to some degree in the behavior targeted for change, only the *behavioral* dimension is tapped for practice. The modification of internal processes is based on their reflection in specific behavior—behavior that can be discerned readily and reliably through the worker's senses. This behavior is of two classes: operant or respondent. *Operant behavior* (such as a child's cry for attention) is normally considered voluntary but tends to be controlled by its consequences in the environment. *Respondent behavior* (such as a child's hunger cry) is considered involuntary and is controlled mainly by stimuli. *Symptoms* are responses that are viewed as problematic or deviant—either by the person or by others in the person's environment. In applying modification techniques, both operant and respondent behavior sometimes receive attention. Simultaneously, there is alteration of both the stimuli and the consequences of behavior: "For any behavior which is identified as a problem, it is absolutely essential to identify its reciprocal—a response which can be strengthened, the occurrence of which will preclude the occurrence of the problem behavior."[44] In brief, then, both the cause and effect of behavior are controlled for its change.

Values

The primary value behind this concept of human behavior and techniques for changing it is the *predictability* of behavioral change. Confidence in the ability to assess behavioral stimuli and consequences directs the use of behavior modification. Inherent in this approach is the need for individualization. Only the study of the individual and his or her situation can determine the specific stimuli and consequences that control behavior. The individual's interdependence with the environment is also assumed in this perspective.

With its emphasis on changing individual behavior, particularly with involuntary consumers, and with its assumption of environmental determinants of behavior, sociobehavioral theory places secondary value on acceptance and self-determination. Very little value, in turn, is placed on the individual's autonomy and need for an intense emotional relationship with the worker or for gaining insight into behavior through the expression of feelings. The relationship is primarily conceived as a medium for social influence that can also be used in behalf of the consumer's behavioral change. The worker's basic stance is therefore that of teacher and expert guide rather than process-oriented helper. The worker determines who will be included in the treatment, where behavioral change will be directed, and the specific techniques for change. The worker teaches consumers the logic of intervention in order to make them effective allies in changing their behavior.

Techniques

Techniques of the sociobehavioral approach fall primarily into three categories: assessment, intervention, and evaluation. The techniques used most are direct influence and reflection on behavioral antecedents and outcomes. Most techniques are related to specification and quantification of problem behavior and its change. Behavioral assessment begins with the selection of target behavior. This assessment involves the stimuli and consequences attending the behavior and the rate of behavior—its frequency, magnitude, and duration. Assessments are often made by charting baselines for which information is gathered by experimenting with systematic variances of either stimuli or consequences, detailed observation of the behavior in natural settings, consumer self-reports, and such electrical and mechanical devices as stopwatches and tape recorders.

The stimuli considered include objects on which the behavior depends, rules for behavior, efforts to strengthen the consequences of behavior through "rewards," and *discriminative stimuli* associated with certain consequences in the past. The major question explored is: What specifically is needed to elicit the desired response? The consequences are positive reinforcement (rewards toward which responses are directed), punishment (events that inhibit the response which produces them), negative reinforcement (removal of adverse consequences following desired behavior), and extinction (following a problematic behavior with consequences that are essentially neutral with respect to the behavior). In most cases, there is an emphasis on positive reinforcement. Punishment, negative reinforcement, and extinction are used only in conjunction with the positive reinforcement of alternative behavior.

The intervention and modification techniques depend on the assessment. These techniques are based on whether the worker or another in control of aspects of the consumer's environment will be the primary modifier, the behavior targeted for modification, and the control over positive reinforcement that can produce the change most promptly. Among the techniques used to modify *operant* behavior are the following:[45]

1. *Positive reinforcement* to increase the future rate of an operant response. Example: Showing approval to a mental patient who has just made his bed with the result that in the future he makes his bed more frequently.

2. *Negative reinforcement* to increase the future rate of response through the removal of an aversive stimulus following a response. Example: An

increase in self-feeding by fastidious mental patients who were unwilling to feed themselves but found it aversive to have nurses systematically spill food on them in the course of spoon feeding.

3. *Extinction* to reduce the rate of response by withholding the reinforcer when the response is emitted. Example: The reduction of tantrum behavior that was established as an operant response and sustained by parental attention.

4. *Differential reinforcement* to encourage a desired response and discourage a problem response by presenting a stimulus following the first and withholding reinforcement following the second. Examples: Demonstrating approval when the client gives concrete details concerning a contemporary problem (with a consequent increase in such responses); withholding verbal reinforcement when the client discusses remote and nonspecific matters (with a consequent reduction of such responses).

5. *Response shaping* to present stimuli following desired responses and withhold reinforcers for undesired responses to increase the probability of desired behavior. Example: The reinforcement of sensible speech of a psychotic who has been mute for years, beginning with reinforcement of mouth movements, then sounds, utterances of words, sentences, and finally sensible speech (combined with no reinforcement for psychotic language).

6. *Punishment* to present an aversive stimulus after a response in order to reduce the frequency of the response. Example: Having the child sit in a chair in an isolated room every time he hits another person (with a consequent reduction in hitting).

For *respondent* behavior—intense anxiety, for example, or deviant sexual arousal—there are other behavior modification techniques. *Systematic desensitization* counterconditions anxiety responses with incompatible relaxation responses; *operant desensitization* uses the specific operant conditions during graduated exposure to stimuli that elicit the respondent behavior; *covert sensitization* extinguishes respondent behavior by having the subject imagine noxious stimuli during relaxation. Other general techniques include token exchange systems, verbal instructions on behavioral assignments, role-played rehearsals of behavior, rule making, and exemplary models of desired behavior.

Focus and Phases

Measurement of progress is related to the baseline data. Change is charted with ongoing evaluation and perhaps redesign of the modification plan. During the assessment process the desired behavior is specified as well as its rate, allowing a mutual determination of success by worker and consumer. The emphasis is on assessment, determination of goals, selection of an interventive plan, formulation of a contract, and evaluation. Thomas suggests twelve procedural steps to this casework process:

1. Inventory of problem areas

2. Selection and contract

3. Commitment to cooperate

4. Problem specification

5. Baseline of problem behavior

6. Identification of probable controlling conditions

7. Assessment of environmental resources

8. Specification of behavioral objectives

9. Formulation of a modification plan

10. Intervention

11. Monitoring outcomes

12. Maintenance of change[46]

Empirical Support

This practice theory has the highest empirical status of the casework approaches. The baseline and evaluation data readily lend themselves to empirical verification. The outcome is behaviorally defined and therefore measurable. Although this approach involves much research documentation, specific procedures have not been related to specific problems.

Consumers

The sociobehavioral approach is deemed appropriate for all consumers if their goal is specific behavioral change. It has been used with voluntary and involuntary consumers, including children, adolescents, and adults, and the severely emotionally disturbed and mentally retarded. Stuart has used the approach with dyadic marital and parent–child relationships. It has not been used (nor does it suggest propositions) for work with the family as an interactive system, although family members have been used to alter a person's behavior.

Casework Theories in Action

The setting is a public child welfare agency in a county seat of about 15,000 population. You are the child welfare protective service worker who received Mrs. Green's case from your supervisor along with the intake worker's report.[47] This report gives you the following information about Mrs. Green and her situation.

Mrs. Green is twenty-eight years old, divorced and remarried, and the mother of three children: Darlene, age ten; Jake, nine; and Linda, four. They live with her and Darlene and Jake's stepfather—Mr. Green. Mrs. Green believes she is literally at her wit's end with Jake, her only son. She sees Jake as distinctly different from her other two children and admits, after some talk, that she cannot stand him. She believes she should do something about this situation, but she does not know what. She is afraid the other children will follow Jake's example. An acquaintance suggested foster care but noted that Mrs. Green should talk to the child welfare agency first. She is fearful that she could physically abuse Jake and has beaten him severely in the past, although not in the last year.

During the initial interview, the intake worker was struck by Mrs. Green's vigor and the stream of words that flowed from her. She mentioned that she had not received help for Jake. In fact, she was very put off by the few minutes she had with the doctor when Jake was seen at the child guidance clinic for a medication appointment last year. There, as in other contacts, she was angry that her description of Jake's behavior was ignored.

Mrs. Green said that she was wasting money on Jake's medication. It does not seem to do any good. Jake was much better behaved in school, while always terrible at home—until two weeks ago. The teacher called her and said she was definitely wasting money on his medication, that Jake is very disruptive and acts up in school. While Mrs. Green labeled Jake as "hyperactive," she is certain there is much more than this at fault. She believes he is not a normal child and repeatedly returned to this point in the intake interview.

Additional information gathered during the intake interview concerned the history of her relationship with Jake and the current problem behavior at home. At the time of his birth, Mrs. Green felt Jake was a very aggressive child. She said he literally chewed up her breasts when she tried to nurse him, so she stopped breastfeeding him. During his infancy, Jake had intestinal virus throughout his whole body, which Mrs. Green believes accounts for brain damage and his hyperactivity. Jake was two years old when his parents separated. Prior to that time the home was marked by much arguing and physical fighting—including one incident, witnessed by Jake, when her husband tried to strangle her. Mrs. Green admitted she has always viewed Jake as looking and acting just like her ex-husband. She denied, however, that she sees him in the same light or that she transfers her feelings about her ex-husband onto her relationship with Jake.

Mrs. Green noted several times that her mother often tells her that she has always rejected Jake, that she never wanted him, and that she should not treat him the way she does. These comments began when Jake was two, and his hyperactivity appeared to increase during his parents' separation. After the death of her third child at birth, when Jake was one, Mrs. Green was deeply depressed—she did not even know what day it was. Her husband rejected her altogether through this period. At the time, she frequently went to her family physician, who told her to become pregnant immediately and replace the baby she had lost.

Mrs. Green thinks Jake and his stepfather have "good rapport" and get along well. In her view, Jake likes men and gets along with them fairly well; but he dislikes girls and is frequently assaultive, antagonistic, and irritating to her and to his sisters. In fact, Darlene and Jake are intense rivals. Both are bright, but Darlene does very well in school. Jake was said to pick on Linda constantly, pinching her when Mrs. Green leaves the room. In his mother's words, "he is a walking problem whenever he is at home." Jake was encopretic until about six months ago, but only at home. He does not get along well with other children in school or in the neighborhood. In games, he must win at all costs. When he loses, he gets angry and violent. His temper tantrums were described as "frequent and severe."

Mrs. Green recognizes her influence on Jake's behavior. She has stopped disciplining him because she is afraid of literally killing him. She confided that as a child her father would beat her if she misbehaved. At one time she could not walk as a result of his beating and was confined to bed for a while. This abuse is constantly on her mind. Since she fears doing the same with Jake, she keeps her feelings in and leaves the room.

She spoke of the girls in a sweet and patronizing way, saying "I have to get better results from the girls and I do." She explained at length that she loves children and would probably be regarded crazy for abusing Jake. She loves being pregnant. She especially loves the attention and the physical aspects of delivery. When she discovered she was pregnant a fifth time, out of wedlock, by her husband shortly before their marriage, she was panic-stricken, fearing she would have another boy like Jake. She lost the baby through a natural abortion at three months, and this was a relief to her. Now she and her husband are fighting frequently about Jake.

Mrs. Green commented further in the intake interview that she knows she is not a good mother to Jake but she is one to Darlene and Linda. The relationship between her and Jake is so hostile that she does not know where to begin. She stated with guilt that she should be able to communicate with him—he is her son—but she cannot. She knows at times that she hates him because she feels he has rejected her as a mother. She also knows that she should be mature and get over this, but she cannot. She was promised service to learn to cope with Jake and prevent further abuse.

Your supervisor in the protective services unit has accepted this case based on the intake information. The goal is to prevent abuse of Jake by working with Mrs. Green. You have contacted Mrs. Green, arranged a home visit with her to begin work on her relationship with Jake, and are on your way to this first interview. What are your goals? What are your plans? Where will you begin? The answers to these questions could depend on the casework practice theory you have evolved for working with Mrs. Green and others.

Suppose we consider four different workers as they approach this initial interview with Mrs. Green. The first worker uses a psychosocial casework approach. The second uses a problem-solving approach; the third uses a functional approach; and the fourth uses a sociobehavioral approach. Each is relating to the same events but tends to view them differently (concepts), connect them differently (hypotheses), and find different directions for strategies (principles) in working with Mrs. Green and her situation.

Psychosocial Approach

The first worker, using the psychosocial approach, is particularly attuned to Mrs. Green's potential insights regarding her relationship with Jake and the defenses she uses to block the actual experience of these insights. This worker particularly notes the possibility of Mrs. Green's transferring her feeling of pain and resentment toward her own father and Jake's real father onto Jake and her denial of this transference. Mrs. Green's ego seems vulnerable to facing this insight at this point. She will need support while she explores her mixed feelings about Jake and reflects on her different relationships with Jake and her other children. The worker believes that at some point this insight will cause significant changes in Mrs. Green's feelings about Jake and her behavior toward him.

In this first interview the worker will want to discuss with Mrs. Green, and to assess further, the pressures of her current situation (her difficulties with both Jake and her husband) as they relate to her own social history (her infantile needs reflected in her perception of and feelings about her own abusive father and other men in her life). These current pressures and earlier unmet needs will be related both in discussion and in assessment to aspects of Mrs. Green's own faulty ego functioning—her projections of hostility and aggressive behavior from Jake; her distorted attitude toward men in general; her likewise distorted attitudes toward her daughters, mothering, and women in general. At some point, certain interacting forces will be used to understand Mrs. Green and plan the approach to a more satisfactory relationship with Jake: "infantile needs and weaknesses in libidinal functioning [with males] deriving from childhood, current life deprivations and pressures, and nonadaptive ego functioning that united with childhood remnants to create additional [problems in relating responsively to Jake]."[48]

The strategy of this worker might be to focus first on how these forces affect Mrs. Green's self-satisfaction in personal development. Then Mrs. Green may be shown how these forces affect her relationship to Jake. The worker will also be noting how the stress of the treatment process as well as situational pressures are affecting Mrs. Green's potential for physically abusing Jake and her ability to cope. Finally, the worker must be prepared to prevent abuse—either through specific insight with Mrs. Green or through direct action to protect Jake from physical harm.

Depending on the specific results of this assessment, the *dynamics of treatment* are planned. Mrs. Green's effort to improve her functioning as Jake's mother will most likely be responded to by *sustainment* techniques. There will be early attempts to lessen her anxiety through support and a sympathetic hearing. Some *direct influence* via suggestion and advice may also accompany the worker's responses to Mrs. Green's concerns about dealing with Jake's behavior. As the treatment relationship is developing, the worker may use more *exploration/description/ventilation*—communications designed to elicit descriptions and explanations from Mrs. Green and help her relieve tension through pouring out pent-up feelings and emotionally charged memories in the interview. There will also be some *person–situation reflection* directed both outward ("What does Jake say that angers you so much?") and inward ("What feelings does Jake's behavior set off in you? How do these feelings affect your reactions to him?")

Certainly at some point, based on the diagnostic impression that Mrs. Green's reactions to Jake are transferences of her feelings and thoughts regarding her own father, her first husband, and men in general, the worker will use both *pattern-dynamic reflection* and *developmental reflection*. Pattern-dynamic reflection would encourage Mrs. Green to reflect directly on some of the internal causes for her actions toward Jake and to examine their influence on others' behavior (her perception of Mr. Green's growing hostility toward her related to her expectation of hostile behavior from Jake). Developmental reflection would help Mrs. Green consider the relation of past experiences (her own father's abuse; her first husband's rejection) to her responses to current situations (her expectation of a rift with Mr. Green; her rejection of Jake).

Finally, the worker will be alert to points when *environmental treatment* is needed—such as contacts with Mr. Green to increase his support for Mrs. Green's functioning, contacts with Jake to communicate his effect on the problem, or even the *aggressive intervention* of removing Jake from the home temporarily and placing him in a foster home if abuse should increase during the treatment process.

Problem-Solving Approach

The worker using the problem-solving approach, especially one whose practice is informed by its task-centered branch, would find different meanings in the intake information about Mrs. Green and her situation. Above all, the worker would note the variety of problems Mrs. Green perceives in her situation and the variety of their causes, as well as the fact that she seems to be placing priority on her need to find more effective ways of dealing with Jake as his mother. Certainly she believes much of the problem lies within Jake and the inability of others to change his behavior—both of which may be at some point "problems for work." She does appear motivated, however, to relate in a less stress-producing manner with Jake. This worker wants to help Mrs. Green deal with the specific problems of most concern to Mrs. Green, yet try to establish a contract that specifies problem-solving tasks which will protect Jake from abuse and increase the resources (especially Mrs. Green's relationship with him) to meet his needs.

The first interview will entail a statement of the worker's concern for both Jake and Mrs. Green and a specific exploration of the problem as Mrs. Green is experiencing it. Mrs. Green's feelings and behavior—and their consequences in her relationship with Jake—will be specifically discussed. At some point there will be explicit agreement by the worker and Mrs. Green about the problems to be worked on, their priority, and a specific statement of the goals to be achieved by Mrs. Green through this work. Further work would be based on agreed-upon tasks toward solving this problem in a series of time-limited casework sessions (probably no more than ten in a three-month period).

The target problems in the initial contract might be summarized as follows:

1. Mrs. Green does not know how to cope with Jake's behavior.

2. Mrs. Green is dissatisfied with the diagnosis and treatment Jake has received for his hyperactivity.

For the first target problem, the goal may be stated as "coping with Jake's behavior." The goal for the second target problem may be stated as "getting a comprehensive medical and psychological assessment of Jake and deciding on appropriate treatment." These problem areas would be explored in detail from the point of origin to the current situation. The worker's attention is on objective facts and subjective feelings about them (the "subjective reality"), as well as the obstacles to be overcome in the situation.

Especially important in specifying the problem and planning the tasks to resolve it are the events that are currently influencing the problem. For instance, Mrs. Green's description of Jake's hostile behavior toward her should be specified in detail. The worker should determine what Jake says or does to express this hostility and how his actions relate to Mrs. Green's reactions. Have there been times when she and Jake could relate without fighting? Times when they may even have enjoyed each other's company? What was going on then? Basically, the worker's question will be: Who says or does what to whom and in what order? From this exploration of the problem will evolve a general statement of the difficulty and a list of conditions the worker and Mrs. Green will attempt to change.

In the first target problem (coping with Jake's behavior), the specification of conditions may be as follows:

> Jake frequently agitates Darlene and Linda, through verbal assault and physical jabbing, when they are together. When he does, the girls cry for Mrs. Green to control him. When she tells him to stop, he becomes belligerent and loses his temper with her and picks on the girls more, leaving them in tears. Mrs. Green feels like "shaking him senseless" but, fearing she might strike him, she walks out of hearing distance and lets them alone. Mr. Green, when he is home, can stop this situation by taking Jake with him, but then he tends to be angry with Mrs. Green for not caring about Jake and settling him down herself. There have been three such incidents, one in which Mr. Green was present, during the past week.

This specification can then lead to the determination of what Mrs. Green may be able to do, and wants to do, in conjunction with the worker to change this situation—that is, the tasks. Mrs. Green, for instance, may decide to ask Jake to sit quietly with her in another room for half an hour if this behavior occurs. In their next interview, the worker will discuss what happened when Mrs. Green used this approach and might decide to get Jake's view of this situation and try to locate comprehensive diagnostic services for him. The worker would continue to use this problem-solving process consciously in light of the contracts for target problems, goals, and tasks.

This contracting process will continue throughout the ten interview sessions held in their three months of work together. Throughout this work, the original concept of an effective helping relationship, first proposed by Perlman[49] and then developed by her,[50] has at its core both support and expectation. In fact, in the task-centered approach where "the context of a treatment relationship . . . is problem-focused, task-centered, and highly structured,"[51] it is the worker's expectations that are often the basis of action in relation to specific changes in the situation. These expectations become the basis for developing the ego strength to cope effectively, perhaps without help, with the inevitable problems of living. The intent throughout is to provide the relationship and the interventive strategies for what William Reid calls "a constructive problem-solving experience."[52]

Functional Approach

The worker who uses the functional approach to casework practice may be particularly struck by the fact that Mrs. Green has come for service. In this sense, her will has been mobilized to deal creatively with her relationship to Jake and others. The worker will want to focus this energy on Mrs. Green's choices and actions in relation to the reality of the casework process and her relationship with Jake, since the agency's function is to protect Jake from abuse. Moreover, the worker will expect the process to intensify Mrs. Green's growth crisis and enable her to overcome her resistance to change, experience her own needs as well as Jake's more fully, and act more responsibly and creatively toward getting these needs met.

This worker, in the first interview, will attempt to communicate clearly that the purpose of their work together is to understand Mrs. Green's current situation in a way that will help her to choose more effective ways of promoting Jake's development. Likely, too, the worker will offer Mrs. Green a series of weekly interviews (perhaps three to five of them) to explore her situation together. At that point they can decide what further work they may want to do with each other in behalf of Mrs. Green and her situation. Throughout this first interview and their relationship process, the worker will respond often to Mrs. Green's feelings and help her experience them more fully: her love/hate ambivalence for Jake, her guilt, her anger, her pain, her fears. As these feelings are reached for, expressed, and responded to, the worker will try to learn what Mrs. Green wants to do about the situation.

The worker stands firm in the expectation that Mrs. Green will use the relationship and its focus to determine ways to meet her needs in her relationship with Jake, Mr. Green, her daughters, her mother, and so on—and not as a substitute for involvement. If this substitute involvement occurs, as well might happen for someone with Mrs. Green's dependency needs, the worker will confront this situation directly yet sensitively, suggesting that she is avoiding the use of help, is afraid of responsible change, and has the strength to become more involved with her family and her own growth outside the relationship.

Subsequent interviews will begin with Mrs. Green's *current* feelings and choices and progress toward achieving her own growth. As Mrs. Green becomes more willing to move from feelings to wishes to wants to decisions and then to actions that are more self-satisfying and promote the growth of others, expecially Jake, the use of the relationship process will be terminated with an affirmation of her own effort toward growth.

This worker learns most about Mrs. Green in terms of how she actually uses the agency service and the helping process—how she tackles a problem, what she wants to do, the strength of her new commitments to change and growth, her abilities to maintain what they have begun together. Mrs. Green also learns this about her own unique self as projected on the concrete reality of service. As Keith-Lucas expresses this underlying dynamic of functional casework help: "[Mrs. Green] is actually trying out in a protected situation a way of life, that later [she] can live by [herself]. The helping situation then becomes a kind of laboratory for testing out ways of doing things and, indeed, for finding out whether one can or wants to do them."[53]

Sociobehavioral Approach

The worker with a sociobehavioral orientation may pay more attention to Jake's behavior than to Mrs. Green's as a way of helping to change the conflicts in their relationship. This worker will look for ways in which Mrs. Green can begin to cope more effectively with Jake through modification of his behavior.

In the first interview Mrs. Green may concentrate on ranking the specific aspects of Jake's behavior that upset her. A second interview may then be held with both Mrs. Green and Jake to determine his willingness to alleviate the conflicts in their relationship by changing specific behavior and also to learn his reactions to Mrs. Green's ranking. If, for instance, agreement on specific behavior is discovered—Jake does not want to be yelled at while watching TV with the girls; Mrs. Green wants to stop yelling at Jake but wants Jake to stop poking the girls—the worker can suggest a specific approach to this problem. For three nights next week, Mrs. Green is to observe Jake and the girls for half an hour while they watch TV. She is to count the times each night that Jake pokes the girls and to note what happened immediately before and immediately after each incident. Perhaps Jake pokes at Darlene and Linda seventeen times and Darlene verbally snaps back and slaps him, increasing the frequency of his pokes.

From these data, a behavior modification plan can then be derived along with a discussion with Jake and Mrs. Green about the things Jake especially enjoys that could serve as rewards *(reinforcers)* for changing his behavior. Mrs. Green may be instructed to watch Jake for another week. For a half-hour period on three separate nights, she is to observe him while he is watching TV and praise him every ten minutes in which he does not poke at the girls. Darlene can be instructed by Mrs. Green to ignore him altogether if he pokes at her *(extinction);* she is to be mildly scolded if she does not. While this positive reinforcement of praise is used during these assigned times, Jake is informed that if he goes a week without poking he can go to the movies with Mr. Green, something he greatly enjoys. But if he is observed poking his sisters more than ten times during this period, he will be confined to his room Saturday morning at the end of the week and not permitted to watch his favorite TV shows while he is confined *(negative reinforcement)*.

The worker will monitor changes in the frequency, magnitude, and duration of the baseline behavior as reinforcements are used and help Mrs. Green and Jake to use this approach effectively in changing any behavior (temper tantrums, hostile remarks, and so on) that affects their relationship. The expectation is that changes in behavior will create natural reinforcement of mutually pleasant interactions between Mrs. Green and Jake.[54]

Which Approach Is Best?

As these examples indicate, the practice theory does affect the worker's selected goals, intervention hypotheses, and style of working in practice situations. They spotlight different aspects of the consumer's social reality, they affect the way the casework process begins, and they inform the ongoing work in a manner that makes a difference in the worker's use of generic and specific practice skills (and perhaps in the consumer's situation). The basic question at this point is not which approach works best with Mrs. Green, but which approach seems most compatible with your own assessment of Mrs. Green's needs and your own preferred modes of working with people like her. The careful selection and use of an approach is the first step in contributing to the knowledge base (and its validation) for your practice. Thus the essential question is: Which approach works best for you in working with Mrs. Green and others like her?

Summary

The four casework practice theories—psychosocial, problem-solving, functional, and sociobehavioral—can be compared for selective use in practice. Since these approaches differ regarding the primary goals they are designed to accomplish, the *consumer's* goals should be the primary criteria for selecting an approach. Other criteria include the theory's compatibility with the worker's values and style.

The approaches differ in their basic values, the worker's basic stance, and the personality dimensions of the consumer that are focused upon and tapped for achieving the goals. Other elements for comparison include their time duration, their basic techniques, their emphasis on the phases of the practice sequence, their empirical status, and the types of consumers from which the theoretical propositions have derived and with whom the approach has been used.

The psychosocial approach is a medical model that emphasizes the worker as an expert who can assess, prescribe, and implement treatment. The primary goals are insight, relationship, and environmental change. The worker is a helper who can direct the process of goal achievement. The behavior base is ego psychology, and the concepts of psychoanalysis dominate assessment and treatment. Its techniques have been empirically studied; its outcomes are less validated. The primary consumers have been voluntary adults, and there has been specific documentation of its use with children, adolescents, dyads, and families.

The problem-solving approach is an educational model that emphasizes the worker as a teacher of a problem-solving process and skills. The major goals are related to the consumer's present problem and include strengthening the ego's capacity to cope with problems in interpersonal relationships and social roles. The worker is a teacher who also helps and guides the consumer in a problem-solving process. The behavior base is primarily ego psychology; the basis of work comes from understanding the cognitive and reality-testing functions of the consumer's ego. The crisis intervention and short-term variants of this approach have been put to empirical test. Change in interpersonal relationships has been validated in this work. The primary consumers have been voluntary adults, but the approach has been used with involuntary consumers, adolescents, and hard-to-reach multiproblem families.

The functional approach is a growth model that emphasizes the worker as a guide and helper in providing a specific agency service to a consumer in crisis. The primary goals are providing a sustaining relationship in which the consumer can achieve self-actualization by mobilizing growth impulses in relation to the current demands of social reality. The behavior base is existential and humanistic psychology, particularly the work of Rank. The approach's creative orientation does not lend itself to empirical research methodology, and it has not been validated through research. The practice theory has derived from a variety of individuals: voluntary and involuntary; children, adolescents, and adults; the emotionally disturbed and the mentally retarded. It has not evolved theoretical propositions to direct its use with dyads or families as interactional systems.

The sociobehavioral approach is a technology model used for the specific goal of behavioral change. The worker is primarily an expert who controls the stimuli and consequences of operant and respondent behavior for predicted and measurable changes in behavior. The behavior base is learning theory and behavioral psychology. Assessment includes specification of behavioral causes, effects, and rates; from this assessment a strategy for modification is planned and implemented. The method has been empirically validated, and for specific behavioral change in controlled situations, it is most effective. This approach is not restricted in its application with the exception of work with the family as an interactional system.

All four approaches have evolved from social work practice when casework is the generalist's method of choice. They can serve as a base, however, for the integration of compatible theoretical approaches that have evolved outside of social work.

Suggested Learning Experiences

The important learning activities for Part 3 are those that enable students to refine their understanding of practice theories as a basis for selecting those they wish to study further. For a comparative understanding of the casework approaches the following charts are useful. They can be filled out individually, discussed in small groups or in the entire class, and used for understanding the similarities and differences of the approaches.

Chart 9.1   View of Human Nature

Directions: In the space provided, list key phrases and words to summarize the view of human nature and basic assumptions underlying each casework approach. Review the text *after* you have completed this exercise.

Psychosocial Approach	
Problem-solving Approach	
Functional Approach	
Sociobehavioral Approach	

Chart 9.2   Key Concepts

Directions: In the space provided, give in *your own words* a brief summary of the key concepts of each casework approach. Include such concepts as dimensions tapped, focus, and major theoretical propositions. Review the text *after* you have completed this exercise.

Psychosocial Approach	
Problem-solving Approach	
Functional Approach	
Sociobehavioral Approach	

Chart 9.3   Goals

Directions: In your own words, briefly summarize the basic goals of the casework approaches. Review the text *after* you have completed this exercise.

Psychosocial Approach	
Problem-solving Approach	
Functional Approach	
Sociobehavioral Approach	

Chart 9.4   Procedures and Techniques

Directions: In your own words, summarize the key procedures and techniques used in each casework approach. Review the text *after* you have completed this exercise.

Psychosocial Approach	
Problem-solving Approach	
Functional Approach	
Sociobehavioral Approach	

Chart 9.5   Key Applications

Directions: In a few summary statements, cite in your own words the areas where you think each casework approach is most applicable— where, with whom, and when is it likely to work best? Follow these statements with your assessment of the major strengths and limitations of each approach.

Psychosocial Approach	
Problem-solving Approach	
Functional Approach	
Sociobehavioral Approach	

Suggested Case Studies

To determine how these practice theories actually affect practice, case studies demonstrating their use are invaluable. The following list includes classic examples of casework practice theories in use.

Cormican, Elin J. "Task-Centered Model for Work with the Aged." *Social Casework* 58(8)(1977): 490–494. Use of the problem-solving approach.

Council on Social Work Education. "Helping a Neglectful Mother Choose What Help She Wants for Herself and Her Children." Teaching Record 68–340–82. New York: CSWE, 1968. Use of the functional approach.

Hollis, Florence. "Some Examples of Casework in Practice." In *Casework: A Psychosocial Therapy,* ed. 2nd. ed. New York: Random House, 1972. Use of the psychosocial approach.

Perlman, Helen Harris. "Two Cases: Mr. Grayson and Mrs. Whitman." In *Social Casework: A Problem-Solving Process.* Chicago: University of Chicago Press, 1957. Illustrates the problem-solving approach.

Stein, Theodore J. and Eileen D. Gambrill. "Behavioral Techniques in Foster Care." *Social Work* 21(1)(1976): 34–39. Use of the sociobehavioral approach.

Chapter Ten   Families

Introduction

All the casework practice theories described in the last chapter recognize the family and other primary-group influences on the individual's development. For the most part, however, the family or group system is a backdrop behind the main drama—the face-to-face contact with the individual. "How did it go with your husband and children this week?" "You want to make friends with your neighbors but you're afraid of telling them so." And so on. At times interviews may be arranged with two or more family members in behalf of the individual who has contracted a casework service, but these theories were not designed for face-to-face work with the family as a whole group.

Once the social worker in partnership with the individual has identified both the "consumer system" and the "target system" as the individual and others like him or her (Quadrant B of the generalist framework in Chapter 2), family group work and group work are the methods of choice. The major unit to which the worker's activities are directed and in which growth is desired is the interactional *system* rather than one individual. Practice theories are indispensable for understanding interactional systems, or groups, and for informing the methods for working face to face with members of the system.

Practice theories for working with the family and other primary groups are based on the conception of these units as *social systems*—systems that involve patterned transactions with members toward growth-promoting satisfaction of needs or growth-inhibiting frustration of needs. Alan Klein explains this social system concept of families and groups:

> A social system consists of a number of people who have established more or less regularized patterns of interaction with each other based upon a defined social structure and operative through shared expectations and symbols. Group interaction . . . tends to develop uniformities or habitual modes over a period of time, and the relationships between and among the people tend to become structured. Therefore, social systems have structure and some degree of stability.[1]

Interaction refers to events in which one member influences the actions, emotions, and thinking of another. In a group or family social system, this interaction is always reciprocal and interdependent. And as there are common feelings and goals, usually some degree of intimacy ensues and results in a specific group identity: a bond.

The definition of a *group* implies the significance of family and group systems as primary self-actualizing human relations resources for members:

> A group is a social system consisting of two or more persons who stand in status and role relationships with one another and possessing a set of norms or values which regulate the attitudes and behaviors of the individual members in matters of consequence to the group.[2]

In other words, a group is a statement of relationship among persons. A person becomes a member when he or she internalizes the major norms of the group, other members become a part of the person, and the person carries on the responsibilities and meets the expectations for the position and status he or she occupies. Identity, self-image, security—all are related to the person's status and role in the group, and these determine the person's attitudes toward self, others, and the world outside the group.

This concept of group is built on the ideas of George Mead and Charles Cooley, the symbolic interaction sociologists, who were among the first to develop the primary-group relationship to the development of self.[3] The self evolves in relationship with significant others in primary-group systems. *My* family, *my* friends, *my* colleagues is a statement about *my* self as well as about others. The worker who deals with families and other primary-group systems needs a method for influencing processes toward self-development. These processes involve such ideas as patterned interaction, group goals, structure (position, status, roles, norm), cohesiveness or group bond, group homeostasis, interpersonal communication, members' needs, and self-concept in addition to the psychological concepts of human growth and development. In short, if we are to use practice theories for work with families and other groups we need to describe a healthy system in terms that are different from the words that describe a healthy person. Moreover, work with both families and groups requires knowledge of group process and methods for influencing self-actualizing human relations. In both cases, the primary consumer is the group and the group process is the major means to social work's ends.

The family is a group of persons united by ties of marriage, blood, or adoption, constituting a single household, and interacting in their roles as family members. It is the primary institution for meeting the material, emotional, security, and growth needs for members of our society. A list of the major propositions found in the social work literature on families includes:[4]

1.   The family is a social system that is more than the summed qualities of each of its members.

2.   The family is a group with stages of development that can be traced as inevitably as those of the individual. This development includes:

   a.   Formation of the family, including determination of its membership and the formulation of individual and family goals
   b.   Development of family group structure both formal and informal (division of labor, positions, statuses, roles, subgroups)
   c.   Development of interpersonal relationships and patterns and development of leadership and followship
   d.   Development of group controls and the distribution of authority among family members and various family roles
   e.   Development of communication, deliberation, and decision making within the problem-solving process essential for day-to-day living
   f.   Development of cohesion and morale
   g.   Development of norms and values

3.   The family is a group in which conflicts inevitably occur.

4.   The family is a group with a unique history, and members can know themselves better than outsiders can know them.

5.   The family is a group in which relationships with other social systems are in a constant state of change.

6.   The family is a group that carries the weight of the world upon its collective shoulders—the basic social institution for the development of individual autonomy and interdependence.

These group process elements can be seen in the following vignette of a family in conflict: the Goulds.[5] Mrs. Gould's son, Sammy, age eleven, was having difficulties in school. His mother, who wants him to be a famous scientist, brought him to the clinic when he failed two subjects. He was placed in a group of boys his own age but was unable to get along with them or to find any activity for solitary pursuit. His father, although he had no college education, is employed as an electronics engineer in a plant where all his colleagues are college-trained.

As the social worker listened to Mrs. Gould's explosive account of her troubles, it became evident that to Mrs. Gould everything else was at fault. The subject that occasioned the greatest hostility was her husband; and the problem as she saw it was the failure of her son, Sammy, to get an A average. This month something had to be done because Sammy had not only not made A's but had failed two subjects. When the social worker suggested a family interview, Mrs. Gould did not think that her husband would participate. The appointment for the first interview was canceled because Mrs. Gould "forgot" to tell her husband the time and the place where the family was to meet.

The family conference was finally held in order to clarify the quality of the family relationship, help the family see that the immediate problem might be a *family* problem, and obtain the parents' cooperation if a family approach seemed necessary. The worker started the interview by saying that it was important to discuss, as a family, everything that was concerning them and then try to find a solution. The worker added that a good place to begin was to look at the reason that led them to ask for help. Mrs. Gould immediately said that the problem was her son's school performance, on which subject she elaborated a great deal. The worker at length turned to Mr. Gould and asked him if this was the way he saw the problem. Mr. Gould agreed that Sammy was having trouble in school and said that he gave the boy a good beating once. This resulted in improvement, he said, but it did not last long. The worker then asked Sammy how he saw the situation. The boy was reluctant to say very much; he appeared to accept the criticism as justified. With some prompting, however, he began to complain about the school and to put the blame there instead of on his parents.

When the worker asked about their son's homework, both parents moved in at once. The hot argument which ensued reflected two quite different methods of teaching and the fact that each parent criticized the other's ways of helping Sammy do his homework. Then Sammy became involved, and a three-way argument developed. Mrs. Gould again moved in aggressively, criticizing her husband and son for a variety of things. By this time, Sammy had pushed his chair back until he was against the wall. Mrs. Gould continued to criticize Sammy, saying that he allowed himself to be pushed around by smaller kids; she added that when some children chased him home, she made him go out and fight them. The worker asked the father if he remembered the situation. He said he did because he was told his son had gotten into a fight. When the worker inquired how Mr. Gould had handled this, Sammy blurted out "He got mad at me!" Mr. Gould agreed and said that he did not believe in fighting. The worker asked Sammy where this put him. He threw up his arms and said "I'm confused!" Sammy continued angrily that his mother would tell him to do something and his father would beat him for doing it. This led to further statements on the disagreements between Mrs. and Mr. Gould on how things should be handled.

A further brief exchange among the three involved school friends and fighting. The worker interrupted to point out the conflict between Mr. and Mrs. Gould over how the boy should behave. They both agreed. The worker asked them if they would like to continue having family conferences. The worker felt it would be more helpful to work with the entire family. Mr. and Mrs. Gould agreed. Sammy was noncommittal. It was evident to the worker that the interview with this family of three provided more clues to Sammy's difficulties than had been secured from individual interviews with Mrs. Gould and Sammy.

Comparison of Family Group
Work Theories

The practice theories compared in this chapter involve methods for working with the Goulds as a family group. These methods, here called *family group work,* are often referred to as family treatment, family counseling, or family therapy. These terms are considered more or less synonymous when working with the family as a system.

Two recent schemes have been developed for comparing methodological approaches for working with groups. In combination, these two approaches provide a useful framework for comparing the different practice theories for social work with families and other groups. They have demonstrated validity and reliability in discriminating among different approaches in relation to values, goals, focus, and techniques in group work practice. Now let us turn to the first scheme.

Jacob Lomranz, Martin Lakin, and Harold Schiffman have derived a three-valued framework that differentiates group work approaches.[6] Variant A values effectiveness in participation in interpersonal and group systems. Its overriding goal is the development of social competence. Its major theoretical base is the conceptual language of group dynamics; in practice, the focus is on interpersonal dynamics, group structure and process development, and the interactional conflicts and problems of the group as a social system. Techniques are interpersonal and group-oriented.

Variant B values individual change through group interaction. Its overriding goal is the emotional reeducation of members. Its major theoretical base is dynamic psychology; in practice, the focus is on intimacy and authority, personality dynamics in interactions, and the development of trust and reality testing. Techniques are individual and interpersonal.

Variant C values personal expressiveness. Its overriding goal is self-actualizing expression and experiences. Its major theoretical base is humanistic psychology and communication theory, with special emphasis on authentic emotional communication. In practice, this variant focuses on emotional expression, development of trust in relation to the member's self-concept, intuitiveness in interaction, and sensory awareness experiences. Techniques are individual, interpersonal, and group-oriented.

These three general types of practice theories differentiate family and group work approaches on the basis of the variables mentioned. In addition, the approaches are contrasted through the worker's basic stance, the characteristic interventions in group process, and the structural elements used in intervention.

The second scheme for comparing group work approaches is the attempt to identify the *curative factors* or *change mechanisms* in group process.[7] Twelve factors have been identified. They are the elements of process that can be influenced toward achieving major goals. These twelve factors tend to receive different emphasis in the various practice theories:

1. *Altruism:* helping others by putting their needs ahead of one's own in the group

2. *Group cohesiveness:* belonging to a group of people who understand and accept one

3. *Universality:* feeling less different and more like others in the group

4. *Interpersonal learning (input):* getting information on how one affects others in the group

5. *Interpersonal learning (output):* experimenting with different ways of relating to others in the group

6. *Guidance:* getting prescriptive ideas about one's own behavior from others in the group

7. *Catharsis:* expressing feelings in the group

8. *Identification:* imitating behavior of other group members

9. *Family reenactment:* understanding the family's past influence on behavior in the present group

10. *Insight:* getting information and emotional understanding on how one's interpersonal behavior is influenced by subtle intrapersonal dynamics in the group

11. *Instillation of hope:* being encouraged for one's own change by experiencing change in others

12. *Existential factors:* recognizing the inevitability of life's isolation, pain, and death balanced with our interdependence with others in the group

In this chapter and the next, elements of the three basic variants and these twelve curative factors are used for a comparative analysis of both the family group work and group work approaches. As with the casework approaches, this analysis should help the social worker to select practice theories appropriate to the group's goals for change and compatible with the worker's own values and style.

One review of the practice theories for family group work identified three main approaches: psychoanalytic, integrative, and communicative-interactive.[8] The psychoanalytic approach is similar to Variant B described above; the integrative approach is similar to Variant A; the communicative-interactive approach is similar to Variant C. All three approaches have elements from the other variants, however, and in family group work they are not so clearly differentiated. Nevertheless, the basic differences between these three practice theories are reflected in Table 10.1.

Psychoanalytic Approach

The progenitor of psychoanalytic practice theory for working with the family as a group is Frances Scherz.[9] The primary proposition for practice is: *If a social worker can help the family as a whole to develop insight (bringing unconscious material to consciousness) into their interpersonal transference and resistance, then the family can help members master their normal developmental tasks toward satisfying loving and working.*

Goals

The goal is emotional reeducation for family members in relation to current problems in family functioning. In Scherz's words:

> Family therapy is a clinical approach in that it is based on assessment of the unique family relationship systems and their conscious and unconscious implications for the individual members. Because it is concerned with understanding what the individuals bring to the family system and its problem and what their needs are, it relies on psychoanalytic personality theory in a special way. That is, the approach views the individual not solely as an individual but also as a part of a system.[10]

Focus

Psychoanalytic family group work focuses on observed and latent feelings in communication and how they may interfere with each member's life tasks. It is a group approach in that it deals with more than one family member at a time. It operates by a three-pronged approach: the *content* (data); the *process* of interaction (transaction); and the family *structure*— the rules, roles, identifications, and alliances revealed in the family's communication patterns.

This practice theory therefore focuses on the intense emotional and intrapsychic personality processes of family members. It is based on Freud's definition of the therapeutic process as the analysis of transference and resistance in bringing unconscious material to consciousness. The emotional intensity of family group interaction in the presence of the worker is believed to heighten tensions that create favorable conditions for developing insight into current needs and behavior. The emotional intensity comes from the worker's therapeutic alliance with the family group and his or her focus on the emotional and intrapsychic dimensions of their interaction.

Table 10.1 Characteristics of Practice Theories for Family Group Work

Characteristic	Psychoanalytic Approach	Integrative Approach	Communicative-Interactive Approach
Goals			
Socially competent person	M	H	M
Emotionally reeducated person	H	M	M
Self-actualizing person	L	L	H
Main dimensions			
Emotionality	H	M	H
Cognitive	H	M	M
Interpersonal	L	M	H
Intrapsychic	H	M	L
Behavioral	L	M	H
Worker's focus			
Focus on interpersonal; participating more effectively; developing communication skills	L	M	H
Focus on family as group; group organization and dynamics; group problem solving; learning about group pressures	L	H	M
Focus on interactional problems of family as social system; increasing interpersonal competence in role relationships	L	H	M
Focus on emotional aspects; coping with hostility, dependency needs, feelings of acceptance and rejection	H	M	M
Focus on intrapsychic dynamics; exploring defense mechanisms in interpersonal interaction; diagnosing and evaluating personal conflicts	H	M	M
Focus on trust and self-concept of members; exploring impact of others on self and discrepancy between ideal and real self	L	M	H
Focus on expressiveness; disclosing one's self; becoming intimately known to others; eliciting involvement and confrontation; expressing love and joy	M	M	H
Focus on expanding and fulfilling experiences; increasing use of intuition; increasing ability to enjoy aesthetic-natural experiences	L	L	M
Focus on sensory awareness in order to expand senses; overcoming alienation; developing nonverbal and tactile communication	L	L	M

Worker's stance			
Teacher	L	L	H
Helper	H	M	L
Guide	L	M	H
Intervention			
Observation and analysis	H	M	H
Group dynamics	L	H	M
Psychodynamically oriented	H	M	M
Emotionally expressive and experientially oriented	M	L	L
Individually directed	H	M	H
Group-directed	L	M	H
Structure			
Family group discussion	H	H	H
Program activity	L	L	M
Cognitive input	M	M	H
Fantasy and sensory awareness exercises	L	L	M
Curative factors			
Altruism	L	M	M
Group cohesiveness	L	M	H
Universality	L	H	M
Interpersonal learning (input)	M	M	H
Interpersonal learning (output)	L	L	H
Guidance	M	M	H
Catharsis	H	M	M
Identification	H	M	L
Family reenactment	H	M	L
Insight	H	M	H
Instillation of hope	M	M	M
Existential factors	L	M	M

H = high emphasis; M = moderate emphasis; L = low emphasis.

Stance

The worker's basic stance is that of helper. While workers need to be more active and less anonymous than in individual psychoanalytic approaches, they still control their own interventions. The worker establishes a permissive atmosphere that encourages emotional expression of socially undesirable feelings and the latent (or hidden) meanings of verbal and nonverbal communication. The worker's interventions are individual and intrapsychic-oriented observations and analysis. Workers do not give advice or answer questions, they remain noncritical, and they listen a good deal more than they talk.

Intervention

A typical procedure is to hold the first interview with the whole family to establish a therapeutic alliance of trust and explore the family's major complaints. Moreover, there is an attempt to demonstrate that the present complaint is indeed a family problem; that family members are tied together in their emotional reverberations; and that they have developed defensive and dysfunctional patterns. The worker also attempts to prevent projection of the family's problem onto a particular member or outside system such as school or work, to increase family members' trust in each other to resolve the problem, and to determine who needs to be involved (marital pair, children, individual members) and when. Often the second interview is held with the marital pair, who tend to be conceived as an alliance in which children become focal points for resolution of neurotic conflicts that have not been resolved in the marriage. In this process, the children, dependent for survival on the parents, enter actively into the marital projection system, often becoming symptomatic of the expression of their own and the parents' conflicts. Thus a mutual projection system develops and becomes stabilized.

From these interviews, data about family interactions and difficulties are gathered in a way that encourages the family to observe the process of its feelings and its fears about them. This observation is viewed as the core of therapeutic exploration and treatment. A special observation is how the family "works the worker"—attempting to develop coalitions, to be directive, and so on. The ongoing work is based on techniques for dealing with the family's resistance and transference in the interview situation. In other words, the worker

> deals with resistances to change, with fears of feelings, and with fears of extinction of the family and marriage by helping the family expose and examine hidden feelings and immobilizing secrets. He deals with transference reactions, when addressed to him by individuals, not only by relating these to the individual but also by redirecting them to the family interaction. The treatment emphasis is always on getting the family to observe and to deal with its own processes, the relationship between feelings and behavior.[11]

Empirical Support

The empirical status of the psychoanalytic approach to family group work is low—it has not been put to empirical test. This approach has been used with crisis, short-term, and long-term situations and with a variety of complaints and sociocultural family groups. The therapeutic alliance of trust and the family's "experienced problem" as preconditions for the work has tended to limit the use of this approach to voluntary consumers.

Integrative Approach

Integrative practice theories for family group work have been developed by Sanford Sherman[12] and William Jordan.[13] The major contribution from outside social work has come from Nathan Ackerman.[14] The primary proposition for practice is: *If a social worker can help the family as a whole to develop more effective problem-solving patterns, then the family will increase its capacity to deal with instrumental and affective threats for members.*

Goals

The overriding goal of the integrative approach is the development of social competence. This competence includes interpersonal sensitivity and effective social roles in the family. In other words, members are helped to achieve the family's instrumental and affective goals.

Focus

This approach integrates psychoanalytic and social system elements of the family through the concept of social roles. Family members are viewed as one another's need-satisfiers in the major family function of bridging the processes of intrapsychic life and social participation. In mediating between the needs of its members and society, the family must achieve both instrumental and affective goals. *Instrumental goals* refer to material aspects of living such as economic security and physical health. *Affective goals* refer to emotional aspects of family members. The effectiveness of the family's organization and communication for problem solving determines the family's response to such instrumental and affective threats as an unemployed father, a chronically ill child, an emotionally disturbed child, or an unsatisfying marriage. The primary focus in working with the family as a group is on interpersonal role relationships and their effect on problem solving. This focus involves concern about the intrapsychic and emotional dynamics reflected in family communication and problem-solving patterns.

Stance

The worker's basic stance when meeting with the family as a whole is one of helper and guide. A wide range of interventions are used in family discussions. Most of these are directed to the family's observation and analysis of its own group process. Special emphasis is placed on learning how family members affect each other in their contribution to the perceived family problems.

Intervention

The major strategy of confronting the family's problem-solving patterns is designed to increase their discomfort with maladaptive patterns. This process begins at intake; at this stage the family "diagnosis" is a matter of getting information on how the family deals with instrumental and affective stress. The worker expects the family to resist open discussion of the problem and explains how resistance is one of their strategies to maintain homeostasis (the status quo). The major principle in helping the family develop more adaptive patterns is for the worker to follow family interaction until there is an impasse in communication and then to elicit "psychodynamic" or family history material that may explain the impasse. The impasse is the point where family members restrict their emotional involvement with each other or do not clarify their role expectations. Often this is the point of immediate stress in affective and instrumental areas of functioning.

In the integrative approach, communication patterns tend to be classified into four types, depending on their clarity and directness. Clear and direct communication is essential for instrumental and affective problem solving among members and in the family as a whole. The other three patterns—unclear and direct, clear and indirect, unclear and indirect—are all dysfunctional. Figure 10.1 shows these four types in the communication of anger among family members.

Effective problem-solving techniques are based on clear and direct communication that increases members' autonomy and interdependence.

	Direct	Indirect
Clear	"I'm angry at you" directed to person	"I'm angry at you" directed to person other than the one intended
Unclear	"I don't like the way you comb your hair."	"People are so lazy" when intended for a certain person

Figure 10.1 Communication of Anger in the Family

This balance of autonomy and interdependency is expected to be transferred from the family system to life outside the family. The problem-solving process often begins with the worker's focus on how the family projects its problems onto a certain family member, perhaps an emotionally disturbed or "acting out" child.

In describing these techniques, Ackerman depicts the family worker in the symbolic position of a relative, possessed of goodwill and wisdom, intervening protectively in the family conflict. In this role the worker seeks emotional contact with each family member and encourages their emotional involvement with each other. Moreover, the worker constantly encourages members to undo their distorted perceptions of themselves and other family members, to dissolve their confusion and collusions, and to clarify their views regarding central family conflicts.

Empirical Support

The empirical testing of this practice theory has been negligible. The approach has been used with a variety of problems and with voluntary consumers from diverse cultural, ethnic, and racial groups. The primary use of this approach, however, has been with families in mental health settings where a preadolescent or adolescent member's social functioning is the family's chief complaint.

Communicative-Interactive Approach

The communicative-interactive approach to family group work has been developed in social work by Virginia Satir.[15] Donald Bardill and Francis Ryan have also contributed.[16] Outside of social work the primary theorists are Don Jackson,[17] Jay Haley,[18] and Salvador Minuchin.[19] The major proposition is: *If a social worker can help a family develop its observational capacity, establish a flexible need-meeting homeostasis, and clarify its communication system, then the family can increase each member's self-actualization, problem solving, and perception of self and others.*

Goals

The overriding goal is the liberated self-actualization of family members. This goal requires that members develop the ability to express needs directly to others in the style of "I want this from you in this situation" both inside and outside the family system.

Focus

Human behavior is viewed primarily as an ecological communication system, as originally conceived by Gregory Bateson.[20] The central hypothesis is the double-bind communication in families with a schizophrenic member. The double-bind hypothesis derives from the observation that the talk of schizophrenics leaves out, or leaves ambiguous, the signals or *metamessages* that communicate how the message is to be taken—serious or playful, real or imaginary, ironic or direct, literal or metaphoric. This lack of metacommunication is viewed by Bateson as a logical consequence of a mother who continually puts her child in a paradoxical bind by (1) giving him mutually contradictory messages while (2) implicitly forbidding him to recognize what she is doing. Bateson further specified what sort of mother this is: one who is made anxious and hostile by closeness to her child but finds it intolerable to acknowledge this. When the child approaches, she withdraws. When the child then moves away, she becomes pseudoaffectionate and accuses him of being unloving.

In this approach, work with the family system focuses on present communication as it relates to the clarification of emotional messages and their effect on members' self-concepts. In this context, every family member's communication functions as both a *report* and a *command*. As a report, communication gives literal information. As a command, each communication can be viewed as redefining one's relationship with another. Every relationship (husband–wife, parent–child, family member–worker) is seen in this practice theory as an implicit power struggle over *who* defines the relationship. All members' symptoms are regarded as logical strategies that control relationships which cannot be controlled by other means. They are command communications. Therefore work with the family's communication and interaction system is the means of altering individual behavior.

These family members' symptoms are viewed as being especially reinforced through the family system's homeostatic mechanisms, which reestablish the status quo. Whenever Mrs. Black shows a certain degree of resentment, for example, Mr. Black disparages himself. Whenever Mr. and Mrs. Black quarrel, their child Jack diverts them by becoming troublesome. Whenever their other child, Jill, shows a certain degree of independence, Mrs. Black labels it dangerous or disturbed. In these examples, communicative-interactive practice theorists would say that simultaneous "system-maintaining" and "system-maintained" symptoms arise from each family member's circumstances. They are reinforced and supported, however, by the family system itself.

Stance

The worker's basic stance is one of teacher and guide. The characteristic interventions are system observation and analysis through action techniques geared toward the curative factor of interpersonal learning. It is assumed that if one family member is hurting then all family members are hurting. All have to work toward creating a system that meets their needs.

Intervention

This practice theory places little reliance on insight as an agent of change; rather, insight is viewed as a by-product of the family system's change. Much of the intraobservation (observation of one's own family system in action) comes from confronting the family with its attempt to prevent a member from changing. The worker deliberately disturbs the system's homeostasis to highlight their resistance to change. In other words, families are asked to behave differently in the family sessions. Children are asked to sit with their backs turned while their parents continue a quarrel, for instance, or homework tasks are assigned—such as having family members shut a bedroom door two hours daily to ensure a member's privacy.

There are two special techniques for influencing family communication and perceptual change: prescribing the symptom and relabeling. *Prescribing the symptom* is the technique of encouraging family members to increase their communication patterns related to a particular member's symptom. For instance, parents concerned with an adolescent daughter who has run away from home on several occasions are instructed to treat their daughter just as they have been doing—and then some. The aim is to try to produce a runaway to increase their awareness of their own interpersonal dynamics as "causes" of the problem.

In *relabeling,* disturbed family members are relabeled as normal; symptoms are relabeled as rational tactics; and wherever possible what looks negative is relabeled as positive. For instance, Don Jackson used relabeling with two parents whose daughter had just had an acute schizophrenic episode. The mother, who plays the martyr, starts to cry:

Father:	I certainly am [*sighs*] sorry to see, ah, Mrs. Starbuck hurt by, ah, things that Sue was saying.
Sue:	Oh, I don't mean to hurt her. . . .
Therapist (Jackson):	I wonder that she was crying necessarily because she was hurt. Has that been established? . . . [To mother] . . . Because you responded to your daughter with I think a rather touching closeness, I don't think it was just a hurt.[21]

As Jackson explains this technique: "This is simply taking the motivation that has been labeled in a negative way and labeling it in a positive way. . . . If they have been defining what they are doing in one way for many years, and if I can suddenly define it another way, it shocks them a little out of believing that they're always right.[22]

Another example reported in the literature is the work with a hardworking black mother of four, more relieved than sorry that her ex-husband no longer visits the family.[23] She comes to the clinic because her seven-year-old daughter Mandy has, for the second time, set fire to the mother's bed. The worker praises the child for her competence in putting out the fire. He notes silently that the mother tends to use Mandy, who has been the father's favorite, as a scapegoat. During this discussion Mandy hides behind a book and the mother reprimands her. The worker deliberately misunderstands and asks Mandy to read aloud: "She was reading OK." The worker then gives a prescription: The mother is to spend ten minutes a day teaching Mandy to light matches safely. Her teacher is to encourage her reading. Throughout, the worker is purposefully low-key. As a result of this relabeling and the change in the communication–interaction system, the arson ceases.

Satir has summarized the basic concepts of the communicative-interactive approach in a videotaped training session. After explaining her concept of the family as a group that needs each other for validating their feelings of self-worth or value, she states:

> I believe people are like flowers and flowers grow because they have sunshine, fertilizer, and water. . . . What provides nurture for the human being? It is his own ability to ask for what he needs and to be in touch with himself. . . . The water for our human "plant" consists of the senses. These are not merely mechanical systems, but dynamic in that they can learn and grow in effectiveness. What is poisonous to the plant within us are the inhuman rules we have about how we should be and how we should act. Getting rid of those poisonous rules will help restore health in the person.[24]

Empirical Support

The communicative-interactive approach attempts to help families uncover their interaction and communication rules and see their effect on each other's self-concepts and growth. The liberated self-actualizing goal of this approach has not been put to empirical test. However, the model has been tested in relation to specific behavioral changes, especially by Minuchin and Haley. The literature reflects more use of this approach than the others with a variety of problems and with families in a variety of cultural, racial, and ethnic groups. It has been used in short-term, crisis, and long-term situations. It has been used most, however, with families in which one member has been diagnosed as schizophrenic—which is consistent with the basic hypothesis of double-bind relationships in the family system.

Family Group Work Theories in Action

Now let us return to the Green family. As you recall, Mrs. Green came to the child welfare agency because of her problems with Jake, her nine-year-old son. Also in the family were Darlene, ten years old; Linda, four years old; and Mr. Green, the father of Linda and stepfather of Darlene and Jake. The case was assigned to you by the protective service supervisor to prevent abuse of Jake by improving the relationship between him and Mrs. Green.

Through casework, informed by the practice theory of your choice, there have been results. Mrs. Green has begun to cope more effectively with Jake's behavior, to become more sensitive to his special needs as a developing person, and to believe that their relationship, for the first time, has a basis for growth in mutual respect and closeness. Jake's behavior has changed also. He is more relaxed; he has stopped fighting with his sisters and Mrs. Green; and he is particularly concerned about growing up—especially about doing better in school and making friends. These changes have occurred in two months' work, including ten interviews with Mrs. Green, three with Jake, and one with both Mr. and Mrs. Green. Moreover, there have been a number of telephone contacts with Mrs. Green and brokerage, or linkage, activities with the private Children's Diagnostic Center in the county to arrange for a comprehensive assessment of Jake's current functioning. The diagnostic services could not find a physiological basis for Jake's behavior. They confirmed Jake's intellectual potential, related Jake's problems to his scapegoat role in the family, and recommended family counseling.

With this recommendation and your support, Mrs. Green has increased her efforts at understanding Jake's behavior, and, indeed, the results of this action (Jake's behavioral changes) have reinforced her understanding and effort. Now, however, at the end of these two months of hard work, new problems have evolved. They have become more serious in the last two weeks. As often happens when a family member improves his or her behavior and thus deflects the scapegoating process in the family system,[25] other family members' behavior began to change and alarmed Mrs. Green. Darlene is suddenly belligerent with Mr. and Mrs. Green; she is reportedly becoming withdrawn in the classroom; she refuses to go to bed at night, suffering insomnia when forced to go. Mr. Green has been particularly taken aback by Darlene's behavior. He has overreacted by severely limiting her after-school play and TV watching, and has been arguing often with Mrs. Green about her siding with Darlene. The new tension in the family has become so serious that over the last weekend Mr. Green would not talk to either Mrs. Green or Darlene.

You have suggested to Mrs. Green that perhaps the family as a group could use help, since their relationships seem to be changing as a result of Jake's changes. She agreed and asked if you would help them determine what is wrong and what they want to do about it. Because you know that you have a relationship with several members of this family and there is no one better able to help them at this time, you agree to meet with them. Your supervisor approves this plan, believing there must be more stabilization in this family system before the case can be closed.

Mrs. Green has arranged this first meeting at their home with everyone in the immediate family present. You are on your way to meet with them. What are your goals? What are your plans? Where will you begin and how? Your practice theory for family group work can answer these questions as it guides your use of self as the instrument for this service.

Now let us see how each of the three practice theories in this chapter affects this work differently. The first worker uses the psychoanalytic approach; the second worker, the integrative approach; and the third worker, the communicative-interactive approach.

Psychoanalytic Approach

The worker using the psychoanalytic approach encouraged Mrs. Green to have Linda, the four-year-old, stay with Mrs. Green's mother during this first interview. This worker believes that Linda is too young for her developing ego to deal with the information about the family that may arise in these sessions. The first family group meeting takes place in the Greens' living room with the family and worker seated in a circle. At the center of the circle, in order, is Mrs. Green, then Jake, then Mr. Green. Darlene is sitting away from the others, to Mrs. Green's right, and the worker sits by her, almost directly across from the three in the center. The worker initiates the meeting by saying that although this family has worked hard so that Mrs. Green and Jake could get along better, there seems to be increased tension among them. The worker then asks them to tell their own story about what has been happening in the family recently and how they feel about it.

Mr. Green initiates the discussion. He says there has indeed been a great deal of tension in the family over the last couple of weeks and he knows it is related to what is going on between him and Darlene. He feels confused by Darlene's turnaround and wants to "nip it in the bud" before she hurts Mrs. Green as much as Jake has. He wonders why they cannot be a normal family without someone acting strange. The worker notices that Darlene cringes at these words and asks her to share her reaction with them (encouraging her emotional expression). Darlene is hesitant at first; a silence ensues; and then she begins to talk. She says she is not strange. Everyone seems to pick on her lately, she says, and she is tired of the fuss everyone is making over Jake, who is only pretending to have changed.

A discussion follows among Mrs. Green, Jake, and Mr. Green about Jake's new behavior. Mr. and Mrs. Green take turns defending the sincerity of Jake's behavior; Jake does not say much but agrees that he is no longer the problem. The worker ends this discussion by noting that in this family it seems that someone always has to be "the problem." The worker wonders why that is. Mrs. Green suggests that maybe it is the only way they can get attention. Jake says, "Yeah, the *wrong* kind." And Darlene retorts in anger, "If you mean me, forget it. I don't need anyone's attention!'' Mr. Green says that's good, because she certainly will not get his. The worker comments that Mr. Green really seems angry at Darlene and wonders how this anger has affected his behavior with her (relating emotions to behavior).

This response brings forth a good deal of discussion about the punishment he has been giving Darlene by restricting her play and TV time. Mrs. Green and Darlene describe him as an unbending tyrant. Mr. Green tries to defend himself by referring to Darlene's behavior and the fact that she really needs something "desperate" to put a stop to it. The worker mentions the rift this punishment is creating between Mr. and Mrs. Green and suggests that perhaps he is also angry at her. He agrees, but believes he has to take charge of this situation, as Mrs. Green has always been too "soft" with the girls, especially Darlene. Jake quickly agrees, but Mrs. Green says she has had no reason to be hard on the girls. Darlene blurts, "And you still don't!'' To which Mrs. Green says, "Yes, I do. I am really worried about you. That's why I wanted this meeting."

At this point the worker remarks that people in this family seem to have to take sides: "It seems that people in this family have a hard time trusting each other and feeling a part of it unless they are teamed up with one member against another. Does it seem that way to you?'' (The question promotes insight into self, interaction, and system.) The worker's question stimulates more discussion about Darlene's behavior and how it has "created" this situation, yet the family agrees that taking sides does seem to be a dynamic factor in their relationship. The worker concludes by asking what purpose taking sides may serve in this family and suggests that they think about this question before they meet again (demonstrating defensive and dysfunctional patterns; defocusing projections; increasing trust in each other to resolve the problem). The worker then asks each family member if they would be willing to reflect on his question and then meet again. They agree, and the worker sets up an appointment to meet with Mr. and Mrs. Green before their next group session.

The second interview is held with Mr. and Mrs. Green. In this interview the worker discusses the history of their relationship, their hopes and fears about rearing children, and the transference of their feelings about each other onto the children. The latter topic is explored in relation to Mr. and Mrs. Green's secret fears that both Jake and Darlene have too much of their real father in them and that is why at times they can be so cruel. At one point in this interview Mr. Green painfully admits he does not believe the two older children have ever accepted him as their father. Mrs. Green is upset by this revelation. The worker sensitively suggests that perhaps he has never accepted himself as their father and is projecting his feelings about Mrs. Green's first husband onto them. Mrs. Green then begins to respond to her husband's anxiety about their current relationship and his resentment about her past. Her understanding, and the worker's, encourage Mr. Green to express his feelings openly and honestly, and Mrs. Green reassures him about her love for him.

In this interview and subsequent family sessions, the worker continues to deal with resistance to change, fear of feelings, fear of extinction of the family and marriage by helping the family expose hidden feelings and secrets, and transference reactions. The emphasis is always on getting the family to deal with its own processes—the relationship between feelings and behavior.[26]

Integrative Approach

The second worker, using the integrative approach to family group work, wants to assure that all members of the immediate family are present for the first meeting. In fact, this worker discussed the possibility of Mrs. Green's mother being present, as she has been very close to all family members although she does not live in the household. Mrs. Green suggested that her mother's presence might deter her own participation, so the decision was made not to include her in this first meeting but to consider strongly inviting her to a later one or perhaps having Mrs. Green and her mother meet separately with the worker. This worker is particularly concerned about how members of this family define and perceive each other's reciprocal role relationships and realizes that Mrs. Green's mother is a significant role-definer, at least for Mrs. Green, in this family.

In the first meeting at the Greens' home, the family members sit as they did for the psychoanalytically oriented worker. However, this second worker asks them to move closer to each other to make the circle a true one in which they can relate to each other face to face. The intent is to encourage interpersonal connections in relation to the content of their discussion. The worker, therefore, "must energize dormant interpersonal conflicts, bringing them out into the arena of family interaction, thus making them accessible to solution . . . must lift concealed intrapersonal conflicts to the level of interpersonal relations where they may be coped with more effectively . . . [and] must activate an improved level of mutual support in family relationships."[27]

The worker begins this first meeting by stating that this is an opportunity for them to discover, together, the conflict in this family, why it is occurring, and what they want to do about it. With this introduction, Mr. Green begins exactly as he did with the first worker. He says there has indeed been a great deal of conflict in the family, especially over the last couple of weeks, and he knows it is based on what is going on between him and Darlene. He feels confused by Darlene's turnaround and wants to "nip it in the bud" before she hurts Mrs. Green as much as Jake has. He wonders why they cannot be a normal family without someone acting strange. The worker responds that it must be hard to be a good father (refers to role) while protecting Mrs. Green from harm (another role)—especially when these two roles are in conflict. The worker then asks how he has tried to deal with this conflict. At this point Mr. Green describes his recent punishment of Darlene, and the family, except for Jake, begins to discuss the matter. When Mrs. Green comments that Mr. Green has been a "tyrant" with Darlene, the worker suggests that she really seems to be put on the spot between them (empathy for her mother–wife role conflict) and asks what Mr. Green should be doing to be the good father he wants to be with Darlene. Mrs. Green replies, "I don't know for sure, but I believe he could understand her more and not be so hard on her, much as he used to be with Jake when he was misbehaving so often." Mr. Green replies that maybe he is being too hard on Darlene but that is because *someone* has to be firm. Mrs. Green has always been so soft on the girls, he says, that they get away with almost anything. Jake agrees strongly; the girls protest. Mrs. Green looks at the worker and asks, "What do you think? Am I so soft on the girls that he has to be hard on Darlene?"

The worker recognizes this question as both an impasse in the communication process (Mrs. Green restricts her emotional connection to Mr. Green's message) and a resistance to facing the immediate conflict together. Therefore the worker confronts Mrs. Green: "I think you want me to resolve a conflict between you two as partners that only the two of you can resolve yourselves. However, I would like to help you with this if I can. When in your marriage did this conflict about disciplining your kids begin?" (The question is reaching for family history material.) This question stimulated a long and active discussion between Mr. and Mrs. Green on their problems with Jake. Mrs. Green discussed her fear of physically abusing him if she let herself go, and she recognized how well Mr. Green could discipline Jake by having clear and consistent expectations of his behavior. Mr. Green acknowledged Mrs. Green's fears of abusing the children, as she had abused Jake in the past, and could understand how these fears prevented her from disciplining any of the children now. He again complained that this responsibility seems to have fallen on him.

His remarks prompt Darlene to ask, in an angry tone, "Why don't you just leave me alone then?" The worker attempts to clarify this communication of anger by suggesting that Darlene try to tell her father directly that she is angry at him and what she really wants from him. Darlene follows the suggestion and tells Mr. Green she is "really mad" at him and wishes he would let her mother handle her. The worker tells Darlene that her comments were clear and that this kind of communication seems difficult in this family—especially people telling each other what they want. Then the worker asks each family member to think of one thing they could do before the next meeting to help another member and strengthen that person in the family (establishing family awareness of each other as significant role reciprocators). The remainder of this first meeting is spent reporting on these ideas and getting a commitment from each member to implement them.

This worker, too, will meet with Mr. and Mrs. Green and other individual family members as well as with the whole family in the subsequent work together. Later the worker serves as a catalyst to bring individual problems into their relationship to the family system. In this family,

intervention may center on the family's scapegoating related to the anxiety
in Mr. and Mrs. Green's relationship and their current inability to give
their love to each other as well as the children. In this sense, the worker
"provokes increasingly candid disclosures of dormant interpersonal conflicts. . . . In due course, he can trace significant connections between
family disorder and the intrapsychic anxiety of individual members. Often
one part of the family armors itself, prejudicially attacks another part.
When needed, the [worker] intervenes . . . by counteracting scapegoating
as a specific defense against anxiety."[28]

Communicative-Interactive Approach

The third worker uses the communicative-interactive approach. This
worker views the Green family as having created patterns of communication, and rules for these patterns, so that interactions protect members'
low self-esteem. These patterns maintain the status quo, which depends
on one member as a scapegoat. When Jake changed and his self-esteem
increased, the family and Darlene began to recreate the old system.
Therefore this worker wants to meet with all the family members and
help them communicate with each other and change their rules for interaction and communication so they can increase their self-esteem without
needing a scapegoat. As Satir notes, "If illness is seen to derive from
inadequate methods of communication (by which we mean all interactional behavior), it follows that [we] attempt to improve these methods."[29]

This worker meets with the whole family throughout their work. As
in the previous case, the first meeting begins in a tight face-to-face circle.
At the beginning of the meeting this worker states: "We are here because
there seems to be some pain in this family, which hopefully we can express,
understand, and resolve. This will not be an open-ended process, one
which will drag on forever. The total number of work sessions will be five.
At the end of five sessions, we will evaluate what has been accomplished
and where we want to go. I believe it will be helpful for each of you to
tell me what you see as the problems in the family, starting with you, Mr.
Green. What are the problems as you see them?" Mr. Green, true to the
form established with the first two workers, proceeds by saying that there
has indeed been a great deal of pain in the family, especially over the last
couple of weeks. He says it is based on what is going on between him and
Darlene. He feels confused by Darlene's turnaround and wants to "nip
it in the bud" before she hurts Mrs. Green as much as Jake has. He
wonders why they cannot be a normal family without someone acting
strange. This worker, modeling clear communication, responds: "I heard
you say quite a bit—especially that you are concerned (relabeling the
symptom) about your family, your wife, and Darlene. Now I want to hear
from others to check out how they see the problem. Darlene, I am
wondering what you think about this, as your father particularly singled
you out." Darlene answers that she does not believe she is so strange—

what is strange is the sudden change in Jake and everyone's thinking he is so good when she knows otherwise. The worker, again modeling the importance of clear and direct communication, asks Darlene what she means by "everyone." Darlene responds, "My Mom."

At this point the worker turns to Mrs. Green and says she thinks Darlene has a message for her. What has Mrs. Green heard and how does she see the current problems in the family? Mrs. Green says that if she is "everyone," then Darlene is right. She does think—in fact, she knows— that Jake has changed. The problem now is that Darlene is suddenly misbehaving and Mr. Green is overreacting to this change. She, too, is concerned, but she does not believe that severe punishment is the answer. When the worker asks Mrs. Green to be more specific (another communication technique) about this "overreacting" and "severe punishment," Mrs. Green describes the restrictions her husband has placed on Darlene. The worker then asks Mr. Green how he feels about what he just heard. Mr. Green, with a painful look on his face, replies, "I feel OK. I expected her to say that." The worker, noting the double-level message (pained look; the phrase "OK"), shares this reaction: "You know, Mr. Green, I got two messages from you. You really looked hurt, yet you said you felt OK. I wonder how you do express your pain in this family so that other members know when you are hurting."

With this the family begins a long and energetic discussion of how Mr. Green and others express pain. They decide that they really do not communicate pain directly to each other. Mr. Green gets firm. Mrs. Green and Jake get angry. Darlene and Linda sulk. At the conclusion of this discussion the worker notes that they do have trouble expressing their pain in a way that others can get their message and respond to their needs. The worker also notes that this is unfortunate, as there does seem to be real care and concern for each other that they could give to those who are hurting (relabeling).

With these words, Darlene begins to cry. The worker's arm goes around her. When Mrs. Green gets up to go to her, the worker moves away to let Mrs. Green sit beside her and put her arm around Darlene. There is a long silence as the worker and family give supportive attention to Mrs. Green and Darlene. The worker then asks Darlene if she would like to talk about her feelings. She sniffles and says she was hurt because she has been picked on so much lately. Mr. Green responds to this with surprise and warmth. He says, "I didn't know you felt that way. I thought you were just being more defiant and didn't care what I did." The worker asks Darlene if she can repeat what Mr. Green said. She does, and the worker asks her if she knows *why* he saw her behavior that way. When Darlene says "No," the worker asks Mr. Green to tell her. Mr. Green then describes her behavior toward him, and Darlene agrees that she did not really tell how hurt she was. The worker concludes the session with a summary of the family's difficulty in communicating feelings to each other. The worker suspects this may explain why some of them act out—

to get attention when they are feeling down about themselves rather than expressing their pain and their need for each other. The family agrees. And they decide to work on the matter individually, as well as in future sessions.

Further work with the family is similar to this first session. The worker models functional communication and demands it of family members. The criterion for ending this work is the ability of family members to be clear and direct in their communication—especially to express their feelings honestly. As Satir writes: "In short, [family group work] is completed when everyone . . . in the setting can use the first person 'I' followed by an active verb and ending with a direct object."[30]

Which Approach Is Best?

Like the casework practice theories of the last chapter, these approaches to family group work regard the same situation, or practice events, differently. Moreover, they inform different practice strategies and require a different use of generic and specific practice skills. Finally, they emphasize different goals for the family group and demand different styles of working. Before a choice can be made, these differences in theory must be understood and related to one's own preferences and style. The question here, as in the previous chapter, is: Which approach do you prefer for informing your work with the Greens and others like them? Selecting an approach is but the first step, however, in beginning to answer the most important question of all for accountable service to families: Which approach *works* best for you with the Greens and people like them?

Summary

Social work methods with family processes are guided primarily by three practice theories: psychoanalytic, integrative, and communicative-interactive. This chapter has compared these practice theories in light of their major propositions and their procedures for accomplishing family member goals through family group processes. These practice theories, as well as those presented in the next chapter, inform the goals and activities in Quadrant B of the direct-service generalist framework.

The psychoanalytic approach is basically a remedial model. Its goal is to reeducate family members emotionally; its techniques focus on developing insight into emotional aspects of intrapsychic and interpersonal dynamics. The integrative approach is more of an educational model. Its goal is to develop socially competent family members; its techniques focus on family problem-solving and role relationships. The communicative-interactive approach, particularly as developed by Satir, tends to be more of a growth model. The goal is to develop self-actualizing family members; the techniques focus on rules and communication skills that enhance personal expressiveness and meet the family's needs. None of these models has been carefully tested empirically, though all have been used fairly extensively in social work practice.

Suggested Learning Experiences

As in the last chapter, the major learning activities are those that enable students to see the differences in practice theory approaches. The use of comparative charts like those presented at the end of Chapter 9 can help the student recognize the similarities and differences between family group practice theories. The use of case studies can aid comparisons between theory and practice.

Suggested Case Studies

Council on Social Work Education. "The French Family." Teaching Record 169. New York: CSWE, 1965. A case study using the psychoanalytic approach.

Orcutt, Ben A. "Family Treatment of Poverty Level Families." *Social Casework* 58(2)(1977):92–100. Use of the integrative approach.

Satir, Virginia. "A Simulated Family Interview." In *Helping Families to Change,* ed. V. Satir, J. Stachowiak, and H. A. Taschman. New York: Jason Aronson, 1975. Illustrates the communicative-interactive approach.

Chapter Eleven Groups

Introduction

The three practice theories examined in Chapter 10 apply to social work with the family. All note the uniqueness of the family as a group. Many worker activities, however, are with other kinds of groups that fall in Quadrant B of the generalist's framework. These activities, which include work with the individual and others like the individual in their own behalf, are guided by the traditional methods of group work. This chapter compares the practice theories for group work as we compared the family work approaches in the last chapter.

Group work was defined in Chapter 2 as "a method for engaging a group as a whole and its several members in a relationship process with the worker and each other to facilitate use of group experience for achieving individual and group purposes, within the purpose of an agency or service program."[1] What distinguishes group work from casework or family group work is not its purpose for the individual. In all three methods the individual purpose is self-actualizing human relations development. Group work is different from the other methods because of its *additional* purpose of responsible social change and the pattern of relationships through which these purposes are realized—member to group, member to member, worker to group, worker to member.

A group work approach is appropriate when consumer and worker decide to work with others in their own behalf so that members can develop their mutual capacities to help each other with common concerns. All group work approaches are predicated on this objective.

Comparison of Group Work Theories

Several writers have identified the basic group work approaches.[2] There is a general consensus that four different theories inform social work practice with groups: social goals, developmental, interactional, and social treatment. These theoretical approaches are well differentiated by the criteria developed by Jacob Lomranz, Martin Lakin, and Harold Schiffman and the studies isolating the curative factors in group process (see Chapter 10). As Table 11.1 indicates, the gestalts of these four approaches evolve from their goals, the elements of the individual's process, the worker's focus and characteristic interventions in group process, and the specific curative factors.

Social Goals Approach

The social goals approach for work with groups has derived from a variety of sources. Early contributors were Gracy Coyle,[3] Gisela Konopka,[4] and Gertrude Wilson and Gladys Ryland.[5] Recent theoretical contributions have come from Alan Klein and those at the Boston University School of Social Work.[6] The major hypothesis of this theory is: *If a group and its members are influenced by a worker to establish a common cause and to convert self-seeking behavior into a social contribution in group process, then members will develop their skills for meaningful and responsible social participation.*

Goals

The overriding goal for the group experience is to develop each member's social competence. The primary theoretical base is developmental psychology (especially the work of Erik Erikson), the educational theories of John Dewey and his students and colleagues, and social systems theory.

Focus

The members' interpersonal interactions are the primary focus—at the cognitive, emotional, and behavioral levels. The worker's influence on group process is focused on interpersonal communication skills, the group as an evolving social system, interactional problems and potential within this system, and the development of members' self-disclosure and self-concept. The worker's basic stance is conceived as an influencer, enabler, or guide—one who uses self and a variety of programming skills to promote the development of intermember closeness and the group's awareness of its needs, goals, and resources in relation to members' tasks inside and outside the group. The major curative factors to which the worker's activities are directed are member altruism, group cohesiveness, interpersonal learning (input and output), instillation of hope, and such existential factors as freedom, autonomy, interdependence, and responsibility.

Intervention

In Klein's recent work on social goals theory for work with groups, he develops the generic aspects of the approach for work with a variety of consumers for a variety of purposes. It is the group's *purpose* that informs its composition and method. Developmental friendship and task groups can be as large as fifteen members and composed on the basis of sociometric choices. Treatment groups are best kept at a size of eight to ten members and composed on the basis of homogeneity (similarities) with regard to developmental task, heterogeneity (differences) with regard to coping and defense patterns, and such variables as member's "social hunger" and willingness to communicate with fidelity. Before a group begins, members are seen in a brief interview to clarify the group's purpose, to begin a contract of mutual expectations for the experience, to express anxieties about the experience, and to decide about joining the group.

Subsequent work is based on the worker's knowledge of his or her own function, goals, beliefs, and self, their natural expression, and the worker's influence of the developmental sequences of the group's process. The first meeting is marked by feeling out and testing the social situation. Anxiety is paramount. Behavior reflects this anxiety as members are cautious of one another and of close interpersonal relations. The climate is tense, reserved, and hostile; fearing rejection themselves, members often reject other members. While the atmosphere often appears accepting and sociable, it is not.

> The themes in the first phase are anxiety, a desire for but fear of closeness, a desire to reveal oneself and be known but a fear of being vulnerable, a desire to be helped but a reluctance to pay the price. The worker must be responsive to these feelings as he conducts himself and as he considers program. This phase may last for several weeks or it may go on for a long time depending upon how mistrusting the people are and also how trustworthy the situation proves to be.[7]

As members develop trust in one another and a feeling of security about the group experience through the worker's establishment of a democratic climate, the focus shifts to the evolving power structure in the group—especially the threat of the worker. Conscious (stated), unavowed (conscious but unstated), and unconscious (neither conscious nor stated) goals of the group and its members are sought in the context of testing who is going to control the group. Members find their niche in the group. They learn that they truly are free and that what happens in the group is up to them. At this point, the social competence skills are developed with a recommitment to the group's purpose and goals.

Once the members are relieved of this struggle, they can move on to planning group events. There is a reclarification of their purpose. This period is characterized by the establishment of direction and motivation. A unique group culture is now discernible. The collection of people has become a group, ready to work on its tasks. Members can accept and trust each other and the worker; personal involvement can increase. There is a strengthening of cohesion and a desire to achieve group goals. "It is toward the end of the third phase of group development that the question

Table 11.1 Characteristics of Practice
Theories for Group Work

Characteristic	Social Goals Approach	Developmental Approach	Interactional Approach	Social Treatment Approach
Goals				
Socially competent person	H	M	H	L
Emotionally reeducated person	M	M	M	H
Self-actualizing person	M	H	M	L
Main dimensions				
Emotionality	M	H	H	M
Cognitive	M	M	H	H
Interpersonal	H	H	H	L
Intrapsychic	L	M	L	H
Behavioral	M	L	M	H
Worker's focus				
Focus on interpersonal; participating more effectively; developing communication skills	H	H	H	L
Focus on groups; group organization and dynamics; group problem solving; learning about group pressures	H	H	H	M
Focus on interactional problems of social system; increasing interpersonal competence in role relationships	H	M	M	M
Focus on emotional aspects; coping with hostility, dependency needs, feelings of acceptance and rejection	M	H	M	M
Focus on intrapsychic dynamics; exploring defense mechanisms in interpersonal interaction; diagnosing and evaluating personal conflicts	L	M	L	H
Focus on trust and self-concept of members; exploring impact of others on self and discrepancy between ideal and real self	H	H	M	L
Focus on expressiveness; disclosing one's self; becoming intimately known to others; eliciting involvement and confrontation; expressing love and joy	H	H	M	L

	1	2	3	4
Focus on expanding and fulfilling experiences; increasing use of intuition; increasing ability to enjoy aesthetic-natural experiences	M	M	M	L
Focus on sensory awareness in order to expand senses; overcoming alienation; developing nonverbal and tactile communication	M	M	M	L
Worker's stance				
Teacher	M	M	H	H
Helper	L	L	L	H
Guide	H	H	H	L
Interventions				
Observation and analysis	H	H	H	M
Group dynamics	H	H	H	M
Psychodynamically oriented	L	L	L	H
Emotionally expressive and experientially oriented	H	H	M	L
Individually directed	L	L	M	H
Group-directed	H	H	H	L
Structure				
Group discussion	H	H	H	H
Program activity	H	M	L	M
Cognitive input	M	L	M	H
Fantasy and sensory awareness exercises	L	L	L	L
Curative factors				
Altruism	H	H	M	L
Group cohesiveness	H	H	H	L
Universality	M	M	M	L
Interpersonal learning (input)	H	H	H	M
Interpersonal learning (output)	M	M	M	H
Guidance	M	M	M	H
Catharsis	L	L	M	M
Identification	M	M	L	H
Family reenactment	H	H	L	H
Insight	H	H	H	H
Instillation of hope	M	M	H	L
Existential factors	H	H	H	L

H = high emphasis; M = moderate emphasis; L = low emphasis.

of what members are really there for is raised even though purpose has been discussed before and a contract negotiated."[8]

Helping members to resolve the conflicts of earlier phases of the group's development requires the worker's calmness and perceptiveness. It also requires the worker's feedback to the group about its evolving structure and process. The social worker refuses to sanction autocratic members. All members are validated in the worker's interaction with the group. The worker supports mutual aid and interpersonal closeness, ignores non-productive contributions, and teaches members to perform in ways that benefit the entire group. The worker consistently refuses to allow dependence on him or her. Feedback to the group and its members is based on the worker's attention to what is being reinforced in the group. The worker personally reinforces egalitarianism, person-to-person relationships (rather than power and domination), and mutuality and intimacy.

A major aspect of this approach is feedback. Feedback helps members to be aware of their conflicts and tactics, to compare their behavior with their contract for the group and their desire for help, and to become empathic to the needs and hurts of others. Another major part of the approach is the worker's personal demonstration of how one behaves toward others and especially how people in positions of authority can act in behalf of others. The problems of the group, for instance, are made *group* problems, and the group is expected to deal with them.

At the point the group establishes its own purpose and assumes responsibility for achieving it, the group can mobilize its own resources in behalf of its needs. These resources include choice, problem solving in the here-and-now relationships within the group, support for increased personal freedom and risk, social action, shared responsibility, self-expression, and the discovery of one's own values.[9]

Empirical Support

This practice theory has been used with a great many consumers of varying needs and degrees of illness and health. Most research on this model has been in the form of case studies. Because the main outcomes are social consciousness and social responsibility, there is some difficulty in measuring the results when this practice theory is applied. The aim of social goals theory is expressed in the words of Gracy Coyle, its foremost pioneer:

> It is not enough . . . for man to seek enjoyment in isolation from others. Because of his essentially social nature his fullest growth comes only as he uses his expanding powers in conjunction with and for the benefit of others . . . to use his capacities in part at least for social ends beyond himself. Each man must find for himself the objects of his social devotion, but to discover them is as essential to fulfillment as to find the objects of his more personal loves.[10]

Developmental Approach

The developmental approach to group work evolved from the earlier work of Helen Phillips[11] but is primarily the product of one person: Emanuel Tropp.[12] The central hypothesis is: *If a worker can influence a group and its members, brought together around a significant common concern, to develop the group's potential for task accomplishment and empathetic interpersonal relationships, then the group can achieve its goals, members can increase interpersonal relationship skills, and individuals can further their self-actualization.*

Goals

The overriding goal for members is self-actualization: enhanced awareness of self and others; enhanced ability to place value on self and others; and enhanced ability to mobilize oneself, activate oneself, and interact with others. The basic theory informing this approach is developmental, humanistic, and phenomenological psychology and the social systems theory of social action.

Focus

In practice, the worker is concerned especially with group members' emotionality in interpersonal relations in the here and now of group events. The focus is on interpersonal communication, group dynamics and processes, emotional conflicts, cohesiveness in relation to trust development, and self-expression. The worker tends strongly toward the stance of guide; there is authentic use of self within the limits of the group's purpose and the worker's leadership function. Interventions and program activity are directed predominately to the group as a whole and to the experiential-enhancing dynamics of the process. There is a strong emphasis on the curative factors of altruism, universality, interpersonal learning (input), member-to-member guidance, identification, and such existential factors as choice and responsibility.

Intervention

Tropp has developed this practice theory from work with a large variety of consumers in natural groups and formed groups, voluntary and involuntary. Group formation begins with identification of the target population and the purpose of the group experience. The next decision regards the type of group experience needed: activity (common interests), counseling (discussion), or action (task of environmental change). The type is based on members' needs, their common interests, age, sex, cultural variants, abilities and limitations, physical location, and availability for meetings. The group's size and composition are based on its purpose and type.

Work in the group is guided by the worker's basic presentation of self and the worker's influence on the lines of action that flow during the development of the process. Tropp has identified sixteen implicit messages that constitute the worker's "professional presentation" with a developmental practice theory:[13]

1. *Compassion*—"I care deeply about you."

2. *Mutuality*—"We are here on a common human level; let's agree on a plan and then let's walk the path together."

3. *Humility*—"Please help me understand."

4. *Respect*—"I consider you as having worth. I treat your ideas and feelings with consideration. I do not intrude upon your person."

5. *Openness*—"I offer myself to you as you see me, real, genuine, and authentic."

6. *Empathy*—"I am trying to feel what you are feeling."

7. *Involvement*—"I am trying to share and help in your efforts."

8. *Support*—"I will lend my conviction and back up your progress."

9. *Expectation*—"I have confidence that you can achieve your goals."

10. *Limitation*—"I must remind you of your agreed-upon obligations."

11. *Confrontation*—"I must ask you to look at yourself."

12. *Planning*—"I will always bring proposals but I would rather have yours."

13. *Enabling*—"I am here to help you become more able and more powerful."

14. *Spontaneity and control*—"I will be as open as possible, yet I must recognize that, in your behalf, I need to exercise some self-control."

15. *Role and person*—"I am both a human being like you and a representative of an agency with a special function to perform."

16. *Science and art*—"I hope to bring you a professional skill based on organized knowledge, but I am dealing with people, and my humanity must lend the art to grace the science."

The *lines of force*, or lines of action, to which the worker pays attention throughout the process are relations—between each member and the group as a whole, between each member and each other member, between each member and each subgroup, between each subgroup and each other subgroup, and between each subgroup and the group as a whole. All these forces are operating at all times in the group. If they are ignored for any length of time, they may influence the group as a system to increase in entropy—that is, to lose the energy, order, and differentiation needed for growth.

The worker's foremost activity is directed toward the group as a whole: its goal-achieving process, deliberations, and decision-making actions. In the beginning stage, this influence requires the worker to (1) clarify purpose, function, and structure; (2) establish an agreement to proceed; (3) support early efforts; (4) offer convictions; and (5) encourage task selection and unification. Much of the early work is perceiving what is happening in the group, clarifying and evaluating communications among the various lines of forces, and helping the group link its actions to its common goals. Special attention is given to helping the group convert long-range goals into planned activities for each session together. Throughout these activities, the worker in partnership with members evaluates the group's functioning in relation to its potential maturity. Maturity is conceived as a state in which the group is achieving its purposes. Members are imbued with a vital responsiveness to each other and accept responsibility to each other, the agency, and the community.

In the middle stage of the group's development, the focus stays on the building of an optimum group experience as the vehicle for the self-actualizing growth of its members, but the worker now pays more attention to members' autonomy and interdependence. As Tropp sums up the worker's activities in this stage: "The leader is guiding the group toward goal focus, clarifying tasks completed and still to be accomplished, facilitating the group's ability to do more for itself, supporting the group in its growing ability, and helping the group to recognize time limits and the approaching termination for achievement."[14]

The focus on interpersonal behavior in the group is guided by an assessment of its *instrumental* (task) and *expressive* (emotional) elements in relation to the common goals. The intent is always to deal with expressive behavior (likes and dislikes, attraction and repulsion, anger, resentment, distrust, affection) in the interests of more effective instrumental (conscious goal-seeking) interaction. For instance, expressive behavior that obstructs the instrumental process is confronted by questions: What is happening here? How is this affecting our goal-achieving efforts? Individual behavior is dealt with like interpersonal behavior. The emphasis is on enabling members to perform their group functions as effectively as possible. Feedback rather than interpretation is the worker's preferred response. The attempt is to grasp what a person is doing, or expressing, in feeling. This behavior is available for all to see and to reflect back to the member just how the actions appear.

Empirical Support

The empirical status of developmental group work has been summarized by Tropp:

> The developmental group work theory for practice is . . . based on its consistent application, its evolving systemization and internal coherence, and its demonstrated usefulness in a great variety of settings, over many years with different kinds of populations. The fact that gains have only been subjectively perceived by group leaders and members but not confirmed by objective research requires attention. However, in view of the comparable situation in other behavioral professions, it is still necessary and worthwhile to live by the conviction that direct personal experience with this method brings, and to keep working at sharpening it for more effective service.[15]

Interactional Approach

The practice theory for interactional group work has been called interactionist, mediating, and reciprocal. It is primarily the work of one person—William Schwartz.[16] Other significant contributions to this approach have been made by Lawrence Shulman[17] and Alex Gitterman.[18] The major practice hypothesis is: *If a worker can engage group members with each other and the worker and with the performance of selected tasks as independent actors in an organic mutual aid system, then members can accomplish their goals in a manner that increases their skills for mutual aid transactions in the various systems through which they carry on their relationships with society.*

Goals

The overriding goal is nonspecified social competence, reflected in increased mutual aid relationships with others. Basic theory comes from systems theory and field theory.

Focus

The primary dimensions of group members are the cognitive and emotional elements of interpersonal transactions: "The interactionists emphasize experience and affect, step-by-step process, and situational rather than structural descriptions of people in difficulty."[19] Emphasis is on communication skills and group problem solving in interactional and self-concept-building experiences. The worker serves as a teacher and guide who uses observation and group-directed intervention in group discussions. The main curative factors in group process include group cohesiveness or "symbiosis," interpersonal learning, the instillation of hope in mutual aid relationships, and such existential factors as power (or autonomy) orientations and intimacy (or interdependence) orientations toward self and others in social systems.

Schwartz's basic model of the mediating function for the social worker influencing group process is shown in Figure 11.1. Social work with any consumer system is based on a two-client concept for the interactionists: the individual and the social system. In relation to group work:

> If each [group] system is thus regarded as a small version of the individual-society relationship, the worker's skills are fashioned by two inter-related responsibilities: he must help each individual [member] negotiate the [group] system immediately crucial to his problem and he must help the [group] system incorporate the [member], deliver its service, and thus carry out its function in the community.[20]

The worker's skills with the group flow from this function and four phases of work: preparation, beginnings, substantive work, and endings or transitions.

Intervention

The *preparation phase* is a "tuning in" period marked by the use of a variety of empathic skills. The preliminary empathy is getting in touch with the imagined life processes of group members and anticipating their needs, resources, and obstacles for engagement with each other and the worker. Human behavior hypotheses suggest that the worker consider coded styles of communication, increased wishes and fears related to new experiences, ambivalence regarding authority, and the need for clarity of purpose and function. Other skills include, according to Schwartz, both connecting and partializing data—organizing bits of information into a pattern of expectations and breaking down one's knowledge into smaller propositions that are relevant both to the class of clients ('the aged') and the individual members ('these aged'). In addition, the worker must be able to retain his peripheral vision for events to which he has not tuned his perceptions.[21] In this early phase there is no prior prescription for group composition. This practice theory asserts that only one criterion is useful for forming a group: common tasks in relation to service needs.

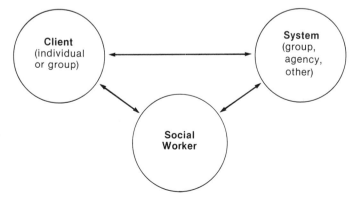

Figure 11.1 Social Worker as Mediator

The *beginning phase* of group work is the formation of a working contract. Contract negotiation requires a clear understanding of the conditions of work together and consensus about the members' needs and the agency's stake in offering the service. In the beginning phase the worker must understand the members' needs and the agency's service in order to make a simple statement of their connection. The worker's skills also demand an ability to elicit responses and encourage specific communication. The worker refuses to allow comfortable yet vague formulations to rest undisturbed. Moreover, the worker challenges members to abandon their timidity and express their problems and desires directly without disguising them in euphemisms. In this stage, the worker prepares to monitor the terms of the contract; later, the worker may have occasion to ask both group and agency to renegotiate this contract as they pass through the various stages of the work.[22]

The *work phase,* or middle phase, deals with the main problems and tasks of the helping process. Full use is made of the common mediating tasks. First is the search for the common ground between members' needs and the needs of the systems, inside and outside the group, they are required to negotiate. Second is the process of challenging the obstacles that come between members and their social tasks, both inside and outside the group. Third, the worker contributes ideas, facts, and values to members. Fourth, the worker shares his or her own vision, feelings about the process, and faith in the members' mutual aid relationships. Fifth, the worker continually defines the limits and requirements of the situation for the group, including contract renegotiation when warranted.

The *transition or ending phase* is marked by evasion and intensification of individual members' authority (their use of the worker) and intimacy (their use of each other). The worker needs to hold the group to its ending work and encourage the expression of ambivalence regarding dependence and separation. The demand for work is made throughout, and there is emphasis on preparation for future commitments and tasks.

Empirical Support

Interactional group practice theory, like the other approaches, has been used with a variety of consumers in a number of different settings. Research has been predominantly in the form of case studies. One recent study has tested some of the process and outcome hypotheses of this theory,[23] but this work is exploratory at present. More recently, this theory has been developed as a generic approach to social work methods with less attention to its group work uses. Schwartz claims: "As the work continues, it becomes clearer that the interactionist impetus is essentially integrative; its generic core is found not only within the field of social work but in all of the other professions that need to see deeply and precisely into the nature of the helping process."[24]

Social Treatment Approach

The primary theorist for the social treatment approach to group work is Robert Vinter.[25] Other leading theorists are Charles Garvin and Paul Glasser.[26] Additional contributions have been made by others at the University of Michigan School of Social Work.[27] The basic hypothesis for this theory is: *If a worker can use his or her expertise to direct group process and dynamics for specific behavioral change of individual members, then members can become reeducated in areas of social dysfunction.*

Goals

The overriding goal is individual emotional reeducation or remedial behavioral change. Basic theory comes from role theory, sociobehavioral theory, ego psychology, and group dynamics.

Focus

In practice, the group members' intrapsychic, cognitive, and behavioral dimensions are tapped by focusing on personal and interpersonal conflicts and defense mechanisms related to the structural components of group process. The worker is a teacher and helper—a change agent whose interventions are directed to specific goals for individual members through group discussion and program activities. The central curative factors in group process are interpersonal behavioral change, guidance, identification, family reenactment, and insight.

The social treatment approach is built on two levels of analysis: (1) the sequential arrangement of tasks confronting the worker and (2) the levels of social organization the worker seeks to affect in order to accomplish these tasks. The worker's activities and tasks can be expressed in outline form:

1. Study and diagnosis
   a. Preliminary diagnosis and intake
   b. Working diagnosis
   c. Intervention goals
   d. Intervention plan
   e. The helping contract

2. Intervention
   a. Direct means of influence
   b. Indirect means of influence
   c. Extragroup means of influence

3. Evaluation and termination

Preliminary diagnosis is based on the remedial determination of problem behavior translated into specific goals for change. Information on the problem, the circumstances, and the environmental responses it evokes are sought through discussion and observation at the intake stage. Particular attention is paid to the consumer's ability to engage in relationships toward group problem solving. The group's composition is vital. The primary questions for this composition are: What composition will enhance the attainment of individual goals and establish a group purpose consistent with these goals? Given a specific group composition, what purposes can evolve that are consistent with individual goals?

The focus throughout the work is on the individual and his or her goals. The group is only the backdrop. The early part of the group experience continues the study and diagnosis process as members are helped to state their individual goals in precise terms. ("I want to cut my drinking down to one drink per evening.") These individual goals, translated into group goals, become the terms of the contract for group service. ("We will help each member decrease his or her addictive behavior.") The worker's subsequent intervention is based on deliberate use of peer group pressures, modeling among members, legitimating group rules and norms, and generally directing group resources to promote individual goal achievement.

Intervention

Using *direct means of influence,* the worker maintains certain group positions, roles, and statuses throughout the process. In the role of "central person–object of identification and drives," the worker acts as a model, responds to members' feelings, and verbally supports goal-directed activity. In the role of "symbol and spokesman–agent of legitimate norms and values," the worker is continually involved in clarifying policy, setting limits, creating group rules, and confronting members with the long-range consequences of their behavior. In the role of "motivator and stimulator–definer of individual goals and tasks," the worker helps members find new ways of handling problems by giving advice, exhorting, structuring new opportunities, providing psychological interpretations, and giving behavior assignments. Finally, as the "executive–controller of member roles," the worker assigns responsibilities and alters relations (roles, statuses, positions) in the group.

Using *indirect means of influence,* the worker's focus is on creating and modifying conditions within the group system. This influence requires the application of small-group theory and research directed toward such group variables as composition, size, goals, structure, and processes. The worker's major indirect tasks involve the use of selected program activities, behavior modification, the logic of problem solving for conflict resolution, the addition or subtraction of members in the group, and group developmental processes, especially sociometric and cohesiveness development.

Extragroup means of influence are clearly distinguished as a third level of intervention. This task is one of environmental modification. Here the worker focuses on social systems outside the group and works with persons, groups, or institutions in behalf of one or more group members. The worker seeks environmental change in order to modify behavior or to support changes achieved in the group.

Garvin and Glasser summarize the worker-as-expert base of this practice theory:

> The task of the worker, then, is as follows: The worker, with an awareness of appropriate goals, determines which processes enhance or hinder the attainment of goals. The worker develops a series of propositions regarding forces that are maintaining or could maintain such processes. Depending on the goals of the client-worker system, the worker with or on behalf of clients seeks to increase the occurrence of specified processes or to decrease them.[28]

Empirical Support

The social treatment theory has been used primarily with voluntary consumers, since it demands an initial recognition by the consumer of a problem in social functioning. This approach has also been used for working with children in groups.[29] Its empirical status, like that of the other group work approaches, is underdeveloped, though it is based on much empirical work in group dynamics. As Garvin and Glasser concluded: "Further development and testing of propositions related to this approach are clearly required."[30]

Group Work Theories in Action

This section demonstrates how group work practice theories make a difference in the worker's procedures in direct-service social work. Again let us assume you have worked with Mrs. Green and her situation using a casework approach (Chapter 9) and a family group work approach (Chapter 10). During this work, Jake, the nine-year-old son, has initiated a great deal of concern about his inability to get along with peers. He wishes he could make friends with classmates and playmates, but much of his behavior is marked by competition, fighting, and his rejection. You know of five other boys on your caseload, all between the ages of nine and eleven, who have had trouble relating to their peers and wish to make friends. Their problem, like Jake's, is affecting their classroom functioning and self-satisfaction. You believe much of this problem is related to their earlier rejection in their family group, which has been improving for them, but also to their lack of basic interpersonal skills. You know that a directed small-group experience is an excellent laboratory for learning these skills and also that no such resource exists in the community. You have discussed this situation with your supervisor, who has accepted your recommendation that the agency sponsor such a group after school for ten weekly sessions. Your caseload will be lessened during this period to permit you to work with the group.

You then talked to all six boys and their parents, explaining that you will be offering ten weekly meetings for the purpose of helping boys aged nine through eleven to develop skills for working cooperatively with their peers. The group will meet for an hour after school, and parents will be responsible for their sons' transportation. Five of the six boys are interested in joining the group, have gotten their parents' permission, and are planning to attend the first meeting—Tom, Al, Eric, Steve, and Jake. Tom and Al are eleven years old; Eric is ten; and Steve, like Jake, is nine.

You are on your way to this first meeting. What are your goals? What are your plans? How will you begin? Again the answers to these questions may be found in the practice theory you have chosen for working with the group.

The meeting is scheduled to begin at 4:00 P.M. in the agency's conference room. You have soft drinks ready to lessen the formality of the meeting and have arranged the chairs in a circle. The boys begin to straggle in at 3:55 P.M. Al is first; upon being greeted, he slips unobtrusively into a chair. Steve and Eric arrive together rather noisily, say hello to you, and make straight for the soft drinks. Al and Jake come in quietly, scrutinize the others, nod at you, and take a seat. All seem to have settled down as you pass out the drinks. Several minutes after 4:00 P.M., Tom makes a grand entrance, yelling goodbye to his mother in the hallway and stirring things up with some loud comments about how the meeting looks like a school Christmas party with everyone sitting on hard chairs drinking refreshments. Now let us see how four different workers using the four major approaches to group work would handle the meeting.

Social Goals Approach

At this point, the worker using the social goals approach greets Tom, gives him a soft drink, and asks that he join them and be seated so they can get started. The worker begins by telling them that they have all been told individually about this group but they must be wondering what it is going to be like, what they are going to be doing together, and who the others are. The worker then tells them that, together, they can decide what they want to do in their meetings. The worker will try to help them make these decisions in a way that involves everyone. What they do should be related to their purpose of being together—learning to get along better with each other in the group and with classmates and playmates outside the group. The worker asks if there are any questions or comments. There are none. The worker then suggests that perhaps the best way to start would be for them to introduce themselves and tell the others what they hope to get out of this group experience.

The worker is particularly attuned to the members' anxieties and fears and wants this first meeting to be pleasant. The worker assumes that members are also very concerned about who is going to control the group and how much authority the worker will use. Before they can negotiate a contract that specifies individual goals in relation to group goals, there must be some sense of security and freedom for members. As the members introduce themselves and begin to express their hopes toward the establishment of this contract, this worker does not demand anything at this early stage that may embarrass them. The climate must be trusting and trustworthy, protective and permissive. It must permit maximum exploration of each other, the group as a whole, and the worker. As Klein writes, "It is a great and ubiquitous mistake to assume that there is a contract or group goal before the question of whether the worker is going to control the group is partially resolved."[31]

Developmental Approach

The worker using the developmental approach to group work, having settled on a counseling group, wants to establish the identity of the members and the worker and to reach an agreement on the group's purpose, function, and structure. Therefore, this worker begins the group with the following activity, which he introduces as soon as Tom is seated: "As you know, we will be meeting from 4:00 P.M. to 5:00 P.M. every Tuesday for the next ten weeks. You have all been informed why this group has been established. I think it would help me and all of us if we could give our own ideas of the purpose of this group."

This worker intends to clarify the group's purpose in the first meeting. In this discussion the worker may add information and summarize what everyone has said to state the purpose clearly. The worker will add that their own discussion will determine *how* the purpose is achieved (structure and function). The worker will serve as leader but will not give answers; in fact, the worker expects to learn a great deal from them as they learn from each other.

The balance of this first meeting may be spent building a program for the remaining nine meetings. The boys are asked to list their greatest concerns in getting along with others as potential topics for subsequent sessions. The worker takes these suggestions, suggests some others, and discourages the group from discussing each topic immediately in the interest of discovering the whole picture for building their program. Then, as Tropp notes, "he states at the conclusion of this process what the group has achieved by way of program-building, that it is now *their* program, and he asks agreement to the total plan of operation."[32] The worker gets their agreement on major topics and then asks the group to decide on the topic it wishes to discuss at the next meeting. Subsequent meetings are devoted to the topics the group selects.

Interactional Approach

The worker using the interactional approach, like the last worker, has three things to accomplish in this first meeting. All are related to negotiating a contract with the boys. These three aims are clarity about purpose, clarity about roles, and feedback from group members. This worker, however, will emphasize the agency's stake in their work together, the common ground among them in the group experience, and their reason for joining the group. Therefore this worker begins by stating that the agency and the worker would like this group experience to help them work cooperatively so that they can get along better with their classmates and playmates. The worker will help them try new ways of working together; but they will have to be willing to talk about their problems in making friends inside and outside the group. Moreover, they will have to be willing to help each other. The worker then asks for their reaction to what they just heard.

The next step for this worker may be to answer their questions about the purpose of the group, to clarify how they can proceed, and to elicit their agreement on these points. The worker then begins to deal with specifics. The following example shows how one worker using the interactional approach moves in the first meeting from clarification to the specifics of work with preadolescents having problems in school:

> I asked if they wanted to see what it would be like. They all anxiously said they would. I asked if anyone right now could think of anything bothering him in school. They all thought it was too difficult for them. I asked if they wanted to give me an example. All said, "Yes." "Okay," I said. "Suppose I was in your school and had something on my mind. Maybe I had a fight with my brother. Even if I wanted to think about my studies, I can't because I can't stop thinking about how I would like to get even with my brother." Bill broke in and said, "You can't do the writing." I continued, "Okay, I can't think about the writing. And the teacher comes along and I get into trouble. I get mad because she doesn't understand that I have something that bothers me." Every ear was involved and it seemed real to them. Their remarks came fast. "Those teachers are mean sometimes." "Yeah, that Mr. Johnson, he's mean."[33]

By offering a specific example (prepared by "tuning in"), the worker helps the group to *experience* the kinds of material pertinent for discussion. The contract is tested and, if needed, renegotiated in subsequent meetings.

Social Treatment Approach

The worker using the social treatment approach to group work will base his or her procedures on the preliminary diagnosis determined from extensive intake interviews with the boys. This worker, too, will be interested in determining the group's goals and rules as they relate to individual needs. This worker welcomes Tom warmly; then, mildly but firmly, points out that even though the boys will have a lot of freedom to do what they want in the group, they must follow certain rules—not wandering about the halls, not playing with agency material in the conference room, and keeping noise down. This worker then asks each boy to make a name tag giving his name and one thing he is interested in talking about in the group. The worker's tag notes an interest in talking about their individual problems in getting along with others. The worker then reminds the boys that in the individual interviews they decided a group could help them with their personal problems. The worker adds, "And I've found that groups can work together only when everyone knows each other and what they want to do. Why don't we finish going around, introducing ourselves, and explaining our tags?" After this exercise, the worker summarizes their common problems and asks which ones they want to discuss the following week. The discussion ends when the worker believes the group has specified what they want to discuss and members have committed themselves to work together on this decision.

Later meetings will be based on these plans. Specific problems will be elicited and discussed. The group will be encouraged to think of solutions and rehearse them in the group, perhaps through role playing. The worker will also frequently take stock of what each member, based on his stated goals, is getting from the group and giving and how the group is achieving *its* stated goals. Janice Schopler and Maeda Galinsky summarize the principles of the social treatment approach to group work as guidelines for this first meeting:

> As the members come together at the first meeting, the social worker relates to their preoccupation with self-interest and mistrust . . . to help members become acquainted and reveal their commonalities. . . . As members begin to express themselves, the social worker needs to focus the discussion on the members' reasons for meeting . . . insures that each member's interests are considered and shares her own views with the group. . . . When members reach agreement on goals, the social worker makes certain these are clear, realistic, and representative of members' mutual interests. . . . In addition to helping members formulate goals, the social worker needs to provide direction in developing and clarifying responsibilities, expectations, and ways of proceeding. . . . Social workers use a variety of styles and techniques as they help groups form and begin to work together. Whatever the approach, it is important to remember that the way social workers carry out their tasks during the first few meetings sets the stage for later group development. Thus, during this beginning phase, social workers must be aware of the potential impact of their actions and vary their interventions to meet the particular needs of the members.[34]

The worker's subsequent tasks in this approach are related to these group maintenance and group achievement objectives.

Which Approach Is Best?

The approaches to group work probably reflect more similarity to each other than do the casework and family group work approaches. Some of this similarity is a result of their common roots[35] and the generic aspects of groups,[36] which include similar, almost universal, processes and dynamics. The differences, however, are real. The contract and specificity, for instance, guide the worker's strategy much more in the interactional and social treatment approaches than in the social goals and developmental theories. The developmental and social treatment approaches require much more planning of activities. The developmental and interaction-oriented workers will direct more initial comments to the group as a whole, whereas those using the social goals and social treatment approaches will direct many comments to individual members. Each approach is unique when considered in its entirety. Each tends to inform the worker's use of self differently and is directed to somewhat different goals. The choice of approach again depends on your goals and your preferred styles of using your self to achieve professional purposes through group process.

Summary

Social work methods with group processes are currently informed by four practice theories: social goals, developmental, interactional, and social treatment. In this chapter we have compared these practice theories in light of their major propositions and procedures for accomplishing individual goals through group processes. These practice theories guide the goals and activities in Quadrant B of the direct-service generalist framework.

The social goals approach is designed to increase group members' social competence by focusing on aspects of group structure and member-to-member and member-to-worker interaction in the group process. The developmental approach is based on the specific goal of self-actualization. It focuses on interpersonal relationships in the group as they relate to specific group tasks. The interactional approach, like the social goals approach, sets priority on achieving social competence for members. The focus is on problem-solving skills in the group and with social systems transacting with the group. The social treatment approach is the most remedial of the four. Its goal is primarily the emotional reeducation of group members; its focus is on organizational influences, both inside and outside the group, upon members' dysfunctional behavior. All four approaches require knowledge of group development and demand skills in influencing group process in behalf of members.

Suggested Learning Experiences

To compare the differences and similarities of group work approaches, charts can be designed as in Chapters 9 and 10. Case studies can be used to demonstrate these similarities and differences in practice.

Suggested Case Studies

Council on Social Work Education. "Natural Mothers' Club—Brookwood Child Care." Teaching Record 68–340–87. New York: CSWE, 1968. Use of the developmental approach.

Council on Social Work Education. "The Jiggers: Social Group Work with 'Hard-to-Reach' Acting Out Adolescent Girls." Teaching Record 8–52–2. New York: CSWE, 1958. Illustrates social goals approach.

Gitterman, Alex. "Group Work in the Public Schools." In *The Practice of Group Work,* ed. W. Schwartz and S. R. Zalba. New York: Columbia University Press, 1971. Use of the interactional approach.

Schopler, Janice H. and Maeda J. Galinsky. "Guiding Group Development: An Illustration." In *The Field of Social Work,* ed. A. E. Fink. 7th ed. New York: Holt, Rinehart and Winston, 1978. Employs the social treatment approach.

Stempler, B. L. "A Group Work Approach to Family Group Treatment." *Social Casework* 58(3) (1977): 143–152. Use of the interactional approach.

Sundel, Martin and Harry Lawrence. "Behavioral Group Treatment with Adults in a Family Service Agency." In *Individual Change Through Small Groups,* ed. P. Glasser, R. Sarri, and R. Vinter. New York: Free Press, 1974. Illustrates the social treatment approach.

Chapter Twelve   Organizations

Introduction

All social work involves organizations. Moreover, all methods are affected by the organizational context. And when the direct-service generalist works with indirect consumers in behalf of the individual (and often other direct consumers), the focus is directly on the service network. The major methods in this case are organizational development, brokerage, and case advocacy (Quadrant C and Quadrant D of the generalist framework presented in Chapter 2). The practice theories for these methods are based on an understanding of organizational functioning in general and the functioning of human service organizations in particular. The objective is to develop effective and humane resource systems.

An organization has been defined as "the rational coordination of the activities of a number of people for the achievement of some common explicit purpose or goal, through division of labor and function and through a hierarchy of authority and responsibility."[1] In social work practice, formal and informal processes constitute both major resources and major obstacles to the delivery of services. Therefore the development of the *organization* is a simultaneous outcome of effective service to each individual, family, or group. At points, the organization becomes the major target and its change becomes a major goal.

The formal processes of organizations have evolved in modern society into a structure known as *bureaucracy*. The evolution, efficiency, rationality, and equity of the bureaucratic organization were originally investigated by Max Weber, the sociologist.[2] According to Weber, these are the ideal criteria of bureaucratic effectiveness:

1. Staff members are free from constraints on their personhood and subject to authority only in relation to their impersonal work obligations.

2. Staff is organized in clearly defined and hierarchical offices.

3. Each office has a clearly defined sphere of competence.

4. Offices are assumed by choice and are therefore based on a contractual agreement regarding their terms.

5. Staff members are selected on the basis of their technical qualifications
   for the office, not on the basis of personal status or prejudice.

6. The positions in the system constitute a career for the occupant.

7. The staff's work is separate from the ownership of the means of
   administration.

8. Staff members are subject to strict and systematic discipline in the
   conduct of their offices and are therefore accountable for the organization's effectiveness in achieving goals.

To Weber, the central dynamics of bureaucracy are the "specialization
and standardization of tasks" and the "rational allocation of these tasks"
in relation to an overall plan. These assumptions have been challenged
by others. Rational organization is greatly affected by the purposeful, yet
not necessarily rational, underside of bureaucracy—informal structure and
processes, vaguely defined goals, and changing needs.

Human service organizations, for instance, often do not have a clear,
consistent, comprehensive, and accepted definition of their ultimate goals.
Agency functions are more often defined in general, unmeasurable terms
("contribute to youth and family development") or defined by program
("day care" or "crisis intervention") rather than by standard consumer
goals. Further, in reality, consumer tasks and goals are individualized to
the point that rational, standardized tasks of organizational staff are an
impossibility. Thus it is through the creative and informal process of
mediating between organization and individual that services get delivered.
In other words: "A profession works by applying principles and methods
to resolve problems determined by unique client input and professional
judgment rather than by employing standardized procedures toward some
predetermined goal established by a hierarchical authority."[3]

The direct-service generalist in the organization must deal with the
strains between the profession and the bureaucracy. The social worker
must be a bureaucratic professional, not a professional bureaucrat. As
Harold Weissman has noted in *Overcoming Mismanagement in the Human
Services:*

> Professionals . . . expect a large degree of autonomy from organizational
> control; they want maximum discretion in carrying out their professional
> activities, free from organizational interference or confining procedures.
> In addition, professionals tend to look to other professionals to gain
> some measure of self-esteem, are not likely to be devoted to any one
> organization, and accept a value system that puts great emphasis on the
> client's interest.[4]

The bureaucrat is different. Bureaucrats perform specialized and routine activities under the supervision of a hierarchy of officials. Their

loyalty and career are tied up with their organization. Therefore conflict is bound to result when professionals are required to perform like bureaucrats.

Weissman further indicates that one of the crucial functions of professionals is to work for bureaucratic change in the inevitable strains between individual self-actualization and organizational achievement. A major problem in this work is the social worker's failure to distinguish between nonprofit and profit-making organizations: "Money serves as an alarm system in private enterprise: Ford sooner or later must respond to the tension caused by lack of Edsel sales."[5] Yet we in the human services have continued to sell Edsels without an alarm system. Many agencies are judged by the number of Edsels they turn out (the *effort* expended in service), rather than by the consumer's support of the product (the *effect* of services in relation to consumers' needs). Without an effective means of accounting for services offered, nonprofit agencies may not know their problems or how to solve them. Administration has little need to consider the views of lower-level staff, since it will not be penalized if it is not effective. Thus it is essential that all social workers have skills for promoting organizational change and development.

Organizational Change and Development

To make an organization effective requires the use of organizational development methods. A comprehensive definition of organizational development has been devised by John Sherwood:

> Organizational development is an educational process by which human resources are continuously identified, allocated and expanded in ways that make these resources more available to the organization and therefore improve the organization's problem-solving capabilities. The most general objective of organizational development—OD—is to develop self-renewing, self-correcting systems of people who learn to organize themselves in a variety of ways according to the nature of their tasks, and who continue to expand the choices available to the organization as it copes with the changing environment.[6]

There are no specific social work practice theories for organizational development. Most of the recent work, of which there has been an increase in volume, has been primarily in the "pretheory" stage of examining organizational practice and using general management and community organization knowledge to formulate strategies, principles, and skills for changing human service organizations. The major thrust of this recent work is to provide conceptual frameworks for the direct-service staff's development of the organization from within.[7] There are three basic approaches to organizational change and development: (1) rational-empirical, (2) normative-reeducative, and (3) power-coercive.[8]

Rational-Empirical Approach

Behind the rational-empirical approach for organizational change and development is the assumption that people "are guided by reason and . . . will utilize some rational calculus of self-interest in determining needed changes in behavior."[9] The primary proposition is: *If empirical knowledge is made available to all staff in an organization and systems of using this information are established, then the organization will increase its effectiveness by closing the gap between its goals and its means for achieving them.*

In social work, this method requires the dissemination of basic research both to the agencies and to the public at large. On this research are based decisions affecting organizational goals, resource allocation, and the selection of consultants for ongoing evaluation and "action research" (research in which findings are immediately used for change). This approach in social work is perhaps best represented in the works of Howard Freeman and Clarence Sherwood[10] and Carol Weiss.[11]

Normative-Reeducative Approach

The normative-reeducative method rests on assumptions about social action. People are viewed as inherently active and driven by both rational and irrational (yet purposeful) forces. People are in constant transaction with their environment "in the process of shaping organism-environmental relations toward more adequate fitting and joining of organismic demands and environmental resources."[12] In this process, people are guided in their actions by "socially funded and communicated meanings, norms, and institutions, in brief by a normative culture"—that is, by a consensus about ends and means of their work together.[13] The major theoretical proposition is: *If people are involved in working out programs of change and involvement for themselves in organizations, then reeducation in knowledge, values, and skills can improve their functioning and develop self-renewing processes for organizational change.*

The tasks of this approach are designed to improve the organization's problem-solving capabilities and foster growth in the people who make up the organization. Specific interventions of the normative-reeducative method include team building, intergroup problem solving, confrontation, goal setting and planning, third-party help, and consultation.[14] This social work method was developed by Mary Follett[15] and is reflected in the work of Pruger, Compton and Galaway, Patti and Resnick, Askerooth, and Brager and Halloway.

Power-Coercive Approach

The power-coercive approach emphasizes political and economic sanctions and the exercise of power. The assumption behind this approach is that power is inevitable and therefore needs to be used for desirable rather than undesirable goals by those who can marshal it in societal institutions and organizations. The primary theoretical proposition is: *If political and economic power is brought to bear on the goals that the strategists of change regard as desirable, then organizational change will result.* The three general strategies for this change are oriented toward (1) nonviolence or resistance; (2) the use of existing political institutions to achieve change; and (3) recomposition and manipulation of power elites. In social work the primary theorists of power-coercive methods are Frances Fox Piven and Richard Cloward.[16]

The basic methods for organizational change are the strategies of brokerage, advocacy, and consultation. In social work, the method depends on whether one is attempting to influence one's own organization from within or another organization from without. In either case, the first principle for direct-service generalists is to understand their own organization and others in the service network—that is, to know how their structure and functions have been determined. This task requires sophistication and a willingness to be creative within the organizational network. The prerequisite for this understanding is the realization that social work is itself organizational. Rather than trying to escape the organizational environment that affects them in their professional function, social workers need to develop bureaucratic skills to negotiate that environment in behalf of consumers.

The first step is to remove the chip on the shoulder regarding bureaucracy:

> The tremendous range of unanticipated consequences (in formal organizations) provides a gold mine of material for comics like Charlie Chaplin and Jacques Tati who capture with a smile or a shrug the absurdity of authority systems based on pseudologic and inappropriate rules. Almost everybody, including many observers of organizational behavior, approaches bureaucracy with a chip on his shoulder.[17]

The second step is to understand the strategies available for negotiating the organizational environment—both internal and external. First let us look at the strategies for influencing internal change.

Strategies for Internal Development

Pruger's Approach

Useful strategies for internal organizational development have been developed by Robert Pruger in his concept of "the good bureaucrat."[18] The good bureaucrat is the social worker who is able to manage the organizational environment in a manner that maximizes the worker's ability to provide professional services in relation to his or her position. According to Pruger, the good bureaucrat's strategic concerns are the following:

1. "One important property of the good bureaucrat is staying power." Staying power is based on the recognition that change is slow in complex organizations. Social workers cannot influence these changes if they do not stay in the organization. If good bureaucrats do not stay, the "bureaucratic virtuosos" remain to control organizational resources.

2. "The good bureaucrat must somehow maintain . . . vitality of action and independence of thought." To lend their vision of the organization's mission, the good bureaucrats n ıst resist the pressure embedded in organizational roles that can suppress vital action and independent thought.

3. "There is always room for insights and tactics that help the individual preserve and enlarge the discretionary aspect of his activity and, by extension, his sense of personal responsibility." If autonomy is lost in the organization, it is most often because it was given up, perhaps unintentionally, not because it was structurally precluded. The potential for discretionary action increases in relation to the *use* of autonomy and personal responsibility in the organization—especially in early supervisory conferences when workers can help define their jobs and thus influence their discretionary activities.

4. The social worker needs to understand legitimate authority and organizational enforcement. Regulations and codes are inevitably general. This generality permits a great deal of autonomy for the worker who recognizes and uses it. Organizations do not have the power that most social workers assume. If the limits of legitimate authority are recognized, the social worker is in a position to expand his or her discretionary limits by challenging informal roles and behavioral norms.

5. One must conserve energy. Energy is often wasted when workers expect large organizations to give the support received from friends and family. "Complex organizations are notoriously inefficient distributors of appreciation and recognition. He who expects to receive in the bureaucratic milieu the emotional support that is only possible where relationships are intimate is doomed to suffer disappointment." Much energy is also wasted in resisting such bureaucratic paraphernalia as collecting statistics or using the appropriate form. Excessive reporting and other officious demands "can be absorbed without injury to oneself; forms can be completed with dispatch, rather than left to be around and invite resented reminders. Careful distinctions must be drawn between behavior which is truly impersonal and that which is merely businesslike and humorless. Indeed, a sense of humor, if it can be maintained against the relentless frustration of organizational life, is probably the most useful of all in skills needed to conserve energy."

6. The good bureaucrat's strategy requires him or her to "acquire a competence needed by the organization." These skills include proposal writing, community relations, training, and organizational analysis.

7.   The worker needs to abide by the following prescription: "Don't yield unnecessarily to the requirements of administrative convenience. Keep in mind the difference between that which serves the organization and that which serves the consumer." This requires keeping ends and means in clear perspective. Too often the organization's means (rules, standards, norms, forms, directives) become ends. For example, workers must not be more concerned with reporting their mileage than reporting on what transpired in home visits with consumers.

8.   The good bureaucrat remembers that "the good bureaucrat is not necessarily the most beloved one."

Compton and Galaway's Approach

Beulah Roberts Compton and Burt Galaway have suggested strategies for dealing with the organization's policies and procedures. The first question is whether agency policy or the *interpretation* of agency policy is responsible for the obstacles to service. Brokerage and advocacy, two methods for dealing with problems of access to services, begin with knowing the agency's policies and procedures and how they operate—including a thorough understanding of the limits of policy and the authority for interpretation.

As Compton and Galaway explain this process,[19] the worker and the consumer decide on the resource needed to solve the problem. Then the worker discovers exactly what the written statement of policy says. Next the worker considers what that policy actually means and all the different ways to interpret it. The next step is to select the interpretation that will enable the worker to help the consumer. The worker then writes down the interpretation and the way he or she would apply it to the situation. If necessary, this statement may be submitted to the supervisor for approval. In any case, Compton and Galaway suggest that it ought to be made part of the consumer's record of service. What happens when existing policy, or its interpretation, does not permit adequate service to consumers? This shortcoming needs to be documented adequately. The documentation includes specific details of the problem for rational decision making by agency boards. Rather than eloquent complaints, the worker must present the organized *evidence* of his or her position.

In sum, then, Compton and Galaway offer the following principles of organizational change:[20]

1.   Be clear about goals, obstacles, and costs.

2.   Determine the internal and external forces on the organization that contribute to the problem.

3.   Determine who in the organization is responsible for formal decision making in relation to the problem at hand.

4.   Anticipate the consequences of the solution to the problem.

5.   Time your efforts. Agencies are often open to change during critical periods—when budgets are changing, when the number of consumers is changing, when critical performance reports are due, when new methods of dealing with the problem are gaining supporters.

6.   Understand the change process, including the procedures needed for *initiating* change and then *implementing* change. Though the battle to initiate change may be won, the war to implement it may be lost through lack of persistence.

7.   Consider whether advocacy strategies, collaborative strategies, or both will achieve change more effectively. Tactics for advocacy include "the use of citizen groups, unions, and professional organizations to engage with the social worker in litigation, picketing, bargaining, building pressure alliances, contriving for crises to occur, bringing sanctions to bear through external authorities, and encouraging noncompliance with policy by workers and clients." Collaborative tactics require the worker to "provide facts about the nature of the problem; present alternative ways of doing things; try to develop an experimental project that involves different ways of doing things and get permission to implement it." The worker should also try to establish a committee to study the situation and make recommendations for change. Moreover, he or she should attempt to improve the agency's working climate so that people can look beyond securing their own position to the task ahead. Professional values and ethics should be stressed throughout. Logical argument should be used to persuade. And, finally, the worker must point out what is really happening under the present policy.

Patti and Resnick's Approach

Rino Patti and Herman Resnick have formulated a three-phase method for changing the agency from within: formulation of goals, mobilization of resources, and intervention.[21] During the first phase, goal formulation, the direct-service social worker needs to identify the organizational problem and specify the changes, or goals, desired. Goals must be considered on the basis of *who* influences decisions related to the problem and their resistance or support of the specific proposal for change.

Agreement or disagreement on change is analyzed on the basis of three types: issue consensus, issue difference, and issue dissensus. *Issue consensus* refers to basic agreement among parties on how issues should be resolved. *Issue difference* refers to situations in which decision-makers do not recognize or understand the substance of a change proposal. *Issue dissensus* refers to situations in which decision-makers do not share the interests of those who propose the change. This analysis helps to determine goal feasibility and to test the commitment to work for change.

Resource mobilization, the second phase, requires an analysis of the power available to the social worker and others who support the change. Their power resources include both the *types* of power and the *attributes* of the workers. The five types of power are:

1. *Coercion*—the capacity to reward and punish

2. *Referent*—the ability of a person or group to attract others, to be a role model with whom others wish to identify

3. *Expertise*—the possession of knowledge and information important to others

4. *Legitimacy*—the capacity to invoke authority in the organization

5. *Value*—the ability to express values to which others are drawn

The *source* of power lies in certain attributes of the worker:

1. *Cosmopolitan orientation*—identifying with social causes through professional values and norms

2. *Informal leadership*—being sought out by other staff members for advice and support

3. *Education and experience*—having special skills and prestige needed by the organization

4. *Specialized knowledge*—being able to influence the case made by those who propose change through knowledge

Together these attributes and types of power constitute the real resources available to initiate and implement change. Table 12.1 depicts the nature of these resources.

Table 12.1 Power Resources for
Organizational Change from Within

	Worker's Attributes			
Types of Powers	Cosmopolitan Orientation	Informal Leadership	Education and Experience	Specialized Knowledge
Coercion	M	L	M	H
Referent	M	H	L	L
Expertise	L	M	H	H
Legitimacy	L	H	M	L
Value	H	M	L	L

H = high relationship; M = medium relationship; L = low relationship.

Intervention, the third phase, includes the selection and implementation of change strategies. According to Patti and Resnick, these strategies are based on a continuum ranging from fundamental agreement to fundamental disagreement between the "action system" (those who support the change) and the "target system" (those who must be influenced for change to take place) with regard to the substance of the proposed change. *Collaborative strategies* come into play when action and target systems are in essential agreement about needed changes and are willing to modify their goals to accommodate each other's needs and interests. A collaborative strategy may involve the following activities:

1. Providing information about the problem

2. Presenting alternative courses of action (programs, procedures, and the like)

3. Requesting support for new approaches to the problem (perhaps new forms of service delivery)

4. Seeking to establish a committee to study alternative approaches to the problem

5. Creating new opportunities for members of the action system and target system to express ideas and feelings, build trust, and learn better ways to communicate with one another

6. Making appeals to conscience, professional ethics, and values

7. Persuading by logical argument

8. Pointing out the undesirable consequence of continuing a certain policy

If the action system and target system are not in agreement about the change proposal, *adversary strategies* come into play. In selecting adversary strategies, the action system is convinced that the target system must find it more costly to adhere to the existing arrangement than to adopt the proposed change and that the organization's failure to respond will be more dysfunctional in the short or long term than any negative consequence that may result from instituting the plan. An adversary strategy may involve the following activities:

1. Submitting to the administration petitions that set forth its demands

2. Confronting the target system openly in agency meetings and public forums

3. Bringing sanctions against the agency through external funding, setting standards, and professional agencies

4. Engaging in public criticism and exposing organizational practices through the communications media

5. Encouraging deliberate noncompliance with agency policy or interference with agency procedures

6. Calling strikes

7. Picketing

8. Engaging in litigation

9. Bargaining for the purpose of negotiating differences and developing compromise solutions

Patti and Resnick have developed a basic framework for relating strategies to goals and resources. Collaborative strategies are most effective in situations of issue consensus when the power resources are specialized knowledge, expertise, and education and experience. Collaborative strategies are also appropriate, at least initially, in situations of issue difference when the power resources of cosmopolitan orientation, value, referent, and informal resources are available. When goals are marked by issue dissensus and when coercive and informal leadership power are available, adversary strategies increase in effectiveness. Both strategies, collaborative and adversary, require the systematic use of informal sources of power—referent, value, cosmopolitan orientation, informal leadership, expertise, and education and experience. In all organizational change, the social worker needs to use the full range of strategies available—selecting those that are likely to be effective according to an assessment of the action system's and target system's goals and power resources.

Askerooth's Approach

Gary Askerooth has developed a strategy for changing agencies from within that is based on phasic principles (sequential steps) for practice.[22] His model assumes that the worker has at least a moderate degree of freedom. (Workers at the lowest level of the organizational hierarchy are considered more effective acting *outside* the organization to influence organizational change.) For changing the agency from within, the strategy includes three phases, each continuing as the next is initiated: (1) *preparation,* in which administration's confidence is gained; (2) *process,* during which change objectives are proposed and supported by steady communication; and (3) *establishment,* at which point decision-makers are convinced that changes are useful to them and the formal organization. The following list summarizes the six principles of change that emanate from these phases:

Preparation phase	1. Increase your interpersonal competence.
	2. Make yourself useful (if possible indispensable) to the organization.
Process phase	1. Stress the increase in organizational effectiveness that will result from the desired change.
	2. Maintain a high degree of communication with all levels in the organization.
Establishment phase	1. Gain acceptance of change through professional responsibility and power of ideas.
	2. Gain acceptance of change by reducing managerial insecurity and ensuring that work flow is not disrupted.

These principles are based on a process orientation toward the organization that regards the emotional needs of members as more important than their intellectual needs in the acceptance and rejection of changes. The six principles outlined above use the managers' emotional needs and problems to justify organizational development. As Askerooth notes:

> Increasing interpersonal competence, for example, means the change agent must expand his ability to be responsive to the needs of others within the organization. . . . Simple tactics such as communicating empathy with a supervisor or expressing personal feelings of admiration for a commendable action are extremely useful. This relationship should, however, be cemented by actions that convince the hierarchy of your competence on the job.[23]

Once the social worker has gained the supervisor's confidence, the worker can encourage his or her perception of changes as *solutions* rather than as new problems. For example: "You've been having trouble lately with some clients disrupting the office schedule demanding information about their rights. Why not publish a little booklet that we can give them and cut down on our wasted time?" In follow-up, informal groups can be organized to discuss a proposed change—for example, a workers' efficiency advisory group. These groups can present themselves to management as "concerned members" of the organization. Finally, to establish a change it is often necessary to relieve the administrator's fears that new and greater problems will be created. This can be done by assuring that workers will accept the change as a professional responsibility and by helping to set up a procedure for implementing the change.

Brager and Holloway's Approach

To these schemes for organizational change George Brager and Stephen Holloway add the importance of a *force-field assessment* from which to select change tactics.[24] This assessment begins with the identification of the principal actors in the system who maintain the status quo in reference to change, the driving forces for change, and the restraining forces against this change in the organization. Each force is then evaluated from the perspective of its amenability to change, its influence on the situation, and its consistency as an influence on both the status quo and desirable change. When this balance sheet is totaled, the bottom line suggests the chances of success, primary targets, and appropriate tactics for organizational development.

The change itself follows this assessment. Most often, the process of change includes (1) preparing the organization for change, (2) initiating the change, and (3) implementing and institutionalizing (maintaining) the change. These steps are distinct in the following example of a direct-service social worker who developed organizational resources to meet consumer needs.[25]

A school social worker noticed that some of the foreign students were getting into trouble at the local high school and getting worse grades than might be expected from their school records. As she obtained information on the problem, she soon discovered that no provision was being made for the fact that they spoke little English. She felt that their problems in school were related to this deficit and therefore enlisted the aid of a community worker and three teachers.

After a series of evening meetings and lunchtime sessions, this newly formed group decided on a simple proposal. They would establish an English-speaking class for the eighteen students; involve administrators, parents, teachers, and students to consider their ideas and gain their support; and organize the project so that costs, both financial and psychological, would be minimal. They would consider their job done only when the school system had incorporated this class into the budget for the following year.

The action system group then initiated contracts with the parents of these young people—who were quite enthusiastic about the plan and were able to provide funds for the project. More important, the group found a volunteer who would teach the class twice a week after school. They also met with the building administrators, who, even though reluctant to start such a program in midyear, did provide a room in the basement of the school. Two meetings with the teachers were held to inform them of the project and the reasons behind it. The students themselves were approached individually and in groups to obtain their commitment to participate in this class after school.

These activities took place over a six-week period, and by the seventh week the students were installed in the class. They began their work on the English language with an instructor from the same ethnic background. The action system group then met with the administrators to plan how the course, its finances, legitimation, and instruction would be taken over by the school system next year. This meeting, too, was successful.

In recent years the social work literature has been demonstrating the value of the advocacy methods used in this example of organizational development. They do seem to work. When social workers move beyond mere resentment of bureaucratic constraints to their practice and develop the skills for changing organizations from within, they can translate "organization" into "organizing"—the self-renewing, ever-evolving extension of consumer-centered goals and processes.

Strategies for External Development

One of the basic dilemmas of advocacy is that the worker who has the power to be an effective advocate from within is often cautious when it comes to championing the social victims of organizations from without.[26] Robert MacRae has described this worker: "While his heart may lead him to the barricades, his head will tell him that his contribution will be greater if his effort is directed toward the education of the influential leaders by whom he is employed."[27] In these situations, increasing the power of the powerless requires advocacy methods for changing organizations from without.

Askerooth, among others, has designed a strategy for exerting external influence on organizational development. His social action and conflict strategy is based on two interdependent principles: (1) creating crises for bureaucracies and (2) widening the range of choices for the powerless. This strategy uses competition and conflict tactics related to the escalation of issues in the process of change. Table 12.2 summarizes these tactics and countertactics.

Table 12.2 Escalation in
Changing Organizations from Without

Bureaucratic Tactic	Worker Countertactic	Strategy
1. Appeal to rules	1. Know rules better than bureaucrat	Congruence: The strategy of competition
2. Lack of resources	2. Knowledge of organization; informal contacts in organization	
3. Pseudorealism	3. Knowledge of external power vectors (connections with informal community influentials)	Incongruence: The strategy of conflict
4. Naked power	4. Skilled use of people power	

Askerooth's approach assumes that the bureaucrat will try to avoid any disruptions of routine. Therefore this first tactic, one of legitimacy, will most likely be an appeal to bureaucratic procedure: "Rules are rules. You know this is against the rules. We can't make an exception in your case." Knowing the rules better than the bureaucrat can allow the social worker to refer to a counterrule that authorizes the "exception" sought.

The next bureaucratic tactic may likely be the argument that although the rules do not prohibit serving the consumer, the organization lacks the resources: "Yes, I agree your consumer has a right to this service, but we have no staff or money." In keeping with a competition strategy (neither party challenges the other's legitimacy but questions his or her interpretation of service), the worker responds to this tactic by working from within the organization. This worker attempts to influence opinion leaders in the organization's informal power structure. This worker seeks others in the organization who agree with the requests or are at least ambivalent about their agency's formal stance on the matter. Moreover, this worker gives information on the agency's response as ammunition to cliques within the organization who are contesting the system's manner of operating.

If this tactic does not work, the organization may attempt to create an illegitimate situation by "pseudorealism" tactics: "OK. You caught us. We should be providing this service. But we're not and we won't start now. Be realistic. There's nothing you can do about it. We're big and you're small. Stop wasting your time and energy and go away." This power tactic needs to be counterattacked by a similar tactic. Workers who know the agency well enough can respond with their own call for realism. That is, every organization is vulnerable to outside attack if the worker can prove that it is blatantly nonresponsive to consumers. Powerful figures outside the organization (the board of directors, funding sources, regulatory agencies, respected community influentials, the executive's family) can be used to confront this nonresponsiveness.

If the power struggle escalates beyond this stage (and it seldom does), the bureaucrat's next tactic is often one of "naked power"—that is, a threat of harm (retaliation, tarnishing the worker's professional reputation, and the like). At this point the worker must respond with the best power resource available: people. He or she needs to create a social movement, a group of citizens who are sufficiently moved by the injustices of the organization to expose the situation to the public at large. In view of the organization's illegitimate tactics, public relations are generally easy to come by. No organization is immune to an indignant public. As Watergate attests, not even the most powerful can be sanctioned without public support and trust.

Like organizational change from within, change from without requires a basic acceptance that services are delivered through organizations. The effective generalist will use the strategies for organizational development to work with indirect consumers in behalf of the individual. The social worker will not leave the responsibility of organizational development to the bureaucratic virtuosos who turn organizational means into organizational ends. In a phrase, whether working within or without, the effective generalist will become "a good bureaucrat." Your organizational change skills will increase your ability as a bureacratic professional and decrease your susceptibility to become a professional bureaucrat.

Summary

The direct-service generalist needs skills for working with service networks toward organizational development in behalf of the individual and other direct consumers. This work requires an understanding of organizational dynamics, an attitude of creative challenge to counterbalance the frustrations in dealing with organizational change, and the skills for bringing about internal and external change.

The methods for these changes, while not yet formulated into practice theories, are based on rational-empirical, normative-reeducative, and power-coercive approaches. The methods for organizational development, brokerage, and advocacy have been predominantly normative-reeducative. The best-developed strategies are those of Pruger, Compton and Galaway, Patti and Resnick, Brager and Holloway, and Askerooth. Through their contributions, social work has cemented a foundation on which future practice theory for organizational development can be built.

Suggested Learning Experiences

An excellent resource for organizational development and change skills in relation to theory is William C. Morris and Marshall Sashkin, *Organization Behavior in Action: Skill Building Experiences* (New York: West Publishing Co., 1976). This book and the Instructor's Manual that accompanies it offer conceptual, structured experience, case study, and simulation activities for organizational development. Another useful resource is the work of University Associates, 7596 Eads Avenue, La Jolla, CA 92037. Their six volumes of *Structured Experiences* and the *Annual Handbook for Group Facilitators* (1972–1979) offer a wealth of experiential and conceptual learning skills to influence organizational development. A number of excellent case illustrations can be gleaned from George Brager and Stephen Holloway, *Changing Human Service Organizations: Politics and Practice* (New York: Free Press, 1978).

Suggested Case Studies

In addition to the case studies listed at the end of Chapter 3 are the following. Each includes several examples of organizational change strategies in action.

Gitterman, Alex. "Social Work in the Public School System." *Social Casework* 58(2) (1977): 111–118.

Resnick, Herman. "Effecting Internal Change in Human Service Organizations." *Social Casework* 58(11) (1977):546–553.

Shulman, Lawrence. "Change in the Institutional Community." In *A Casebook of Social Work with Groups: The Mediating Model*. New York: Council on Social Work Education, 1968.

Chapter Thirteen   Communities

Introduction

When the direct-service generalist works with indirect consumers in behalf of direct consumers and others like them (Quadrant D of the framework presented in Chapter 2), the focus is on the community. The method of choice is community organization and development. In this context, community refers to both a "geographic community and a functional community."[1] A *geographic community* is "an aggregation of families and individuals, settled in a fairly compact and contiguous geographic area, with significant elements of common life, as shown by manners, customs, traditions, and modes of speech."[2] A *functional community* is a group of people who share some common interest or function, such as welfare, agriculture, education, or religion. Therefore, for purposes of discussing practice theory, the methods of community organization and development include policy or program development and cause advocacy. The major target systems for all these methods have geographic or functional boundaries equivalent in theory to work with communities.

Arthur Dunham has defined community organization in a manner that specifies its development objectives:

> Community organization . . . means a conscious process of social inter-action and a method of social work concerned with any or all of the following objectives: (a) The meeting of broad needs and . . . maintaining adjustment between needs and resources in a community or other area; (b) helping people to deal more effectively with their problems and objectives, by helping them develop, strengthen, and maintain qualities of participation, self-direction, and cooperation; (c) bringing about changes in community and group relationships and in the distribution of decision-making power."[3]

These three objectives can be designated *task goals, process goals,* and *relationship* (or reallocation of power) *goals.* The different strategies for achieving these goals in work with communities have influenced the development of three different practice theories. In some of these theories, the approaches are distinguished by the emphasis placed on the development of mutual aid systems in the community (process and relationship goals) or on the solution of specific problems (task goals).

Community Organization and
Development Approaches

In a seminal article on community organization and development, Jack Rothman identified three general approaches that differentiate practice theories.[4] He writes: "There appear to be at least three important orientations to deliberate . . . community change in contemporary American communities, both urban and rural. . . . We may best refer to them as . . . models A, B, and C, although they can roughly be given the appellations respectively of *locality development, social planning,* and *social action.*"

These three approaches set priorities on particular goals, tap different dimensions of the community, use different change strategies, and demand different practitioner roles. While there is some overlap among the approaches in these areas, Rothman regards their basic differences as follows. Model A (locality development) presupposes that community change may be pursued through broad participation of a wide spectrum of people at the local level. Model B (social planning) emphasizes a technical process of problem solving with regard to substantive social problems such as delinquency, housing, and mental health. Model C (social action) presupposes a disadvantaged segment of the population that needs to be organized, perhaps in alliance with others, in order to make demands on the community for increased resources or social justice. Table 13.1 presents the characteristics of these three approaches.

Locality Development

Goals

The social work progenitors of locality development approach are William and Loureide Biddle,[5] Murray Ross, Arthur Dunham, and Charles Grosser.[6] These writers place great emphasis on process goals. Their central focus is on the community's capacity to become functionally integrated, to engage in cooperative problem solving on a self-help basis, and to use its democratic processes for decision making and action. The intent is to develop the community's inherent self-actualization processes. Ross, for instance, states this most directly in his definition of community organization as a process by which a community identifies its needs, orders them, develops the confidence to work at them, finds the resources to deal with them, takes action in respect to them, and in so doing develops cooperative attitudes in the community.[7]

Focus

To these process and self-help goals Dunham adds the specific problem-solving process and skills for locality development. His focus is on

Table 13.1 Characteristics of Practice
Theories for Work with Communities

Characteristic	Locality Development Approach	Social Planning Approach	Social Action Approach
Goals			
Self-help	H	L	M
Problem solving	M	H	L
Reallocation of power	M	L	H
Process	H	L	M
Task	L	H	M
Main dimensions			
Anomie/alienation	H	L	M
Interpersonal relationships	H	L	L
Democratic problem-solving capacities	H	L	M
Social problems	M	H	M
Disadvantaged populations	L	M	H
Social injustice	M	M	H
Change strategies			
Broad-based participation in problem definition	H	M	L
Intergroup communication	H	L	M
Small-group discussion	H	L	L
Building consensus	H	M	L
Fact gathering for rational decision making	M	H	M
Conflict intensification	L	M	H
Crystallization of issues	M	L	H
Organization of people against targets	L	L	H
Confrontation	M	L	H
Direct action	L	L	H
Negotiation	M	L	H
Worker's stance			
Enabler-catalyst	H	L	M
Coordinator	H	M	L
Teacher of problem solving skills	H	L	M
Teacher of ethical values	H	L	L
Fact-gatherer and analyst	M	H	M
Program implementer	L	H	H
Facilitator	H	M	L
Activist-advocate	M	L	H
Agitator	L	L	H
Broker	M	L	H
Negotiator	M .	L	H
Partisan	L	L	H
Constituents			
Citizens	H	M	L
Consumers	M	H	M
Victims	L	L	H

H = high emphasis; M = moderate emphasis; L = low emphasis.

Table 13.2 Ross–Dunham Model
of Community Development

Ross's Process Steps	Dunham's Problem-Solving Steps
1. Community identifies its needs.	1. Recognition of one problem
2. Community establishes priority of needs.	2. Analysis (fact finding)
3. Community develops the will to work on needs.	3. Planning
4. Community finds necessary resources.	4. Action
5. Community takes action.	5. Evaluation
6. Community extends and develops cooperative attitudes.	

one specific problem toward which community resources are mobilized in analysis, planning, action, and evaluation.[8] Table 13.2 shows how the works of Ross and Dunham relate to the goals and procedures of locality development.

The perspective on the local community and the dimensions tapped are related to the problem of alienation as a result of technological change in society. The concern is with people's dignity, feelings of belonging, democratic problem-solving skills, and personal self-actualization within a mutual aid community. Ross sums up these basic assumptions about the local community in our postindustrial and urban society: "This is the problem of man's loss of his essential human dignity. For surely man is being overwhelmed by forces of which he is only dimly aware, which subjugate him to a role of decreasing importance and present him with problems with which he has no means to cope. Aspects of this central problem are the difficulty of full expression of a democratic philosophy and the threats to the mental health of individual members of society."[9] The locality development theorists argue that the antidote to this alienation is full participation in community affairs.

Strategies

This perspective on the community suggests change strategies that emphasize the unity of community life and the participation of *all* groups in the community—both sexes, all ages, all racial, ethnic, religious, economic, social, and cultural groups. Rothman depicts the basic change strategy thus: "In locality development the change strategy may be characterized as 'Let's all get together and talk this over'—an effort to get a wide range of community people involved in determining their felt needs and solving their own problems."[10] Toward this broad-based participation in problem definition and solution, much consensus building is developed in intergroup and small-group discussion.

Roles

The social worker's characteristic role in locality development is that of an enabler, facilitator, or encourager. This role involves modeling problem-solving skills and valuing collaborative work. As an enabler, the worker promotes a process of problem solving by helping people express their discontent toward issues, encouraging organization, nourishing sensitive and purposeful interpersonal relationships, and emphasizing common objectives. The emphasis is on procedural issues and not on particular tasks or problems. For instance, Biddle and Biddle regard the encourager as one who "has been responsible for initiating a growth of initiative in others. He has been party to a process of participant-guided learning of the habits of responsibility, of applied intelligence, and of ethical sensitivity. The indigenous process he has started . . . is one of growth in democratic competence."[11]

Grosser has added the roles of broker, negotiator, and advocate to neighborhood organization in urban communities.[12] While his conception of neighborhood responsibility for determining problems, priorities, and objectives is consistent with the locality development approach, he notes the *activist* roles demanded of social workers serving complex urban areas.

In the locality development approach, constituents are likely to be conceived as normal citizens with inherent strengths that are not fully developed. They need the social worker to help them focus these abilities. Biddle and Biddle express this point of view best: "Each person is valuable, unique, and capable of growth toward greater social sensitivity and responsibility. . . . Each person has underdeveloped abilities in initiative, originality, and leadership. These qualities can be cultivated and strengthened."[13] The locality development approach has evolved the participatory means toward these ends.

Social Planning

Goals

The primary theorists for the social planning approach to community organization and development are Robert Morris and Robert Binstock,[14] Roland Warren,[15] Alfred Kahn,[16] and Robert Perlman and Arnold Gurin.[17] They stress task goals oriented toward the solution of substantive social problems. Social planning is the application of a social problem-solving process to achieve particular goals. Kahn's succinct definition of social planning is "policy choice and programming in the light of fact, projections, and application of values."[18] In his model, the planning process includes (1) instigation, (2) exploration, (3) definition of the planning task, (4) policy formulation (the standing plan), (5) programming, and (6) evaluation, monitoring, and feedback.

Focus

This approach focuses on specific social problems. The community is viewed as a collection of social problems or the locus of a specific problem of special interest to the planner, such as housing, health, employment, recreation. All social planning practice theories begin with the definition of the problem to be addressed. The change strategies for social planning are described by Rothman in these terms:

> In planning, the basic change strategy is one of "Let's get the facts and take the logical next steps." In other words, let us gather pertinent facts about the problem and decide on a rational and feasible course of action. The practitioner plays a central part in gathering and analyzing facts and determining appropriate services, programs, and actions. This may or may not be done with the participation of others, depending upon the planner's sense of utility of participation in the given situation and the organizational context within which he functions.[19]

Strategies

The significant skills for social planning are analytical and fact-finding skills. These tasks determine whether conflict or consensus tactics will be used during the interaction with others in the planning process. Perlman and Gurin have related these tasks to social problem solving. Table 13.3 reflects their model.

Roles

The worker's basic stance for social planning is that of technical expert. This role emphasizes fact finding and analysis, program implementation, and relationships with various bureaucratic organizations. Much work is done in influencing formal organizations, especially interorganizational relationships, as well as in data collection and analysis.

In this approach, the constituent is conceived as the consumer of services to which the plan is directed—mental health, health, public housing, recreation, welfare benefits. Morris and Binstock specifically refer to "consumers" rather than "clients" in their social planning framework. But in this case, unlike the other approaches, the planning is done *for* rather than *with* consumers. Morris and Binstock note:

> Opportunities for members and consumers to determine policy are severely limited because they are not usually organized for this purpose. If they are organized, and if the central issue which brings them together

Table 13.3 Social Problem-Solving
Phases and Tasks

Phase	Analytical Tasks	Interactional Tasks
1. Defining the problem	Studying the problematic aspects of a situation. Conceptualizing the system of relevant actors. Assessing the opportunities and limits set by the organization employing the planner and by others.	Eliciting and receiving information, grievances, preferences.
2. Building structure	Defining the planner's relationship to others. Deciding on structures to be developed. Choosing people as experts, communicators, influencers.	Establishing formal and informal communication lines. Recruiting people into structures and roles and obtaining their commitment to address the problem.
3. Formulating policy	Analyzing past efforts to deal with the problem. Developing alternative goals and strategies. Assessing their consequences and feasibility. Recommending options to decision-makers.	Communicating alternatives to others. Determining their preferences and testing their acceptance of alternatives.
4. Implementing plans	Specifying the tasks for achieving goals, by whom, when, and with what resources and procedures.	Presenting requirements to decision-makers, overcoming resistance, obtaining commitment to the program. Marshaling resources and implementing procedures.
5. Monitoring	Designing systems for collecting information on operations. Analyzing data and specifying adjustments needed and new problems that require planning and action.	Obtaining information on others' experiences. Communicating findings and recommendations and preparing others for new decision making.

is sufficiently strong, they are likely to withdraw to form a separate organization. If the issue is weak the opportunity to control policy is short-lived because the coalition will fall apart, lacking sufficient incentive to bind together the otherwise diverse constituent elements.[20]

While consumers are often consulted, there is usually little effort to organize them in their own behalf in this approach.

Recently the theorists of social planning have considered the use of social action strategies to crystallize issues, synthesize differences, and avoid the elitism of planning experts deciding what is best for consumers. For instance, Peter Morris, Martin Rein and Armand Lauffer have analyzed the problem of elitism in planning for social reform.[21] Morris and Binstock emphasize the limitations in community development in their definition of planning as the attempt of a single worker, possessing limited influence, to change the policies of formal organizations in order to improve social welfare. It is in assuring that consumers' needs are represented in the social planning process that the direct-service social worker can contribute to policy development and planning. This task requires an intimate knowledge of planning bodies and their interorganizational functioning in the planning process. The direct-service worker is thus in a strategic position to give flesh and blood to the planners' cerebral concept of priorities.

Warren suggests that the direct-service social worker and the social planner represent the polar extremes of "love" and "truth" in social planning. He states the issue from the social change perspective of the social planner:

> Truth and love come into conflict distressingly often, not least in the field of social change. When we speak of channeling social change, do we really mean getting people to jump through our hoops?
>
> There are at least two issues involved here. One is the question whether we really know enough about social change to know whether it can be channeled, and if so, whether we have the knowledge necessary to do the actual channeling. The other plummets us into the value questions. If we channel change, . . . we must presumably guide change in accordance with some preconceived end. But whose end? On the other hand, if we do not have a preconceived end or goal, can we really be serious when we use a term like channeling, which means guiding?
>
> Finally, if it is our end toward which we wish to bend the course of events, are we not, in effect, saying that we want to get people to jump through our hoops? Are we not, in effect, saying that we want to help people decide things for themselves so long as they decide them in our way?[22]

To integrate these two principles—the principle of self-determination based on love for each individual's dignity and worth and the principle of purposive social change based on the truth of social planning expertise—requires a commitment to *dynamic pluralism.* Dynamic pluralism places a high priority not on smoothing over differences but quite the contrary—on emphasizing differences. To this end the planning process requires creative confrontation of different interest groups within acceptable boundaries. The participatory mechanisms will not necessarily satisfy all parties to every controversy, but they will assure the right of the dissatisfied to be heard.

Social Action

Goals

Practice theories for the social action approach to community organization and development have been proposed by Saul Alinsky,[23] Warren Haggstrom,[24] Roland Warren, Daniel Thursz,[25] and Charles Grosser. In this approach, the primary goals include the shifting of power, resources, and decision making in the community or society, as well as, on a short-term basis, changing the policies of formal organizations. The major objective is system change. Some social action organizations, such as civil rights groups and cause-oriented organizations (for instance, welfare rights), emphasize specific legislation (higher welfare grants) or social conditions (discriminatory practices toward minority groups). These objectives all require change in the policies of formal organizations. Other social action groups emphasize process-related goals, such as the building of a constituency that can acquire and exercise power. Alinsky's Industrial Areas Foundation and militant black power groups are examples. The aim is more the building of local power and decision-making centers than the solution of a specific problem.

Focus

While changing the system is the primary goal, small-scale or short-range problems are often addressed. These tasks are undertaken because they are feasible, they help to build organizations, and they contribute to the participants' self-esteem. Haggstrom cites self-esteem as a major element in his use of social action for the poor: "One way in which the poor can remedy the psychological consequences of their powerlessness and of the image of the poor as worthless is for them to undertake social action that redefines them as potentially worthwhile and individually more powerful."[26]

In the social action approach the community is conceived as a hierarchy of position, privilege, and power in which clusters of the deprived and the powerless suffer from social injustice. In Alinsky's terms, every community has the "haves, the have-nots, and the have-a-little-want-more." The have-nots are particularly oppressed by the haves through such power structures as government, corporations, or social stratification in the community and the society at large. The powerful control the community's resources. The powerless have a right to decide how to live and what services they need in the allocation of these resources. The solution to community development is thus a more equitable distribution of power. Power comes from two sources: money and people. Since most of the powerless groups, such as the poor, do not have money, their only source of power is themselves. Therefore they must organize to use this power for more equitable community development.

Strategies

The basic change strategies are crystallizing issues and organizing people to take action in their own behalf against the targets—those in power. Rothman describes the basic approach:

In social action, the change strategy may be articulated as "Let's organize to destroy our oppressor"—crystallizing issues so that people know who their legitimate enemy is and organizing mass action to bring pressure on selected targets. Such targets may include an organization, such as the urban renewal authority; a person, such as the mayor; or an aggregate of persons, such as slum landlords.[27]

The strategies are often conflict-oriented and include the tactics of confrontation and direct action. The conflict is against the "enemy," which in general is The Establishment. Municipal government, social welfare agencies (viewed as representatives of "welfare colonialism"), big business—all are seen as instruments of exploitation. All strategies include the mobilization of large numbers of people for rallies, marches, boycotts, picketing, public disruptions, and sit-ins. To Alinsky, all social action involves this basic conflict:

> A people's organization is a conflict group. This must be openly and fully recognized. Its sole reason for coming into being is to wage war against all evils which cause suffering and unhappiness. . . . A people's organization is the banding together of multitudes of men and women to fight for those rights which insure a decent way of life. . . . A people's organization is dedicated to an external war. . . . A war is not an intellectual debate, and in the war against social evils there are no rules of fair play. . . . There can be no compromises. It is life or death.[28]

Warren and Haggstrom have both mentioned strategies that supplement direct conflict in their social action approaches. Warren suggests a variation in conflict tactics according to the degree of issue agreement among the parties involved in social change. *Campaign strategies* are more appropriate when there are differences among parties but issue consensus can eventually be reached. *Contest strategies* are more appropriate when the opponent refuses to recognize the issue or opposes the people's organization proposal so that issue dissensus seems strongly entrenched.

Haggstrom notes that organizations which avoid social conflict altogether tend not to be successful.[29] However, he also notes that there are a number of ways of motivating people (in low-income areas, for example), besides conflict. One is self-responsibility—directing the action themselves. Moreover, there are various self-help programs in which they have a stake, such as building their own housing. Finally, he suggests that the social welfare network itself might have a part to play. The network's role is one of innovation, evaluating efforts that are going on, and interpreting the organization of the poor to the remainder of the community. Social welfare organizations in this context are not inherently enemies of the victims of social injustice or instruments of the powerful. They can mediate between community vectors of power in support of social action objectives for community development.

Roles

The social action approach, therefore, incorporates what Grosser has termed "advocate or activist roles." Grosser regards the advocate as a partisan in social conflicts—one whose expertise is available exclusively to serve specific consumer interests. Social action roles require organization of consumer groups to promote their own interests in the community arena. Many activities are geared to creating and influencing mass organizations and political processes. This effort requires such additional roles as agitator, broker, and negotiator in the rough and tumble bargaining that can result in the community's reallocation of resources.

The constituency is normally a community segment that is powerless and disadvantaged (blacks, the poor, migrant workers, women who work, children). They are viewed as victims of various forces in society and the community. It is for this constituency that the social worker works and participates in mass action and pressure group activities.

As Thursz has indicated, social action may be a responsible approach for any social worker—either individually or in conjunction with an organization or coalition of organizations. One channel for this work is local and state chapters of the National Association of Social Workers. This voluntary organization has traditionally given rise to activities that have come to be considered as "social reform" movements in social work practice. The direct-service generalist who uses the social action approach can sometimes find organized support in these professional groups.

Community Practice Theories in Action

How might the direct-service social worker use these approaches to community organization and development? This section demonstrates the application of these approaches by the worker in the county child welfare agency dealing with the Green family. In Chapter 9, we recall, the worker met individually with Mrs. Green, in Chapter 10 with the Green family as a group, and in Chapter 11 with Jake Green in a goup of boys aged nine to eleven. During this work with the Green family and others like them, the worker has learned that many parents could prevent child abuse if they had some instruction in parenthood or participation in a group of parents who would help each other prevent abuse. The worker is aware of communities that have sponsored parenting classes and Parents Anonymous groups to reduce the incidence of child abuse.[30] The Green's community has neither of these resources, however, and the worker wishes to establish them through the community organization method. If you were this worker, what would be your goals and plans? Where and how would you begin? The answers to these questions could depend greatly on the approach you select for working with communities. Now let us see how these approaches might be applied in action.

Locality Development Approach

The worker using the locality development approach would not start with preconceived solutions (parenting classes and Parents Anonymous groups). Rather, this worker would attempt to create a broad-based group concerned with a general problem—for example, the community's responsibility in preventing child abuse. This worker may begin with an open public hearing on the problem—a hearing that has been well publicized in the local news media. From this hearing would emerge not only the participants' agreement on how child abuse could be prevented in this community but also the initial goals, solutions, and strategies.

The hearing might conclude with three major proposals reflecting the general consensus of those in attendance: (1) providing better birth control services to prevent unwanted children through unwanted pregnancies; (2) establishing parenting classes to teach parents such skills as communicating with their children and disciplining them without using physical punishment; and (3) educating the community on the nature of child abuse and the help available from the child welfare agency.

The worker, as enabler and encourager, may suggest that the participants at the hearing organize into three groups based on these three goals. What do they think should be done and who else must become involved to achieve the particular goal? With this initial commitment of participants, the beginnings of an organization, and the seeking of resources, the worker may press for the appointment (or election) of a group leader and subgroup leader to coordinate activities. The worker may serve as a consultant to these leaders in the ongoing activities, continuing to encourage broad-based participation, democratic decision making, and cooperative attitudes and practices.

Social Planning Approach

The worker using the social planning approach would begin with the goals of establishing parenting classes and Parents Anonymous groups. Data would be gathered (from service consumers and other community experts) to document the need. Experts on the use of these programs to prevent child abuse would be consulted. The worker might very well assemble this information in a formal position paper to be discussed with organizations who might sponsor such a program. At this point in the planning process, key decision-makers in these organizations would be targeted for these recommendations and their interest would be tested.

For instance, this community has a Mental Health Association made up of private citizens and professionals who may be influenced to sponsor a Parents Anonymous group. The school systems throughout the county may be considered as potential resources for sponsoring parenting classes as part of their evening adult classes, and superintendents and school boards may be presented with the current position paper. Moreover, this worker may have discovered in the problem definition phase that some states require counties, as part of their child protective services, to offer instruction in parenthood and to develop self-help groups such as Parents Anonymous; in fact, some states even fund these programs.[31] In this case, the worker may recommend sponsorship to key state legislators and administrators concerned about services to prevent child abuse. If there is a commitment to the program by decision-makers at the local and state levels, this worker would most likely bring them together to work out the details for establishing these programs.

Social Action Approach

The worker using the social action approach would be more concerned with the self-defined needs of a disadvantaged or handicapped group—such as abusing parents and their children who lack preventive services. This concern has led to the development of community "child advocacy" programs that sanction an adversary stance to the community power structure.[32] In this approach, the worker may organize the consumers themselves—the abusing parents—and other concerned citizens and mobilize them toward action on behalf of children in need in the community. A child advocacy organization would use social action to confront the existing service system in order to meet their self-defined needs. The target here would be "the planning system, the budget, the nature of service arrangements, or any other service or administrative functions."[33]

As the group is established on a self-help basis to monitor current community services for children and to be involved in both case and cause advocacy, the worker may disengage from the organization (while offering moral support). This worker, remember, is part of the system. As Kahn, Kamerman, and McGowan point out, the most effective child advocacy organizations are led by those who are not part of the service delivery system—even though they may have been given their early impetus by professionals like the generalist social worker in this example.[34]

Which Approach Is Best?

The practice theories for community organization and development, like those for casework, family group work, and group work, apply differently, affecting the worker's goals, strategies, and personal style. More than the other methods, these practice theories are particularly effective for specific goals and specific contexts. As these examples indicate, the locality development approach can create community-initiated programs in particular problem areas. The social planning approach is more effective for establishing preconceived programs initiated by the worker. The social action approach does not necessarily lead to new programs, but it often creates an advocacy organization that can assure more effective and humane delivery of existing services. The choice of approach depends ultimately on how these differences relate to the needs of the direct-service generalist worker.

Summary

When the direct-service generalist has determined the development goals in work with the community, there are three basic practice theories available to guide his or her methods: locality development, social planning, and social action.

In locality development the goals are self-help and the integration of various community groups. The target is the total community. Strategies are directed toward achieving communication and consensus among different community groups. The social worker serves as enabler, catalyst, coordinator, and educator. The community, however, is self-determining.

In social planning the focus is on problem solving in regard to serious social problems. The target is preconceived change in particular situations. The social worker serves as expert, fact-finder, analyst, and program implementer. The constituents are the recipients of services. Strategies may be either consensus-building or conflict-creating, depending on the worker's judgment.

Social action aims at changing power relationships and resources of the community system itself. The constituents are disadvantaged and powerless segments of the community. The social worker uses roles and strategies that help these groups become organized in order to crystallize issues and engage in conflict-oriented action against the power structure.

Rothman has suggested propositions regarding the most suitable practice theory for community organizations and development under given conditions. Locality development appears most appropriate where populations are generally homogeneous and consensus exists on the major goals of community development. Social action is more appropriate in a situation characterized by antagonistic subgroup interests. Rothman notes, however, that the social worker should be able to mix these approaches in a single practice context when problems require a mixed approach and organizational situations permit adaptation. In Rothman's words: "Thus the practitioner would be able to make adjustments in a social planning approach that is heedless of functional participation, a community development approach that stresses endless group discussion at the expense of addressing compelling community problems, or a social action approach that utilizes conflict when avenues are open for fruitful resolution of issues through discussion and negotiation."[35]

Brager and Specht have presented a fruitful integration of these approaches in their phasic model of community organizing.[36] Perhaps more than any of the other methods, the direct-service worker's use of community organization approaches requires specific knowledge of appropriate strategies for particular goals. As Brager and Specht state this position: "The important question is not whether the worker is a 'good' organizer in a particular situation at a particular point. . . . It is, rather, whether he can assess the needs of groups in different developmental states at different stages of the community work process and help them deal with *their* needs, thereby increasing their competence . . . to achieve their goals."[37]

Suggested Learning Experiences

A community study is often a useful way for students to see how community processes relate to consumer needs and community development methods. A good format for an explorative community study is included in Arthur Dunham, *The New Community Organization* (New York: Crowell, 1970), pp. 572–574. An excellent case study source based on the three practice models is Fred M. Cox et al., eds., *Community—Action, Planning, Development: A Casebook* (Itasca, Ill.: F. E. Peacock, 1974).

Suggested Case Studies

Ecklein, Joan Levin and Armand A. Lauffer. "Building Relationships." In *Community Organizers and Social Planners: A Volume of Case and Illustrative Materials*. New York: Council on Social Work Education, 1972. Examples of social action.

Ecklein, Joan Levin and Armand A. Lauffer. "Community Workers in Direct Service Agencies." In *Community Organizers and Social Planners: A Volume of Case and Illustrative Materials*. New York: Council on Social Work Education, 1972. Illustrates social planning.

"Fostering Self-Help and Inter-Agency Coordination." In *Case Reports*. New York: National Federation of Settlements and Neighborhood Centers, 1974. Examples of locality development.

Afterword: Toward the Complete Generalist

The direct-service generalist approach of this book is a current concept of social work. The roots of social work—the human relations profession that mediates between the individual's needs and society's resources—have been planted deeply. In this sense, the social work approach developed here is not new but a rediscovery—a restatement of past efforts to define practice and deepen its direct-service theory base.

There will always be competing approaches, of course. This is the stuff of professional growth. A clash of doctrines is not a disaster but an opportunity for further evolution of the various schools of thought that contribute to professional competence. The healthy tension among competing views has always been a difficult but formative element of social work's development.

Today there are models of practice that differ sharply from the one presented here. Many, for instance, have abandoned traditional practice theories altogether. Most often this abandonment has taken two routes. The first trend is the use of generic problem-solving and system assessment frameworks that are thought to apply to practice with any unit—individual, family, group, organization, community. In this view, a single generic method of practice is assumed to apply simultaneously to both the microlevel and the macrolevel. Once a system has been analyzed, the worker can plug into the framework of all the units chosen for change (whether individual, family, group, organization, or community). This social worker does not identify his or her activities as casework, family group work, group work, organizational development, or community organization and development methods.

The second trend away from traditional practice theories is the use of people-changing approaches that have evolved outside of social work. This concept, individualistic in focus, nudges the idea of social work toward the "fifth profession"—a general psychotherapy profession. The clinical and individual-changing theories range from gestalt therapy and transactional analysis to meditation, yoga, behavior modification, and encounter groups.

The framework of social work methods and processes developed in this book tends to bridge these two extremes. To the adherents of both, the ideas presented here may seem too traditional—a restatement, in a traditional methods and processes manner, of practice theories that do not work as separate specializations and cannot be mastered by the individual generalist.

Yet the direct-service generalist must have basic skills for determining the most appropriate service in behalf of consumers and their social systems. Direct-service social workers must be able to use and test the practice theories behind the methods for helping the individual, family, group, organization, or community. The ideal is to match the best possible people with the best possible means for providing social services. Now let us take a look at this social worker.

You have a stake in both consumers and their social systems. You care about consumers and others who are significant to them. You can help consumers match their needs to resources in a manner that contributes to their autonomous and interdependent development. You are a skillful mediator who helps others work toward their goals with full respect for their dignity and worth, uniqueness, and self-determination.

You can make judgments in partnership with consumers regarding the activities that are appropriate for your goals. You are not committed to any particular methods for practice. You know your own limits and do not do anything that others could be doing. Yet you can determine with others what will meet their needs and be able to work with them in their own behalf, work with colleagues and others in the service network in behalf of individual consumers, and work with community members in behalf of direct consumers and others like them. You have a core of skills that make you effective in working in all these areas.

You have a basic understanding of each individual's needs and can help others to understand these needs. You know about your clients' personal development and how it relates to the situation that has led them to ask for help. You know this because you have done a lot of hard work understanding people in general and discovering each consumer as a person in particular.

You also know *why* you are doing what you are doing. You are not merely experimenting on human subjects. To some degree you may be guessing, of course. You are not a soothsayer. But you do know what your guess is based on. You can tell early on how accurate your guess is, and sometimes you will be wrong. But you and the person you serve will both know *what* was wrong and *how* it may be righted. Because you have this knowledge, you could, more often than not if asked, tell others, including consumers, what you are doing and why. Since you have worked hard to deepen your knowledge of what can be done in situations like this one, you have as much confidence and trust in yourself as consumers do.

You are a social *worker*. What you know has evolved from your work with people in real situations. Whether you are working with the consumer as an individual or a member of a family group or a member of a group of other consumers, whether you are working with organizations or communities in behalf of consumers, you are informed about the many possible approaches to what you are doing. You have studied some extensively and have chosen the ones most applicable for achieving your goals. These approaches have been tested in the field in situations like yours. Most important, they fit the consumer and not vice versa.

Even if you are trying an approach that has not been tested in situations similar to the present one, you are still basing your approach on a solid foundation of experience. Consumers are not totally an experiment. They are people who need help and realize that—because they are unique and the worker never stops growing and learning—some things are bound to be new to the worker. But not *everything*. Certainly you will not ignore what has been learned about working with people like this consumer in this situation.

Finally, you care a great deal about whether this person has been served. Your caring is reflected in your concern for the consumer as a person, your concern for evaluating your effectiveness, your expectations that the consumer will do as much as possible in using the service, and your willingness to fight for the services that the consumer deserves but is not receiving. Above all, you will fight what you consider unjust in the way things are done and even in things the consumer may do. To wage these battles you have knowledge and skills as well as sermons.

While you know a good deal about ways to serve consumers and have the courage to carry your share of the service and even to fight if you believe people are being frustrated in their self-actualization, you have humility. You realize that you may in fact know very little for sure about helping others. You are therefore continually learning more, and are coming to see that many successes are due to what consumers themselves and others put into it—not what you have done yourself.

Alan Keith-Lucas describes some of these basic qualities of the effective worker in the use of social work methods and processes:

> Courage, humility, and concern may give us some characterization of the helping person. Other qualities such as dependability, patience, integrity, or a sense of humor are of course also desirable, or perhaps simply facets of these. Intelligence and imagination can be of help. But the social worker is basically a human being, with many of the faults that all of us share. There is nothing ascetic or infallible about him or about his knowledge. He is disciplined but no automaton, sensitive but no seer, knowledgeable but not necessarily intellectual, unselfish but not self-denying, long suffering but no martyr. When we meet him we will probably like him but not, perhaps, be too impressed.[1]

When others need help, I hope for no less than a social worker who has the ability to use the methods described in the preceding pages. Moreover, I hope that you, the reader, liked the book but are not, perhaps, *too* impressed—that it does not weld you only to the theories presented here. Instead, I hope you have understood, selected, and developed your own personal use of some of these "espoused theories" as direction for your practice and for the careful testing of your own theories in use. The most significant thing I have learned in writing this book is that in the complex arena of social work, the models that inform our practice are never really finished. If they are useful at all, these models are only maps to guide your negotiation of the ever-changing territory of practice. For you and for me, then, I hope this is a beginning more than an end.

Notes

Chapter 1: The Generic Framework

1. For further elaboration of this position see: Harry Specht, "Generalist and Specialist Approaches to Practice and a New Educational Model," in *The Pursuit of Competence in Social Work Education,* ed. Frank W. Clark, Morton L. Arkava, and associates (Washington, D.C.: Jossey-Bass Publishers, 1979), pp. 1–22; and Betty L. Baer, "Social Work Practice," in Betty L. Baer and Ronald C. Frederico, *Educating the Baccalaureate Social Worker: A Curriculum Development Resource Guide,* vol. 2 (Cambridge, Mass.: Ballinger Publishing Co., 1979), pp. 139–162.

2. Transaction has been defined "as a mutual, reverberating process occurring in a system of relations." See John Speigel, *Transactions: The Interplay Between Individual, Family, and Society.* (New York: Science House, 1971), p. 29. Transaction includes the concept of interaction, where processes can be directly balanced in viewing causal interconnections. If Jack enters the tennis court with his partner, Jill, and begins to volley, we need a transactional perspective to view the events. The mutual reverberations are no longer so easy to predict by Jack as the ball bounces toward him. The independent process that is Jill could *choose* to hit the ball to the forecourt or backcourt, to Jack's forehand or backhand, with a slice or with english, etc. This tennis game is more analogous to human transactions.

3. Abraham Kaplan, *The Conduct of Inquiry: Methodology for Behavioral Science* (San Francisco: Chandler, 1964), p. 23.

4. NASW, *Social Case Work: Generic and Specific: A Report of the Milford Conference, 1929* (New York: National Association of Social Workers, 1974); Harriet Bartlett, *The Common Base of Social Work Practice* (New York: National Association of Social Workers, 1970); William E. Gordon, "Basic Constructs for an Integrative and Generative Conception of Social Work," in *The General Systems Approach: Contributions Toward an Holistic Conception of Social Work,* ed. Gordon Hearn (New York: Council on Social Work Education, 1969); and William Schwartz, "The Social Worker in the Group," *The Social Welfare Forum, 1961* (New York: Columbia University Press, 1961), pp. 146–171. For a more recent attempt to identify unitary elements of practice see: Chauncey A. Alexander, "Social Work Practice: A Unitary Conception," *Social Work,* vol. 22, no. 5 (September 1977):407–414.

5. Herbert Bisno, "A Theoretical Framework for Teaching Social Work Methods and Skills with Particular Reference to Undergraduate Social Welfare

Education," *Journal of Education for Social Work,* vol. 5, no. 1 (Fall 1969):1–16; Martin Rein, "Social Work in Search of a Radical Profession," *Social Work,* vol. 15, no. 2 (April 1970):1–17; and Schwartz, "Social Worker in the Group."

6. Leon W. Chestang, "The Issue of Race in Casework Practice," *Social Work Practice, 1970* (New York: Columbia University Press, 1970), pp. 114–126; Jeanne M. Giovannoni and Andrew Billingsley, "Child Neglect Among the Poor: A Study of Parental Inadequacy in Families of Three Ethnic Groups," *Child Welfare,* vol. 49, no. 4 (April 1970):196–204; and John B. Turner, "Education for Practice with Minorities," *Social Work,* vol. 17, no. 3 (March 1972):112–120.

7. Ethnic Affairs Committee, "Beyond Ain't It Awful," mimeographed (Columbus: Ohio State University School of Social Work, 1974).

8. Harold L. McPheeters and Robert M. Ryan, *A Core of Competence for Baccalaureate Social Welfare and Curriculum Implications* (Atlanta: Southern Regional Education Board, 1971), p. 22.

9. For other conceptual frameworks for social work practice see: "Special Issue on Conceptual Frameworks," *Social Work,* vol. 22, no. 5 (September 1977)—especially articles by Minahan and Pincus, pp. 347–352; Reid, pp. 374–381; Gilbert, pp. 401–406; and Alexander, pp. 407–414.

10. Harriet Bartlett, "Social Work Practice," in *Encyclopedia of Social Work,* vol. 16 (New York: National Association of Social Workers, 1970), p. 1479.

11. William E. Gordon, "Fragmentation and Synthesis in Social Work Today," in *Social Work Promises and Pressures,* ed. Sue W. Spencer (Nashville: University of Tennessee School of Social Work, 1968), p. 3.

12. Abraham H. Maslow and John J. Honigam, eds. "Synergy: Some Notes of Ruth Benedict," *American Anthropologist,* vol. 72 (Fall 1970):10–28. For further elaboration of the concept of synergy in social work practice see: Joseph D. Anderson, "What Will Social Workers 'Will'?", *Social Casework,* vol. 60, no. 1 (January 1979):11–18.

13. Baer and Frederico, *Educating the Baccalaureate Social Worker,* p. 12.

14. For an excellent example of a social worker concerned with the developmental quality of matching in a situation similar to Mrs. Woods' and able to mediate in hospital, patient, and family processes toward better matching, see Zelda P. Foster, "How Social Work Can Influence Hospital Management of Fatal Illness," *Social Work,* vol. 10, no. 4 (October 1965):30–35.

15. Schwartz, "Social Worker in the Group," pp. 154–155.

16. Alan K. Klein, *Effective Groupwork: An Introduction to Principle and Method* (New York: Association Press, 1972), p. xv.

17. Donald F. Krill, "Existentialism: A Philosophy for Our Current Revolutions," *Social Service Review,* vol. 40, no. 3 (September 1966):292.

18. Bertha Reynolds, *Social Work and Social Living* (New York: Citadel Press, 1941), pp. 24–25, 162.

19. William E. Gordon, "Toward a Social Work Frame of Reference," *Journal of Education for Social Work,* vol. 1, no. 2 (Fall 1965):9.

20. Emanuel Tropp, "Three Problematic Concepts: *Client, Help, Worker,*" *Social Casework,* vol. 55, no. 1 (January 1974):29.

21. Harold Lewis, "The Cause in Function," *Journal of the Otto Rank Association,* vol. 11, no. 2 (Winter 1976–1977):20–21.

22. Ruth E. Smalley, *Theory for Social Work Practice* (New York: Columbia University Press, 1967), pp. 131–132.

23. George Brager and Harry Specht, *Community Organizing* (New York: Columbia University Press, 1973), pp. 68–69.

24. Arthur W. Combs et al., *Florida Studies in the Helping Professions* (Gainesville: University of Florida Press, 1969).

25. For a discussion of values and their conflict in practice see: F. M. Loewenberg, *Fundamentals of Social Intervention* (New York: Columbia University Press, 1977), pp. 29–45.

Chapter 2: The Generalist Framework (Microlevel)

1. Beulah Roberts Compton and Burt Galaway, *Social Work Processes* (Homewood, Ill.: Dorsey Press, 1975), p. 11.

2. Allen Pincus and Anne Minahan, *Social Work Practice: Model and Method* (Itasca, Ill.: F. E. Peacock, 1973), p. 63.

3. Ruth R. Middleman and Gale Goldberg, *Social Service Delivery: A Structural Approach to Social Work Practice* (New York: Columbia University Press, 1974), pp. 17–24.

4. Ruth Elizabeth Smalley, *Theory for Social Work Practice* (New York: Columbia University Press, 1967), pp. 29–30.

5. Helen Harris Perlman, *Social Casework: A Problem-Solving Process* (Chicago: University of Chicago Press, 1957); and Helen Harris Perlman, "The Problem-Solving Model in Social Casework" in *Theories of Social Casework,* ed. Robert W. Roberts and Robert H. Nee (Chicago: University of Chicago Press, 1970), pp. 131–179.

6. William J. Reid and Laura Epstein, *Task-Centered Casework* (New York: Columbia University Press, 1972), pp. 41–47; and William J. Reid, *The Task-Centered System* (New York: Columbia University Press, 1978).

7. John Mayer and Noel Timms, "Clash in Perspective Between Worker and Client," *Social Casework,* vol. 50, no. 1 (January 1969):32–40.

8. This situation was adapted from Rosemary Chaplin and Nancy Waldman, *The Helping Process* (Minneapolis: Minnesota Resource Center for Social Work Education, 1972), pp. 84–100.

9. Smalley, *Theory,* p. 34.

10. Joseph D. Anderson, "Human Relations Training and Group Work," *Social Work,* vol. 20, no. 3 (May 1975):195–199; and Joseph D. Anderson,

"Growth Groups and Alienation," *Group and Organization Studies,* vol. 3, no. 1 (March 1978):85–107.

11. Grace L. Coyle, "Some Basic Assumptions about Social Group Work," in *The Social Group Work Method in Social Work Education,* Social Work Curriculum Study, vol. 2, ed. Marjorie Murphy (New York: Council on Social Work Education, 1959), p. 91.

12. William Schwartz, "Between Client and System: The Mediating Function," in *Theories of Social Work with Groups,* ed. Robert W. Roberts and Helen Northen (New York: Columbia University Press, 1976), pp. 189–190.

Chapter 3: The Generalist Framework (Macrolevel)

1. John J. Sherwood, "An Introduction to Organizational Development," in *The 1972 Annual Handbook for Group Facilitators,* ed. J. William Pfeiffer and John E. Jones (Iowa City: University Associates, 1972), p. 153.

2. This level of analysis is developed in Peter L. Berger, *Invitation to Sociology: An Humanistic Perspective* (Garden City, N.Y.: Doubleday and Company, 1963), pp. 25–53; and in Paul Lazarsfeld and Herbert Menzel, "On the Relation Between Individual and Collective Properties," in *A Sociological Reader,* ed. Amitai Etzioni (New York: Holt, Rinehart and Winston, 1961), pp. 499–516.

3. Ruth R. Middleman and Gale Goldberg, *Social Service Delivery: A Structural Approach to Social Work Practice* (New York: Columbia University Press, 1974), pp. 175–176.

4. Summarized from Zelda P. Foster, "How Social Work Can Influence Hospital Management of Fatal Illness," *Social Work,* vol. 10, no. 4 (October 1965):30–45.

5. Andrew Weissman, "Industrial Social Services: Linkage Technology," *Social Casework,* vol. 57, no. 1 (January 1976):50–54.

6. Adapted from Patrick V. Riley, "Family Advocacy: Case to Cause and Back to Case," *Child Welfare,* vol. 50, no. 7 (July 1971):374–383.

7. Ruth Elizabeth Smalley, *Theory for Social Work Practice* (New York: Columbia University Press, 1967), p. 42.

8. Murray Ross, *Community Organization: Theory, Principles and Practice,* 2nd ed. (New York: Harper & Row, 1967), p. 6.

9. Kenneth L. M. Pray, "What Makes Community Organization Social Work?", in *Social Work in a Revolutionary Age* (Philadelphia: University of Pennsylvania Press, 1949), p. 276.

10. Violet M. Sieder, "Community Organization in the Direct-Service Agency," in *Social Welfare Forum, 1962* (New York: Columbia University Press, 1962), pp. 90–102.

11. David G. Gil, *Unravelling Social Policy* (Cambridge, Mass.: Schenkman Publishing Co., 1973), p. 24.

12. Harry Specht, "Casework Practice and Social Policy Formation," *Social Work,* vol. 13, no. 1 (January 1968):42–52.

13. Riley, "Family Advocacy."

14. William M. Banks, "The Black Client and the Helping Professions," in *Black Psychology,* ed. R. L. Jones (New York: Harper & Row, 1972), pp. 204–212; Douglas Glasgow, "Black Power Through Community Control," *Social Work,* vol. 17, no. 3 (March 1972):59–64; William G. Mayfield, "Mental Health in the Black Community," *Social Work,* vol. 17, no. 3 (March 1972):32–43; and Dorothy Zietz and Jane L. Erlich, "Sexism in Social Agencies: Practitioners' Perspectives," *Social Work,* vol. 21, no. 6 (November 1976):434–440.

15. Adapted from Francis P. Purcell and Harry Specht, "The House on Sixth Street," *Social Work,* vol. 10, no. 4 (October 1965):69–76.

16. Alfred J. Kahn, *Social Policy and Social Services* (New York: Random House, 1973), p. 69.

Chapter 4: Generic Principles

1. Alfred Kadushin, *The Social Work Interview* (New York: Columbia University Press, 1972), p. 3.

2. Scott Briar and Henry Miller, *Problems and Issues in Social Case Work* (New York: Columbia University Press, 1971), p. 184.

3. William Schwartz, "The Social Worker in the Group," *The Social Welfare Forum, 1961* (New York: Columbia University Press, 1961), pp. 150–151.

4. Ibid., p. 157.

5. For further elaboration of this principle see: Joseph D. Anderson, "What Will Social Worker's 'Will'?", *Social Casework,* vol. 60, no. 1 (January 1979): 11–18.

6. Ruth R. Middleman and Gale Goldberg, *Social Service Delivery: A Structural Approach to Social Work Practice* (New York: Columbia University Press, 1974), p. 431.

7. Recent works on the importance of working with natural networks in social work practice are particularly illustrative of this principle in action. See for example: Alice H. Collins and Diane L. Pancoast, *Natural Helping Networks: A Strategy for Prevention* (New York: National Association of Social Workers, 1977); and Judith A. Lee and Carol R. Swenson, "Theory in Action: A Community Social Service Agency," *Social Casework,* vol. 59, no. 6 (June 1978):359–369.

8. Adapted from Armando Morales and Bradford Sheafor, *Social Work: A Profession of Many Faces* (Boston: Allyn and Bacon, 1977), pp. 135–153.

Chapter 5: Core Interactional Skills

1. Betty Baer and Ronald Frederico, *Educating the Baccalaureate Social Worker: Report of the Undergraduate Social Work Curriculum Development Project* (Cambridge, Mass.: Ballinger Publishing Co., 1978).

2. May Gay Harm, ed., *A Report of the Community Mental Health Practice-Education Project* (New York: Council on Social Work Education, 1978).

3. Carl K. Rogers, "The Necessary and Sufficient Conditions of Therapeutic Personality Change," *Journal of Consulting Psychology,* vol. 21, no. 2 (February 1957):95–103.

4. Robert R. Carkhuff, "Helping and Human Relations: A Brief Guide for Training Lay Helpers," *Journal of Research and Development in Education,* vol. 4, no. 2 (February 1971):20.

5. Robert R. Carkhuff, *Helping and Human Relations,* vol. 1 (New York: Holt, Rinehart and Winston, 1969), p. 180.

6. Ibid., p. 180.

7. Ibid., p. 181.

8. Ibid., p. 187.

9. Ibid.

10. Ibid., p. 121.

11. This discussion of phase-specific skills is based on William Schwartz, "On the Use of Groups in Social Work Practice," in *The Practice of Group Work,* ed. William Schwartz and Serapio R. Zalba (New York: Columbia University Press, 1971), pp. 3–24; and "Between Client and System: The Mediating Function," in *Theories of Social Work with Groups,* ed. Robert W. Roberts and Helen Northen (New York: Columbia University Press, 1976), pp. 171–197.

12. Lawrence Shulman, *A Casebook of Social Work with Groups: The Mediating Model* (New York: Council on Social Work Education, 1968), pp. 75–78; and "Social Work Skill: The Anatomy of the Helping Act," in *Social Work Practice, 1969* (New York: Columbia University Press, 1969), pp. 29–43.

13. This outline is based on Shulman, *A Casebook,* pp. 79–92; "A Study of Practice Skills," *Social Work,* vol. 23, no. 4 (July 1968):274–280; and *The Skills of Helping Individuals and Groups* (Itasca, Ill.: F. E. Peacock, 1979).

14. Lawrence Shulman, *A Study of the Helping Process* (Vancouver: School of Social Work, University of British Columbia, 1977), pp. 184–204.

Chapter 6: Developmental Theory

1. For a sampling of this work see: Henry S. Maas "Social Work, Knowledge and Social Responsibility," *Journal of Education for Social Work Practice, 1969* (New York: Columbia University Press, 1969), pp. 1–14; E. Clifford Brennen, "Defining the Basic Curriculum," *Journal of Education for Social Work,* vol. 14, no. 2 (Spring 1978):24–30; and Harris Chaiklin, "Personality System, Social System, and Practice Theory," in *Social Work Practice, 1969* (New York: Columbia University Press, 1969), pp. 1–21.

2. Chaiklin, "Personality System," pp. 4–5.

3. Ralph E. Anderson and Irl E. Carter, *Human Behavior in the Social Environment: A Social Systems Approach* (Chicago: Aldine Publishing Company, 1974).

4. See: Robert Chin, "The Utility of System Models and Developmental Models for Practitioners," in *The Planning of Change* (2nd ed.), ed. Warren G. Bennis, Kenneth D. Benne, and Robert Chin (New York: Holt, Rinehart and Winston, 1961), pp. 297–312.

5. Heinz Werner and Edward Kaplan, *Symbol Formation* (New York: John Wiley and Sons, 1963), p. 5.

6. George Corner, *Ourselves Unborn* (New Haven: Yale University Press, 1944), p. 122.

7. Lewis Thomas, *The Lives of a Cell* (New York: Viking Press, 1974), pp. 130, 146.

8. Heinz Werner, *Comparative Psychology of Mental Development* (New York: International Press, 1948), p. 11.

9. Jean Piaget quoted in Jonas Langer, *Theories of Development* (New York: Holt, Rinehart and Winston, 1969), p. 93.

10. Werner, *Comparative Psychology*, pp. 458, 467.

11. Abraham H. Maslow, *Motivation and Personality*, 2nd ed. (New York: Harper & Row, 1970), pp. 35–58.

12. Erik H. Erikson, *Childhood and Society*, 2nd ed. (New York: W. W. Norton and Company, 1963), pp. 247–274.

13. Carol H. Meyer, *Social Work Practice: The Changing Landscape* (New York: Free Press, 1976), pp. 70–74.

14. Adapted from Blanca N. Rosenberg, "Planned Short-Term Treatment in Developmental Crises," *Social Casework*, vol. 56, no. 4 (April 1975):197–198.

Chapter 7: Social Systems Theory

1. Jacob W. Getzels and Herbert A. Thelen, "The Classroom as a Unique Social System," in *The Dynamics of Instructional Groups: Sociopsychological Aspects of Teaching and Learning,* ed. Nelson B. Henry (Chicago: University of Chicago Press, 1960), pp. 53–82.

2. Getzels and Thelen, "The Classroom," p. 66. See also: J. W. Getzels and E. G. Guba, "Social Behavior and the Administrative Process," *School Review,* vol. 55, no. 2 (March 1957):423–441.

3. Getzels and Thelen, "The Classroom," p. 68, citing Talcott Parsons and Edward A. Shills, *Toward A General Theory of Action* (Cambridge: Harvard University Press, 1951), p. 114.

4. Ibid., p. 82.

5. For further elaboration of the ecological model for social work practice see: Carel B. Germain, ed., *Social Work Practice: People and Environments: An Ecological Perspective* (New York: Columbia University Press, 1979).

6. Delores G. Norton, *The Dual Perspective: Inclusion of Ethnic Minority Content in the Social Work Curriculum* (New York: Council on Social Work Education, 1978), p. 3.

7. Ibid., pp. 3–4.

8. Ibid., p. 2.

9. Ben A. Orcutt, "Casework Intervention and the Problems of the Poor," *Social Casework,* vol. 54, no. 2 (February 1973):18–28.

10. Ibid., p. 24.

11. Ibid., pp. 25–26.

12. See: James K. Whittaker, "Models of Group Development: Implications for Social Work," *Social Service Review,* vol. 46, no. 3, (October 1972):308–322.

13. These names for the group developmental stages are from James A. Garland, Herbert A. Jones, and Ralph L. Kolodny, "A Model for Stages of Group Development in Social Work Groups," in *Explorations in Group Work,* ed. Saul Bernstein (Boston: Milford House, 1973), pp. 17–71. Some of these ideas about the stages of group development were originally published in Joseph D. Anderson, "Social Work with Groups in the Generic Base of Social Work Practice," *Social Work with Groups,* vol. 2, no. 4 (Winter 1979):281–293.

Chapter 8: From Basic Theory to Practice Theories

1. Michael Polyani, *The Tacit Dimension* (New York: Doubleday and Company, 1967).

2. Chris Argyris and Donald A. Schön, *Theory in Practice: Increasing Professional Effectiveness* (San Francisco: Jossey-Bass Publishers, 1975), pp. 3–34.

3. Scott Briar and Henry Miller, *Problems and Issues in Social Casework* (New York: Columbia University Press, 1971), p. 53.

4. Robert K. Merton, *Social Theory and Social Structure* (Glencoe, Ill.: Free Press, 1957), p. 89.

5. Talcott Parsons, *Essays in Sociological Theory* (Glencoe, Ill.: Free Press, 1954), p. 212.

6. Carl Rogers, "A Theory from Therapy: Personality and Interpersonal Relationships as Developed in the Client-Centered Framework," in *Psychology: A Study of Science,* vol. 2, ed. Sigmund Koch (New York: McGraw-Hill Book Co., 1949), p. 9.

7. Joel Fischer, "A Framework for the Analysis and Comparison of Clinical Theories of Induced Changes," *Social Service Review,* vol. 48, no. 12 (December 1971):41.

8. Donald H. Ford and Hugh B. Urban, *Systems of Psychotherapy: A Comparative Study* (New York: John Wiley and Sons, 1963).

9. Ibid., p. 20.

10. For instance, Francis J. Turner, ed., *Social Work Treatment: Interlocking Theoretical Approaches* (New York: Free Press, 1974), pp. 12–14.

11. See Joseph D. Anderson, "Games Social Work Educators Play in Teaching Practice Theories," in *Teaching for Competence in the Delivery of Direct Services* (New York: Council on Social Work Education, 1976), pp. 1–8.

12. Dorothy D. Lee, "Conceptual Implications of the Indian Language," *Philosophy of Science,* vol. 5 (1938):89–102.

13. Wendell Johnson, *People in Quandaries: The Semantics of Personal Adjustment* (New York: Harper & Row, 1946), p. 76.

14. In social work see: William J. Reid, "Client and Practitioner Variables Affecting Treatment," *Social Casework,* vol. 45, no. 10 (December 1964):586–592; John Goldmeier, "A Study of Selected Personality Attributes and Treatment Preference of Caseworkers and Casework Students," *Social Service Review,* vol. 42, no. 6 (June 1968):232–240; Edward J. Mullen, "Differences in Worker Style in Casework," *Social Casework,* vol. 50, no. 6 (June 1969):347–353; Sallie R. Churchill, "A Comparison Between Two Models of Social Group Work: The Treatment Model and Reciprocal Model," in *Individual Change Through Small Groups,* ed. Paul Glasser, Rosemary Sarri, and Robert Vinter (New York: Free Press, 1974), pp. 266–280; and Dolp Hess and Martha Williams, "Personality Characteristics and Value Stances of Student in Two Areas of Graduate Study," *Journal of Education for Social Work,* vol. 10, no. 3 (Fall 1974):42–49. This latter study suggests that student personality is the primary determinant of choices of both social work as a profession and the preference for specializing in the use of either micro or macrolevel methods for practice. In psychotherapy, Hans H. Strupp, *Psychotherapists in Action: Explorations of Therapists' Contribution to the Treatment Process* (New York: Grune and Stratton Company, 1960), both reviews and extends the research on therapists' style.

15. Adapted from Argyris and Schön, *Theory in Practice,* p. 21.

16. Carl Rogers, *On Encounter Groups* (New York: Harper & Row, 1970).

17. Frederick S. Perls, *Gestalt Therapy Verbatim* (New York: Bantam Books, 1969); and John O. Stevens, *Awareness: Exploring, Experimenting, Experiencing* (New York: Bantam Books, 1971).

18. For this suggested system for organizing Rogers' descriptive work into a theoretical statement, I am indebted to Martin Bloom, *The Paradox of Helping: Introduction to the Philosophy of Scientific Practice* (New York: John Wiley and Sons, 1975), pp. 75–79.

19. Joseph D. Anderson, "Growth Groups and Alienation: A Comparative Study of Rogerian Encounter, Self-Directed Encounter, and Gestalt," *Group and Organization Studies,* vol. 3, no. 1 (1978):85–107.

20. Adapted from Argyris and Schön, *Theory in Practice,* p. 41.

21. Ibid., p. 41.

22. Ibid., pp. 53–55.

23. Johnson, *People in Quandaries,* pp. 169–170.

24. Ibid., pp. 170–171.

Chapter 9: Individuals

1. Robert Morris, ed., *Encyclopedia of Social Work,* vol. 2 (New York: National Association of Social Workers, 1971), pp. 1195–1245; Robert W. Roberts and Robert H. Nee, eds., *Theories of Social Casework* (Chicago: University of Chicago Press, 1970); and Francis J. Turner, ed., *Social Work Treatment: Interlocking Theoretical Approaches* (New York: Free Press, 1974).

2. Otto Rank, *Will Therapy and Truth and Reality* (New York: Knopf and Co., 1947).

3. John Dewey, *How We Think,* rev. ed. (New York: D. C. Heath and Co., 1935).

4. Ruth Elizabeth Smalley, *Theory for Social Work Practice* (New York: Columbia University Press, 1967), pp. 29–30.

5. Bernece K. Simon, "Social Casework Theory: An Overview," in *Theories of Social Casework,* pp. 353–396; Scott Briar and Henry Miller, *Problems and Issues in Social Casework* (New York: Columbia University Press, 1971), pp. 53–78; Joel Fischer, "A Framework for the Analysis and Comparison of Clinical Theories of Induced Change," *Social Service Review,* vol. 52, no. 3 (March 1971):440–454; and James K. Whittaker, *Social Treatment: An Approach in Interpersonal Helping* (Chicago: Aldine Publishing Co., 1974), pp. 62–109.

6. Donald F. Krill, "A Framework for Determining Client Modifiability," *Social Casework,* vol. 30, no. 12 (December 1968):602–611.

7. Values 4 through 8 come from Felix P. Biestek, *The Casework Relationship* (Chicago: Loyola University Press, 1951).

8. Florence Hollis, "Explorations in the Development of a Typology of Casework Treatment," *Social Casework,* vol. 48, no. 6 (June 1967):335–341; William J. Reid and Ann W. Shyne, *Brief and Extended Casework* (New York: Columbia University Press, 1969); and Edward J. Mullen, "Casework Communication," *Social Casework,* vol. 49, no. 11 (November 1968):546–551.

9. Whittaker, *Social Treatment*; Robert W. Klenk and Robert M. Ryan, eds., *The Practice of Social Work,* 2nd ed. (Belmont, Calif.: Wadsworth Publishing Co., 1974); and Beulah Roberts Compton and Burt Galaway, *Social Work Processes* (Homewood, Ill.: Dorsey Press, 1975).

10. Florence Hollis, *Casework: A Psychosocial Therapy,* 2nd ed. (New York: Random House, 1972).

11. Gordon Hamilton, *Theory and Practice of Social Casework,* 2nd ed. (New York: Columbia University Press, 1951).

12. Charlotte Towle, *Common Human Needs* (New York: National Association of Social Workers, 1965).

13. Annette Garrett, *Interviewing: Its Principles and Methods,* rev. ed. (New York: National Association of Social Workers, 1974).

14. Norman A. Polansky, *Ego Psychology and Communication* (Chicago: Aldine Publishing Co., 1971).

15. Gertrude Sackheim, *The Practice of Clinical Casework* (New York: Behavioral Publications, 1974).

16. Francis J. Turner, "Psychosocial Therapy," in *Social Work Treatment,* pp. 84–111. See also: Herbert S. Strean, *Clinical Social Work* (New York: Free Press, 1978); and Francis J. Turner, *Psychosocial Therapy* (New York: Free Press, 1978).

17. Florence Hollis, "The Psychosocial Approach to Casework," in *Theories of Social Casework,* pp. 50–51.

18. Helen Harris Perlman, *Social Casework: A Problem-Solving Process* (Chicago: University of Chicago Press, 1957).

19. Howard J. Parad, "Crisis Intervention," in *Encyclopedia of Social Work,* vol. 1 (New York: National Association of Social Workers, 1971), pp. 196–202.

20. William J. Reid and Laura Epstein, *Task-Centered Casework* (New York: Columbia University Press, 1972); and William J. Reid, *The Task-Centered System* (New York: Columbia University Press, 1978).

21. David Hallowitz, "Problem Solving Theory," in *Social Work Treatment,* pp. 112–146.

22. Kurt Spitzer and Betty Welsh, "A Problem Focused Model of Practice," *Social Casework,* vol. 50, no. 6 (June 1969):323–329.

23. Helen Harris Perlman, "Social Casework: A Problem Solving Approach," in *Encyclopedia of Social Work,* p. 1208.

24. Perlman, *Social Casework,* pp. 89–90.

25. Perlman, "Social Casework," p. 1212.

26. Jessie Taft, "The Relation of Function to Process in Social Casework," *Journal of Social Work Process,* vol. 1, no. 1 (1937):1–33.

27. Virginia P. Robinson, *A Changing Psychology in Social Casework* (Chapel Hill: University of North Carolina Press, 1930).

28. Kenneth L. M. Pray, *Social Work in a Revolutionary Age and Other Papers* (Philadelphia: University of Pennsylvania Press, 1949).

29. Anita J. Faatz, *The Nature of Choice in Social Casework* (Chapel Hill: University of North Carolina Press, 1953).

30. Harold Lewis, "The Functional Approach to Social Work Practice—A Restatement of Assumptions and Principles," *Journal of Social Work Process,* vol. 15 (1965):1–28.

31. Alan Keith-Lucas, *Giving and Taking Help* (Chapel Hill: University of North Carolina Press, 1972).

32. Shankar A. Yelaja, *Authority and Social Work: Concept and Use* (Toronto: University of Toronto Press, 1971).

33. Jessie Taft, "A Conception of the Growth Process Underlying Social Casework Practice," *Social Casework,* vol. 35, no. 10 (October 1950):5.

34. Jessie Taft, "Living and Feeling," *Child Study,* vol. 10, no. 4 (1933):105.

35. Taft, "Relation of Function to Process," p. 8.

36. Keith-Lucas, *Giving and Taking Help.*

37. Edwin J. Thomas, ed., *Socio-Behavioral Approach and Application to Social Work* (New York: Council on Social Work Education, 1967).

38. Richard B. Stuart, *Trick or Treatment: How or When Psychotherapy Fails* (Champaign, Ill.: Research Press, 1970); "Behavior Modification: A Technology of Social Change," in *Social Work Treatment,* pp. 400–420.

39. Morton L. Arkava, *Behavior Modification: A Procedural Guide for Social Workers,* rev. ed. (Missoula: Department of Social Work, University of Montana, 1974).

40. Derek Jehru, *Learning Theory and Social Work* (London: Routledge and Kegan Paul, 1967).

41. Arthur Schwartz and Israel Goldiamond, *Social Casework: A Behavioral Approach* (New York: Columbia University Press, 1975).

42. Frederick H, Kanfer and Jeanne S. Phillips, *Learning Foundations of Behavior Therapy* (New York: John Wiley and Sons, 1970).

43. Albert Bandura, *Principles of Behavior Modification* (New York: Columbia University Press, 1975).

44. Stuart, "Behavior Modification," p. 404.

45. Edwin J. Thomas, "Social Casework and Social Groupwork: The Behavioral Approach," in *Encyclopedia of Social Work,* pp. 1230–1231.

46. Ibid., p. 1233.

47. The basic facts of this case, a real one, are adapted from Maureen C. Didier, "The Use of Self," in *Child Abuse and Neglect: Social Services Reader I.* (Albany: School of Social Welfare, SUNY at Albany, 1977), pp. 37–40.

48. Hollis, "The Psychosocial Approach," p. 43.

49. Perlman, *Social Casework.*

50. Helen Harris Perlman, *Relationship: The Heart of Helping* (Chicago: University of Chicago Press, 1979).

51. Reid, *The Task-Centered System,* p. 88.

52. Ibid., pp. 90–92.

53. Keith-Lucas, *Giving and Taking Help,* p. 127.

54. For an excellent presentation of this approach in work with parent–child behavior problems see: Joel Fischer and Harvey L. Gochros, *Planned Behavior Change: Behavior Modification in Social Work* (New York: Free Press, 1975), pp. 341–365.

Chapter 10: Families

1. Alan F. Klein, *Effective Groupwork: An Introduction to Principle and Method* (New York: Association Press, 1972), pp. 125–126.

2. Ibid., p. 43.

3. George H. Mead, *Mind, Self, and Society,* ed. Charles W. Morris (Chicago: University of Chicago Press, 1962); and Charles H. Cooley, *Human Nature and the Social Order* (New York: Free Press, 1967).

4. Grace L. Coyle, "Concepts Relevant to Helping the Family as a Group," *Social Casework,* vol. 43, no. 7 (July 1962):347–354; Alan F. Klein, "Exploring Family Group Counseling," *Social Work,* vol. 8, no. 1 (January 1963):23–29; Gertrude Wilson and Gladys Ryland, "The Family as a Unit of Service," *Social Work Practice, 1964* (New York: Columbia University Press, 1964), pp. 119–139; and Mary Louise Somers, "Group Processes Within the Family Unit," *The Family Is the Patient: The Group Approach to Treatment of Family Health Problems* (New York: National Association of Social Workers, 1965), pp. 22–39.

5. Adapted from Wilson and Ryland, "The Family as a Unit of Service," pp. 126, 129, 135–136.

6. Jacob Lomranz, Martin Lakin, and Harold Schiffman, "A Three-Valued Typology for Sensitivity Training and Encounter Groups," *Human Relations,* vol. 26, no. 3. (1973):339–358.

7. Irvin D. Yalom, *The Theory and Practice of Group Psychotherapy* (New York: Basic Books, 1970); Morton A. Lieberman, Irvin D. Yalom, and Matthew B. Miles, *Encounter Groups: First Facts* (New York: Basic Books, 1973); William Fawcett Hill, "Further Considerations of Therapeutic Mechanisms in Group Therapy," *Small Group Behavior,* vol. 6, no. 4 (November 1975):421–429; and Michael Rohrbaugh and Bryan D. Bartels, "Participants' Perceptions of 'Curative Factors' in Therapy and Growth Groups," *Small Group Behavior,* vol. 6, no. 4 (November 1975):430–456.

8. Joan Stein et al., *The Family as a Unit of Study and Treatment* (Regional Rehabilitation Research Institute, School of Social Work, University of Washington, 1969).

9. Frances H. Scherz, "Theory and Practice of Family Therapy," in *Theories of Social Casework,* ed. Robert W. Roberts and Robert H. Nee (Chicago: University of Chicago Press, 1970), pp. 219–264.

10. Ibid., p. 236.

11. Ibid., p. 245.

12. Sanford N. Sherman, "Family Therapy," in *Social Work Treatment: Interlocking Theoretical Approaches,* ed. Francis J. Turner (New York: Free Press, 1974), pp. 457–494.

13. William Jordan, *The Social Worker in Family Situations* (Boston: Routledge and Kegan Paul, 1972).

14. Nathan Ackerman, *The Psychodynamics of Family Life: Diagnosis and Treatment of Family Relationships* (New York: Basic Books, 1958).

15. Virginia Satir, *Conjoint Family Therapy,* rev. ed. (Palo Alto: Science and Behavioral Books, 1967).

16. Donald R. Bardill and Francis J. Ryan, *Family Group Casework* (Washington, D.C.: Catholic University of America Press, 1969).

17. Don P. Jackson and John H. Weakland, "Conjoint Family Therapy: Some Considerations on Theory, Technique, and Results," *Psychiatry,* vol. 24, no. 1 (January 1961):30–45.

18. Jay Haley and Lynn Hoffman, *Techniques of Family Therapy* (New York: Basic Books, 1967).

19. Salvador Minuchin, *Families and Family Therapy* (Cambridge: Harvard University Press, 1974).

20. Gregory Bateson, *Steps to an Ecology of Mind* (New York: Ballantine, 1972).

21. Haley and Hoffman, *Techniques of Family Therapy,* pp. 174–264.

22. Ibid., p. 200.

23. Minuchin, *Families and Family Therapy.*

24. Virginia Satir, James Stachowiak, and Harvey A. Taschman, *Helping Families to Change* (New York: Jason Aronson, 1975), pp. 165–166.

25. See: Nathan W. Ackerman, "A Dynamic Frame for the Clinical Approach to Family Conflict," in *Exploring the Base for Family Therapy,* ed. Nathan W. Ackerman, Frances L. Bateman, and Sanford N. Sherman (New York: Family Service Association of America, 1961), pp. 52–67; and Virginia Satir, "Family Systems and Approaches to Family Therapy," in *Family Therapy: An Introduction to Theory and Techniques,* ed. Gerald D. Erikson and Terrence P. Hogan (New York: Jason Aronson, 1976), pp. 211–222.

26. Scherz, "Theory and Practice," p. 236.

27. Stein et al., *The Family as a Unit,* p. 46.

28. Nathan W. Ackerman, "Family Psychotherapy—Theory and Practice," *American Journal of Psychotherapy,* vol. 20, no. 3 (1966):411.

29. Satir, *Conjoint Family Therapy,* p. 96.

30. Ibid., p. 177.

Chapter 11: Groups

1. Ruth Elizabeth Smalley, *Theory for Social Work Practice* (New York: Columbia University Press, 1967), p. 34.

2. Catherine Papell and Beulah Rothman, "Social Group Work Models: Possession and Heritage," *Journal of Education for Social Work,* vol. 2, no. 3

(Fall 1966):66–77; James K. Whittaker, "Models of Group Development: Implications for Social Group Work Practice," *Social Service Review*, vol. 44, no. 3 (September 1970):308–322; *Encyclopedia of Social Work*, vol. 2 (New York: National Association of Social Workers, 1971), pp. 1246–1273; Joseph D. Anderson, "Human Relations Training and Group Work," *Social Work*, vol. 20, no. 3 (May 1975):195–199; and Robert W. Roberts and Helen Northen, eds., *Theories of Social Work with Groups* (New York: Columbia University Press, 1976).

3. Grace L. Coyle, *Group Work with American Youth* (New York: Harper and Brothers, 1948).

4. Gisela Konopka, *Social Group Work: A Helping Process* (Englewood Cliffs, N.J.: Prentice-Hall, 1963).

5. Gertrude Wilson and Gladys Ryland, *Social Group Work Practice* (Boston: Houghton Mifflin Co., 1949).

6. Alan F. Klein, *Effective Groupwork: An Introduction to Principle and Method* (New York: Association Press, 1972); and Saul Bernstein, ed., *Explorations in Group Work* (Boston: Milford House, 1973).

7. Klein, *Effective Groupwork*, p. 83.

8. Ibid., p. 137.

9. Ibid., p. 172.

10. Coyle, *Group Work*, p. 12.

11. Helen U. Phillips, *Essentials of Social Group Work Skill* (New York: Association Press, 1957).

12. Emanuel Tropp, *A Humanistic Foundation for Group Work Practice*, 2nd ed. (New York: Selected Academic Reading, 1972); and Emanuel Tropp, "A Developmental Theory," in *Theories of Social Work with Groups*, pp. 198–237.

13. Tropp, "A Developmental Theory," pp. 222–223.

14. Ibid., p. 220.

15. Ibid., p. 236.

16. William Schwartz, "Social Group Work: The Interactionist Approach," in *Encyclopedia of Social Work*, pp. 1252–1263; William Schwartz and Serapio R. Zalba, eds., *The Practice of Group Work* (New York: Columbia University Press, 1971); and William Schwartz, "Between Client and System: Mediating Function," in *Theories of Social Work With Groups*, pp. 171–197.

17. Lawrence Shulman, *A Casebook of Social Work with Groups: The Mediating Model* (New York: Council on Social Work Education, 1969).

18. Alex Gitterman, "Social Work in the Public School System," *Social Casework*, vol. 58, no. 2 (February 1977):111–118.

19. Schwartz, "Social Group Work," pp. 1256–1257.

20. Ibid., p. 1258.

21. Ibid., pp. 1259–1260.

22. Schwartz, "Between Client and System," p. 190.

23. Lawrence Shulman, *A Study of the Helping Process* (Vancouver: University of British Columbia, 1977).

24. Schwartz, "Social Group Work," p. 1262. For an excellent example of this approach for family group work see: B. L. Stempler, "A Group Work Approach to Family Treatment," *Social Casework,* vol. 55, no. 3 (March 1977):143–152.

25. Robert V. Vinter, ed., *Readings in Group Work Practice* (Ann Arbor: Campus Publishers, 1967).

26. Charles D. Garvin and Paul H. Glasser, "Social Group Work: The Preventive and Rehabilitative Approach," *Encyclopedia of Social Work,* pp. 1263–1273; and Charles D. Garvin and Paul H. Glasser, "The Bases of Social Treatment," *Social Work Practice, 1970* (New York: Columbia University Press, 1970), pp. 149–177.

27. Paul Glasser, Rosemary Sarri, and Robert Vinter, eds., *Individual Change Through Small Groups* (New York: Free Press, 1974).

28. Garvin and Glasser, "Social Group Work," p. 1270.

29. Sheldon D. Rose, *Treating Children in Groups: A Behavioral Approach* (Washington, D.C.: Jossey-Bass Publishers, 1973).

30. Garvin and Glasser, "The Bases of Social Treatment," p. 176.

31. Klein, *Effective Groupwork,* p. 138.

32. Tropp, *A Humanistic Foundation,* p. 110.

33. Alex Gitterman, "Group Work in the Public Schools," in *The Practice of Group Work,* pp. 55–56.

34. Janice H. Schopler and Maeda J. Galinsky, "Common Elements in Group Development," in *The Field of Social Work* (7th ed.), ed. Arthur E. Fink (New York: Holt, Rinehart and Winston, 1978), pp. 279–281.

35. See: Gertrude Wilson, "From Practice to Theory: A Personalized History," in *Theories of Social Work with Groups,* pp. 1–44.

36. See: Joseph D. Anderson, "Social Work with Groups in the Generic Base of Social Work Practice," *Social Work with Groups,* vol. 2, no. 4 (Winter 1979):281–293.

Chapter 12: Organizations

1. Edgar H. Schein, *Organizational Psychology* (Englewood Cliffs, N.J.: Prentice-Hall, 1965), p. 8.

2. Max Weber, *The Theory of Social and Economic Organization* (New York: Oxford University Press, 1947), pp. 333–334.

3. Beulah Roberts Compton and Burt Galaway, *Social Work Processes* (Homewood, Ill.: Dorsey Press, 1975), p. 478.

4. Harold H. Weissman, *Overcoming Mismanagement in the Human Services* (San Francisco: Jossey-Bass, 1973), p. viii.

5. Ibid., p. vii.

6. John J. Sherwood, "An Introduction to Organization Development," in *Sensitivity Training and the Laboratory Approach: Readings about Concepts and Applications* (2nd ed.), ed. Robert J. Golembiewski and Arthur Blumberg (Itasca, Ill.: F. E. Peacock Publishers, 1973), pp. 431–432.

7. Among the most notable of this work are the following: Gary Askerooth, *Advocacy in the Organizational Society* (Minneapolis: Minnesota Resource Center for Social Work Education, 1973); George Brager and Stephen Holloway, *Changing Human Service Organizations: Politics and Practice* (New York: Free Press, 1978); Beulah Compton and Burt Galaway, *Social Work Processes* (Homewood, Ill.: Dorsey Press, 1975), pp. 472–512; Rino J. Patti and Herman Resnick, "Changing the Agency from Within," *Social Work,* vol. 17, no. 4 (July 1972):48–57; Rino J. Patti, "Organizational Resistance and Change," *Social Service Review,* vol. 48, no. 3 (September 1974):367–383; Rino J. Patti, "Limitations and Prospects of Internal Advocacy," *Social Casework,* vol. 55, no. 9 (November 1974):537–545; Edward J. Pawlik, "Organizational Tinkering," *Social Work,* vol. 21, no. 5 (September 1976):376–380; Robert Pruger, "The Good Bureaucrat," *Social Work,* vol. 18, no. 4 (July 1973):26–32; Robert Pruger, "Bureaucratic Functioning as a Social Work Skill," in Betty Baer and Ronald Frederico, *Educating the Baccalaureate Social Worker: Report of the Undergraduate Social Work Curriculum Project* (Cambridge, Mass.: Ballinger Publishing Co., 1978), pp. 149–168; Herman Resnick, "Effecting Internal Change in Human Service Organizations," *Social Casework,* vol. 58, no. 9 (November 1977):546–553; and Weissman, *Overcoming Mismanagement.*

8. Robert Chin and Kenneth D. Benne, "General Strategies for Effecting Changes in Human Systems," in *The Planning of Change* (2nd ed.), ed. Warren G. Bennis, Kenneth D. Benne, and Robert Chin (New York: Holt, Rinehart and Winston, 1969), pp. 32–59.

9. Ibid., p. 35.

10. Howard E. Freeman and Clarence C. Sherwood, *Social Research and Social Policy* (Englewood Cliffs, N.J.: Prentice-Hall, 1970).

11. Carol H. Weiss, *Evaluation Research: Methods of Assessing Program Effectiveness* (Englewood Cliffs, N.J.: Prentice-Hall, 1972).

12. Chin and Benne, "General Strategies," p. 43.

13. Ibid.

14. Sherwood, "An Introduction," p. 435.

15. Mary Follet, *Creative Experience and Dynamic Administration* (New York: David McKay Company, 1924).

16. Frances Fox Piven and Richard A. Cloward, *Regulating the Poor: The Functions of Public Welfare* (New York: Pantheon Books, 1971).

17. Warren Bennis, *American Bureaucracy* (Chicago: Aldine Publishing Co., 1970), p. 5.

18. Pruger, "The Good Bureaucrat" and "Bureaucratic Functioning as a Social Worker."

19. Compton and Galaway, *Social Work Processes,* pp. 490–491.

20. Ibid., pp. 487–488.

21. Patti and Resnick, "Changing the Agency from Within." See also: Patti, "Limitations and Prospects"; and Resnick, "Effecting Internal Change."

22. Askerooth, *Advocacy.* For a similar position see: Brager and Holloway, *Changing Human Service Organizations.*

23. Ibid., p. 23.

24. Brager and Holloway, *Changing Human Service Organizations.*

25. Taken from Resnick, "Effecting Internal Change," p. 548.

26. Frances Fox Piven, "Whom Does the Advocate Planner Serve?", *Social Policy,* vol. 4, no. 3 (May–June 1970):97–104.

27. Robert M. MacRae, "Social Work and Social Action," *Social Service Review,* vol. 40, no. 1 (March 1966):6.

Chapter 13: Communities

1. Murray G. Ross, *Community Organization: Theory, Principles and Action,* 2nd ed. (New York: Harper & Row, 1967), pp. 41–45.

2. R. M. MacIver, *Community,* 3rd ed. (London: Macmillan and Company, 1936), p. 23.

3. Arthur Dunham, *The New Community Organization* (New York: Thomas Y. Crowell Co., 1970), p. 4. Italics omitted from definition.

4. Jack Rothman, "Three Models of Community Organization Practice," in *Strategies of Community Organization: A Book of Readings,* ed. Fred M. Cox et al. (Itasca, Ill.: F. E. Peacock Publishers, 1970), pp. 20–36.

5. William W. Biddle and Loureide J. Biddle, *The Community Development Process: The Rediscovery of Local Initiative* (New York: Holt, Rinehart and Winston, 1965).

6. Charles F. Grosser, *New Directions in Community Organization: From Enabling to Advocacy,* expanded edition (New York: Praeger Publishers, 1976).

7. Ross, *Community Organization,* p. 40.

8. Dunham, *New Community Organization,* pp. 275–290.

9. Ross, *Community Organization,* p. 85.

10. Rothman, "Three Models," p. 27.

11. Biddle and Biddle, *Community Development Process,* p. 82.

12. Grosser, *New Directions,* pp. 155–223.

13. Biddle and Biddle, *Community Development Process,* p. 33.

14. Robert Morris and Robert H. Binstock, *Feasible Planning for Social Change* (New York: Columbia University Press, 1966).

15. Roland L. Warren, *Truth, Love, and Social Change* (Chicago: Rand McNally and Co., 1971).

16. Alfred J. Kahn, *Theory and Practice of Social Planning* (New York: Russell Sage Foundation, 1969), p. 17.

17. Robert Perlman and Arnold Gurin, *Community Organization and Social Planning* (New York: John Wiley and Sons and the Council on Social Work Education, 1972).

18. Kahn, *Theory and Practice,* p. 17.

19. Rothman, "Three Models," p. 28.

20. Morris and Binstock, *Feasible Planning,* pp. 109–110.

21. Peter Morris and Martin Rein, *Dilemmas of Social Reform: Poverty and Community Action in the United States* (New York: Atherton Press); and Armand Lauffer, *Social Planning at the Community Level* (Englewood Cliffs, N.J.: Prentice-Hall, 1978).

22. Warren, *Truth, Love, and Social Change,* pp. 274–275.

23. Saul D. Alinsky, *Reveille for Radicals* (Chicago: University of Chicago Press, 1946).

24. Warren C. Haggstrom, "The Power of the Poor," in *The Mental Health of the Poor,* ed. Frank Reissman et al. (New York: Free Press, 1964), pp. 205–223; and Warren C. Haggstrom, "Impact of New Designs of Community Organization," in *New Trends in Citizen Involvement and Participation* (New York: National Social Welfare Assembly, 1965), pp. 9–24.

25. Daniel Thursz, "Social Action as a Professional Responsibility," *Social Work,* vol. 11, no. 3 (May 1966):12–21.

26. Haggstrom, "The Power of the Poor," p. 207.

27. Rothman, "Three Models," p. 28.

28. Alinsky, *Reveille for Radicals,* pp. 153–155.

29. Haggstrom, "Impact of New Designs," pp. 13–14.

30. For example, Anne Harris Cohn, "Effective Treatment of Child Abuse and Neglect," *Social Work,* vol. 24, no. 6 (November 1979):513–519.

31. As, for instance, in Pennsylvania: "Child Protective Service Regulations," *Pennsylvania Bulletin,* vol. 6, no. 15 (April 3, 1976):837.

32. Alfred J. Kahn, Sheila B. Kamerman, and Brenda G. McGowan, *Child Advocacy: Report of a National Baseline Study* (Washington, D.C.: Children's Bureau, U.S. Department of Health, Education, and Welfare, 1973).

33. Ibid., pp. 65–66.

34. Ibid.

35. Rothman, "Three Models," p. 35.

36. George Brager and Harry Specht, *Community Organizing* (New York: Columbia University Press, 1973).

37. Ibid., p. 87.

Chapter 14: Afterword

1. Alan Keith-Lucas, *Giving and Taking Help* (Chapel Hill: University of North Carolina Press, 1972), p. 108.

Author Index

Subject Index